Wallace Stevens
and the Apocalyptic Mode

MALCOLM WOODLAND

Wallace Stevens

and the Apocalyptic Mode

University of Iowa Press   IOWA CITY

University of Iowa Press, Iowa City 52242
Copyright © 2005 by the University of Iowa Press
All rights reserved
Printed in the United States of America

http://www.uiowa.edu/uiowapress

The University of Iowa Press is a member of
Green Press Initiative and is committed to
preserving natural resources.

Printed on acid-free paper

Library of Congress Cataloging-in-Publication Data
Woodland, Malcolm, 1958–.
  Wallace Stevens and the apocalyptic mode / by Malcolm Woodland.
      p.   cm.
  Includes bibliographical references and index.
  ISBN 0-87745-928-2 (cloth)
  1. Stevens, Wallace, 1879–1955—Criticism and interpretation.   2. Literature and
history—United States—History—20th century.   3. Stevens, Wallace, 1879–1955—
Knowledge—History.   4. Apocalyptic literature—History and criticism.   5. End
of the world in literature.   6. War in literature.   I. Title.

PS3537.T4753Z957   2005
811'.52—dc22   2004058016

05   06   07   08   09   C   5   4   3   2   1

For my mother, and in memory of my father

Contents

Acknowledgments

Thanks are due to Eleanor Cook, whose support and encouragement from the early stages of this project have been invaluable. I owe a similar debt of gratitude to John Reibetanz and Linda Munk.

I would also like to thank Professors Linda Hutcheon and Marlene Goldman, both of the University of Toronto, who both have read portions of the manuscript. Research assistants Rob Mancini and Zachariah Pickard have helped immensely in casting their cold eyes on a manuscript that has at times been much in need of proofreading. Financial assistance from the University of Toronto and the Social Sciences and Humanities Research Council of Canada has facilitated much of the work on this project. Finally, I would like to thank Prasenjit Gupta, Holly Carver, John Mulvihill, and all others involved at the University of Iowa Press for their support of and work on this project.

Introduction

Why has it been possible to read Stevens as both an apocalyptic and an antiapocalyptic poet? Why has it been possible to read Stevens as both a (belated) romantic/modernist and as a poststructuralist/postmodernist? These two questions, I hope to show, are intimately related. To take a stance toward apocalyptic discourse is to take a stance toward the ends and beginnings of historical eras and, by implication, toward the ends and beginnings of cultural and aesthetic eras. For Stevens, confronting the immense sociopolitical upheaval and human suffering of the late 1930s and early 1940s also meant confronting the possible dissolution of the aesthetic principles that guided his creative projects. Stevens's attitude toward the former offers a glimpse of his attitude toward the latter, toward the possibility that the dominant aesthetic modes of the first part of the twentieth century had been shaken to their foundations, were on the verge of collapse or invalidation, and were likely to be replaced by something that as yet had no name or discernible form.

To make such claims is not to suggest that the "dividing line" (if there is such a thing) between modernism and postmodernism should be shifted back twenty or so years from its usual position in the mid to late 1950s; it is, however, to suggest that the practitioners and proponents of an already changing and varied modernist aesthetic—born to a large extent out of a sense of cultural crisis and exhaustion in the early part of the century—were now facing a second crisis that seemed to threaten that same aesthetic. It is to suggest, furthermore, that in most cases these artists were developing strategies of resistance against that threat and were struggling to maintain the aesthetic values in which they had so heavily invested. Stevens's engagement with apocalypse can be understood in relation to this cultural/historical context. His oeuvre, in other words, is in many ways characteristic of late modernism. Tyrus Miller's description of the tensions that mark the cultural artifacts of that period provides some clarification of how my reading of Stevens will proceed: "At first glance, late modernist writing appears a distinctly self-conscious manifestation of the aging and decline of modernism, in both its institutional and ideological dimensions. More surprising, however, such writing also strongly anticipates future developments, so that without forcing, it might easily fit into a narrative of emergent postmodernism" (7). My only disagreement with Miller is over the verb "anticipates," which does not do justice to the subtlety of his study and, in fact, offers a historically displaced version of that early modernist privileging of the "new" that his work seems intended to question. (See, for example, his discussion of the modernist rhetoric of beginnings, on p. 5 of his introduction.) If, as Linda Hutcheon insists (*Poetics* 11, 18, 35), postmodernism is both continuous and discontinuous with modernism, it would make more sense to say that postmodernism echoes certain aspects of late modernism, and that writers who appear to "anticipate" postmodernism are the beneficiaries of that discourse's paradoxically retrospective tendency. In placing Stevens within this context, then, I do not wish to grant him any special anticipatory insight; from my point of view, it would be far more surprising to discover that a much-read, late modernist writer did *not* appear to anticipate some aspects of an emergent postmodernism.

This is not the first critical work to consider the place of apocalypse in Stevens's poetry. A brief summary of the major critics who have dealt with the issue should suffice to reveal the basic positions already taken and the nature of the particular contradiction I wish to explore—the contradiction, that is, between readings that locate an apocalyptic strain in Stevens's poetry and those that find an anti-apocalyptic one. Harold Bloom makes occasional comments on apocalypse throughout *Wallace Stevens: The Poems of Our Climate* (1976), the most intriguing, perhaps, being the observation, in relation to "Saint John and the Back-Ache," that "St. John is . . . the apocalyptic impulse that [Stevens] has dismissed for so long but that will begin to break in upon his reveries in *An Ordinary Evening in New Haven* and *The Rock* and then will dominate the poems composed from 1952 through 1955" (298). In contrast, Eleanor Cook, in *Poetry, Word-Play, and Word-War in Wallace Stevens* (1988), gives a very detailed reading of "An Ordinary Evening in New Haven" as "a purgatorial poem in the antiapocalyptic mode" (273). And Charles Berger's *Forms of Farewell* (1985) actually reverses Bloom's narrative of an increasingly apocalyptic oeuvre: "One can argue that Stevens' late poetry begins in an atmosphere of premature closure, as Stevens fears that the war will bring on a sudden end to civilized life. When these fears subside, we get poems that I have called counterapocalyptic, such as 'Credences of Summer' and 'An Ordinary Evening in New Haven,' poems which begin to see the world as *saved*" (xi). Part of the difference between Bloom and Berger may lie in their respective understandings of "apocalypse." Berger writes of it primarily in terms of events— World War II above all—so catastrophic that they seem to pose an eschatological threat; for Bloom, the primary significance of the term lies in its etymological metaphor of unveiling and in an apocalypse's status as a record of visionary experience. Yet the latter is precisely the understanding of apocalypse that leads to Cook's "antiapocalyptic" reading of "An Ordinary Evening." And Berger's understanding of apocalypse has much in common with the one that underwrites James Longenbach's extended treatment of Stevens's antiapocalyptic stance during World War II in *Wallace Stevens: The Plain Sense of Things* (1991). A recent issue of the *Wallace Stevens Journal* devoted to apocalyptic language in Stevens (23, no. 2, fall 1999) demonstrates a similar range of approaches. It may begin to look as though I am gathering together the sheep and goats for some final eschatological judgment and separation, but my purpose is rather to ask whether both groups might be at least partially "justified" in their accounts of Stevens's (anti)apocalypticism, and whether something irreducibly ambivalent, double, or undecidable in his texts must produce these readings.

In turning to the question of Stevens's place in literary history, I am less willing to leave the poet in an indeterminate space, this time a space between the modern and the postmodern. While remaining attentive, I hope, to the typically Stevensian valuation of process, openness, irony, multiplicity, uncertainty, possibility, and so on, especially as these emerge in his distinctive verbal playfulness and complex poetic texture, I find it impossible to ignore the marks in his oeuvre of a desire for the possibility of stability, and above all for the possibility of a certain kind of poetic power descended from a tradition of "truth," a tradition that is embodied nowhere more forcefully than in prophetic and apocalyptic language. Such a desire cannot easily be subsumed within a reading that insists that Stevens is postmodern. In making this claim, however, I hope to refrain from the value judgments often involved in discussions of Stevens's place in literary history—judgments made by both those who praise and those who damn his work. Angus Cleghorn, for example, enthusiastically reads Stevens as a poet who "practices what is now known as the postmodern enterprise of parodying . . . established ideologies, forms, and tropes" (*Stevens' Poetics* 22), and is disappointed that "Life on a Battleship" "ends by repeating the synecdochic power of one part for the whole" (131). David R. Jarraway, taking a similar approach, finds in "Credences of Summer" the marks of "an argument not carried far enough" (239) for a full deconstruction of the pastoral *locus amoenus*. It seems insufficient to note these contradictions and then set them aside in the name of Stevens's postmodern status. By registering these tensions as momentary failures or marks of incompleteness, critics situate them and Stevens's work as a whole within a teleology whose end—in more senses than one—is postmodernism, and that teleology in turn underwrites a series of judgments as to what is and is not valuable in Stevens's poetry. Such judgments play a similar role in the largely negative assessment of Stevens's work by Lee M. Jenkins, whose "'counter-mutter,' in relation to Stevens and some Stevensians" (7), argues against readings like Cleghorn's and Jarraway's in order to construct a critique of the poet's aesthetics and ideology. Oddly enough, these two opposing approaches share a common assumption: the worth of Stevens's oeuvre depends on its adherence to "our" postmodern values. Such readings tend, in spite of themselves, to reduce or ignore some of the most intense sites of tension—especially of unintentional tension—in Stevens's oeuvre, almost to the same extent as readings that privilege the romantic or visionary aspects of his work (those of Bloom, Carroll, McCann, and so on). My work has its own biases, since it privileges unconscious contradiction over both visionary certainty and postmodern skepticism in reading Stevens. I can only identify that assumption as both starting point and terminus of my study and hope that my own "heavy historical sail" (*CP* 120) will at least end with a renewed sense of the complexity of Stevens's texts.

To claim or even merely assume that a work belongs to one period rather than another is itself a doubled gesture: it facilitates the production of a certain range of interpretations, but also excludes another range, and may have little more than a heuristic value. Periodization takes for granted an ability to search through an impossibly large and heterogeneous array of cultural phenomena and, without the interference of any bias, find some underlying "same" that will "define" an era's conceptual and temporal limits. Obviously, such a search will assume a concept, a set of boundaries, and a whole range of biases in the mere selection of its first object. And even if this initial epistemological difficulty is set aside, the very process of reducing differences to an underlying sameness would remain thoroughly inimical to the bottomless skepticism of postmodernism—so much so, perhaps, that postmodernism should not, by its own logic, "exist" or have a "name" (unless by its own paradoxical logic this is precisely the fate it *should* have come to). One could argue that postmodernism has been spared this fate by the sheer conflicting variety of critical attempts to define or describe "postmodernism." And, of course, there are critics such as Bloom who insist that postmodernism does not exist and never has existed. But even if postmodernism is nothing more than a fiction, even if it is, like all our period concepts, an ideological construct that has been imposed on a diverse body of cultural artifacts that otherwise have no commonality, it seems presumptuous to think it possible to step outside of or annul this history. It was my intention in this study to work with this history and to investigate how it works in our attempts to read Stevens.

My final chapter offers another perspective on Stevens's place in literary history. It examines the work of a contemporary poet, Jorie Graham, who not only reads Stevens but whose poetry quotes from Stevens's oeuvre and shows other marks of his influence. Graham's work is of particular relevance in this context because it consistently and quite self-consciously adopts an antiapocalyptic stance and echoes Stevens's own engagement with apocalypse from Graham's later position in the history of that discourse. I will focus on Graham's 1997 collection, *The Errancy*, and will show that her antiapocalyptic and antieschatological poetry involves a very different attitude toward the possibility of a radical break with a particular cultural or aesthetic dispensation. In addition to the recontextualization of Stevens, then, this chapter also offers a more thorough exploration of my first two chapters' claims about the differences between modernist and postmodernist stances toward the discourse of the End.

The contradictions that interest me demand the closest possible attention to Stevens's texts, and for this reason my discussion is limited to four points of crisis in Stevens's career—two that emerged just before and during World War II, and two that emerged afterward. My first chapter establishes the theoretical framework for the discussion and has four sections. The first and briefest explores Stevens's use of the words "apocalypse" and "apocalyptic" in order to suggest his complex and ambivalent stance toward the terms and all that they signify in his poetry. The second section elucidates the precise literary status of the apocalyptic elements in Stevens's poetry, working largely with Alastair Fowler's deeply historicized understanding of genre and mode. And since to write about a genre or a mode is to write about a textual history, this section is followed by a brief history of the *end* of time, with emphasis on apocalypse as the inscription of a particular discursive power and a particular desire— a power and a desire that are central to Stevens's engagement with apocalypse. Finally, the first chapter discusses the meaning of "anti-apocalypse" and "antiapocalyptic," and, through a consideration of the writings of Jacques Derrida, Frank Kermode, Paul Ricoeur, and others, asks whether an antiapocalyptic discourse might always retain what Derrida calls an "apocalyptic desire" ("Apocalyptic" 82). This last possibility proves crucial to the capacity of Stevens's poetry to generate apocalyptic and *anti*apocalyptic readings.

My second chapter examines Stevens's two wartime essays "The Noble Rider and the Sound of Words" (1942) and "The Figure of the Youth as Virile Poet" (1943), as well as the poems "Extracts from Addresses to the Academy of Fine Ideas" (1940) and "Repetitions of a Young Captain" (1944), with primary emphasis on the first of these texts. The chapter is concerned with the apocalyptic rhetoric that emerges in "The Noble Rider" and in some crucial postmodernist and poststructuralist texts, and asks whether Stevens's stance toward the apparent collapse of modernism is homologous with the stance taken later in the century, especially in the works of Jean-François Lyotard, Derrida, Michel Foucault, and others. My belief is that it is not, and a close reading of the essays' often contradictory figurations of masculinity helps locate the precise points at which Stevens *resists* the possibility of cultural collapse. My third chapter further develops these concerns in relation to a number of relatively neglected wartime poems. I should make it clear, too, that in beginning with works from the period of World War II, I am not claiming that prophetic and apocalyptic elements emerged only at this point in Stevens's career. One need only think of "Sunday Morning," with its proclamation that "The sky will be much friendlier then than now" (*CP* 68) and its absurdist vision of heavenly perfection, to recognize how untenable such a claim would be. These earlier engagements with apocalyptic discourse have more in common with the optimistic, early modernist use of apocalypse as a way of troping modernism's desire to break with the past; it is the kind of apocalypse one finds, for example, in the opening prose sections of Williams's 1923 *Spring and All*. It is only during the war years that this rhetoric takes on a new dimension in Stevens's work. This later version of apocalypse threatens to end the era that the earlier version helped inaugurate, and Stevens's resistance to this end tells us a great deal about his aesthetics and his place in literary history.

The second half of the book considers two of Stevens's major postwar poems, "Credences of Summer" (1946) and "The Auroras of Autumn" (1947), devoting one chapter to each and giving particular attention to how the interaction of (anti)apocalyptic modes with, respectively, pastoral and elegy, involves a historically specific recon-figuration of previous relationships between apocalypse, pastoral, and elegy. My reading of "Credences" suggests that the poem's contradic-tory configurations of pastoral and visionary, apocalyptic topoi reveal an irreducibly doubled stance toward the apocalyptic mode, a mode that the poem simultaneously resists and desires. In "Auroras," Stevens reconfigures conventional relationships among elegy, self-elegy, and apocalypse; here, his investment in a nostalgic fiction of gender marks his final site of resistance to the cultural and aesthetic implications of the poem's strangely postapocalyptic apocalyptic mode.

In locating these points of resistance or contradiction in Stevens's poetry, I am attempting neither to lower nor to raise the value and stature of his work; for me, the question of whether Stevens is mod-ern or postmodern has nothing to do with the quality of his poetry in either aesthetic or moral terms. Obviously, the mere decision to write about Stevens involves many value judgments, and my own desire to avoid making such judgments and particularly to avoid evaluating Stevens according to his status as modern or postmodern has its own ideological assumptions. But I would still like to proceed as though the terms "modernist" and "postmodernist" had a prima-rily descriptive and explanatory power or function. When used in this way, they help to expose and clarify some still unarticulated tensions in Stevens's poetry.

Abbreviations

AW   John Ashbery. *A Wave*. New York: Noonday Press/
Farrar, Straus and Giroux, 1998.

CP   Wallace Stevens. *The Collected Poems of Wallace Stevens*.
1954. New York: Vintage Books, 1990.

EB   Jorie Graham. *The End of Beauty*. Hopewell, N.J.: Ecco
Press, 1987.

LWS   Wallace Stevens. *Letters of Wallace Stevens*. Edited by
Holly Stevens. New York: Knopf, 1970.

M   Jorie Graham. *Materialism*. Hopewell, N.J.: Ecco Press,
1993.

NA   Wallace Stevens. *The Necessary Angel: Essays on Reality
and the Imagination*. New York: Vintage Books, 1951.

OP   Wallace Stevens. *Opus Posthumous*. Revised, enlarged,
and corrected Edition. Edited by Milton J. Bates. New
York: Vintage Books, 1990.

SP   Mark Strand. *Selected Poems*. 1980. New York: Knopf,
2000.

TE   Jorie Graham. *The Errancy*. Hopewell, N.J.: Ecco Press,
1997.

Part I: Stevens and the End of War

chapter one

Past Apocalypse

Stevens, History, Theory

It seems reasonable enough, given my subject, to begin with the End, or at least with Wallace Stevens's attitudes toward the End. Quoted below are three passages that provide some sense of the specific lexical meanings Stevens attached to the words "apocalypse" and "apocalyptic." In each instance, these meanings are anything but fixed and final; Stevens seems to rethink the term and its implications each time he comes to it. The passages quoted below thus register a complex stance or a shifting succession of stances toward these words and their meanings. These stances will be the subject of most of this study. Each of the passages deals in a different way with the immensely troubled political and economic scene of the late 1930s and early 1940s—the depression, the spread of fascism and of communism, World War II; the passages come, respectively, from canto iii of "A Duck for Dinner" (the fourth poem in *Owl's Clover*, 1936), canto vii of "Extracts from Addresses to the Academy of Fine Ideas" (1940), and canto iv of "Description without Place" (1945):

"Is each man thinking his separate thoughts or, for once,
Are all men thinking together as one, thinking
Each other's thoughts, thinking a single thought,
Disclosed in everything, transcended, poised
For the syllable, poised for the touch? But that
Apocalypse was not contrived for parks,
Geranium budgets, pay-roll water-falls,
The clank of the carrousel and, under the trees,
The sheep-like falling-in of distances,
Converging on the statue, white and high." (*OP* 93)

To have satisfied the mind and turn to see,
(That being as much belief as we may have,)
And turn to look and say there is no more

Than this, in this alone I may believe,
Whatever it may be; then one's belief
Resists each past apocalypse, rejects
Ceylon, wants nothing from the sea, *la belle*
Aux crinolines, smears out mad mountains. (*CP* 257)

The eye of Lenin kept the far-off shapes.
His mind raised up, down-drowned, the chariots.

And reaches, beaches, tomorrow's regions became
One thinking of apocalyptic legions. (*CP* 343)

The third passage could initially be written off as an intellectual commonplace, since it recognizes a straightforward homology between the teleologisms of marxism and of Judaic and Christian apocalypse. Such a reading would be concordant with some of Stevens's other comments on communism—for instance, the statement that communism promises "a practicable earthly paradise" (*NA* 143), or the failed socialist apocalypse of the passage from "A Duck for Dinner," both of which suggest that he understood communism to offer a secularized version of the millennium mentioned in Rev. 20:4. More importantly, Stevens's use of "apocalyptic" in "Description without Place" attests in several different ways to the power of apocalypse. There is, no doubt, a certain irony in the suggestion that Lenin, in contemplating the planned communist state that would also supplant the Christian faith in Russia, is nevertheless engaging in the "apocalyptic" thinking so central to that faith; here, apocalypse gets the last word. But Stevens's purpose may involve more than an ironic critique of Lenin's failings: the passage also underscores the sheer longevity and inescapability of apocalypse as a way of thinking about history. The form and force of the apocalyptic narrative is capable of surviving its specific theological contents; those who have most rigorously dismissed such contents may already be burdened with the most intense apocalyptic desires. Above all, Stevens points to a relationship between apocalypse and power: apocalyptic discourse facilitates the creation of powerful narratives of history, and offers a certain discursive mastery over history's complexities. In "Description," it is a discourse mastered by one who desires the highest degree of political power, and it thus has a role in the actualization of that desire.

This combination of apocalyptic motifs in "Description" is entirely consonant with a thematics central to Stevens criticism, one identified by Joseph Riddel when, in *The Clairvoyant Eye*, he finds Stevens "rejecting the illusion of a fixed and final order, either Christ's or Marx's" (126) in canto ii of "Mr. Burnshaw and the Statue." Stevens, writes Riddel, "embraces change and thus chaos, and hesitates to prophesy" (128). Some more recent readings of Stevens, such as Robert Emmett Monroe's "Figuration and Society in 'Owl's Clover,'" Harvey Teres's "Notes toward the Supreme Soviet: Stevens and Doctrinaire Marxism," and Angus J. Cleghorn's *Wallace Stevens' Poetics: The Neglected Rhetoric*, have given still more emphasis to the political and ideological dimensions of this opposition; all three writers show Stevens assigning a critical force to a flexible and open aesthetic, and doing so in opposition to the political rigidity of marxism, fascism, and capitalism. But Stevens's use of the word "resists" in the second of the three quotations suggests that he may have had a more complex stance toward apocalypse. Longenbach's brief gloss on the passage from "Extracts" remains largely in keeping with the work of Monroe and others; he writes that "'Esthétique du Mal' shows how the weight of all previous literature, each 'past apocalypse' (an oxymoron from 'Extracts'), prevents us not only from writing about pain but from knowing the pain of disaster when we experience it" (Longenbach, *Plain* 240). But resistance may be directed against either external or internal forces; and some external forces, such as texts and especially a text that offers "apocalypse," may demand resistance only if they have already been internalized to some extent, only if they appeal to some desire *within* the resister that also needs to be resisted.

The need to resist an internalized apocalyptic urge emerges most clearly in the first quotation, whose words register an apocalyptic desire even as they turn away from that desire. This passage is uttered by "the Bulgar," and the poem's speaker argues against that character's vestigial apocalypticism; but he argues against that desire while still invoking his own tonally complex version of an apocalyptic rhetoric— a rhetoric that half-parodically speaks of "the diverting of the dream / Of heaven from heaven to the future" (*OP* 95), and asks, "Where shall we find more than derisive words? / When shall lush chorals spiral through our fire / And daunt that old assassin, heart's desire?" (*OP* 96). If *Owl's Clover* finally rejects the Bulgar's apocalyptic desires and disappointment, it may well be rejecting a force within Stevens's own creative personality, a tendency toward dissatisfaction with the world of "Geranium budgets, pay-roll water-falls, / The clank of the carrousel and, under the trees, / The sheep-like falling-in of distances," and a corresponding desire for "distances," for "being part, feeling the strength, / Seeing the fulgent shadows upward heaped" (*OP* 93) that form part of the Bulgar's rejected hypothetical apocalypse. The fact that the Bulgar's rhetoric of strength, elevation, and unification appears so frequently in Stevens's wartime poetry may well signify the presence of such a lingering desire in "A Duck for Dinner." To consider this possibility is not to reverse or even disagree with the readings of *Owl's Clover* discussed above, nor to argue against Longenbach's interpretation, which finds an antiapocalyptic force in the poem's final vision of "a future continuous with the past" and its "return to what Stevens had called 'social nature' in 'The Comedian as the Letter C'" (189); nor is it to adopt Janet McCann's account, in *Wallace Stevens Revisited*, of Stevens as a sort of closet or repressed Christian, a poet who found the courage to fully "out" himself only in a deathbed conversion. It is to ask whether Stevens—despite his tenacious adherence to a position of nonbelief, and despite his rejection of Christianity's specific theological contents or articles of belief—nevertheless retains some desire for certain discursive and poetic possibilities that are encoded with particular force in the language of apocalypse, and whether his resistance to apocalyptic discourse can best be understood as a resistance to this lingering desire. My purpose, then, is neither to claim that all of Stevens's reinscriptions of apocalyptic discourse are either straightforwardly apocalyptic, as critics such as Bloom, Carroll, Huston, and others have suggested, or straightforwardly antiapocalyptic, as Longenbach and Cook maintain; nor is it to assert even that Stevens is successively apocalyptic and then antiapocalyptic—the latter being the narrative Berger develops in his study. I wish, rather, to explore the possibility that Stevens's involvement with apocalyptic language is always simultaneously apocalyptic and antiapocalyptic, that his apocalyptic rhetoric is always the mark of a doubled and radically ambiguous desire, the site of an irresolvable tension in his work.

One of the difficulties with previous work on apocalypse in Stevens—indeed with a great many studies of apocalypse in literature—is lack of serious attention to the precise literary status of the terms "apocalypse" and "apocalyptic." This problem may be due to the commonplace use of "apocalypse" to denote any natural or human-caused catastrophe, a meaning that has little to do with the word's origins and etymology (literally an "unveiling" or, as the translators of the King James Bible decided, a revelation), and one that confuses the contents of an apocalypse with the act of divinely initiated "unveiling" by which those contents are made known. My interest here is in "apocalypse" as a classificatory term applied to texts that recount such an "unveiling," that is, in "apocalypse" as a literary term, as the name applied to a genre of texts, the vast majority of which are religious or theological. It is especially important to deal with the generic status of apocalypse, since none of the works I shall consider in this study can be classified as examples of the genre "apocalypse"—in fact, it is not clear that any *literary* text that incorporates apocalyptic elements can be understood as a version of the genre. In Stevens's case, the problem is fairly straightforward, as the following attempt at a definition by J. J. Collins—by no means an ideal or fully satisfying one—illustrates: "'Apocalypse' is a genre of revelatory literature with a narrative framework, in which a revelation is mediated by an otherworldly being to a human recipient, disclosing a transcendent reality which is both temporal, insofar as it envisages eschatological salvation, and spatial insofar as it involves another, supernatural world" ("Introduction" 9). The first and most obvious stumbling block is the word "narrative": none of the poems I shall consider are narrative. Even those that incorporate the largest number of apocalyptic elements do not have the narrative structure characteristic of the genre; they lack, in other words, a crucial aspect of the "overall external structure" (107) of the genre which, for Alastair Fowler, must be present if one wishes to identify a text as an example of a particular genre. In fact, apocalypse as a genre is remarkably rare; the Bible itself contains only two full-fledged examples, in Dan. 7–12 and Revelation, the remainder of such texts being relegated to the apocrypha and pseudepigrapha. Critics struggle with the classification of other apocalyptic passages of the Bible, such as the so-called little apocalypses uttered by Jesus in Matt. 24–25 and Mark 13, or the final chapters of Isaiah, the more elaborately symbolic visions of Zechariah, and so on; R. H. Charles, for example, refers to Isa. 66:6–16 and 18b–22 as "a fragmentary apocalypse" (*Eschatology* 128), and S. D. F. Salmond describes

Ezek. 38, 39, Joel 3, Zech. 14, Obad. 18, and Dan. as prophecies "that are apocalyptic in their character" (1:738). A major topic of debate in studies of apocalypse remains the exact point at which the genre of apocalypse emerges from the prophetic eschatology of the Old Testament, and how these two different kinds of eschatology are to be distinguished from each other, if at all. And Collins's definition of the genre would make a fictional apocalypse an oxymoron. What exactly can critics mean when they speak of apocalypse in a Stevens lyric?

One answer to this question comes from Fowler's definition of mode in *Kinds of Literature*. Fowler describes a mode as an "abstraction with a token repertoire" (191) drawn from its corresponding kind or genre (hence an apocalyptic mode would draw elements from the repertoire of the genre apocalypse), and writes that we usually say that a modulation has occurred when a text brings into play "an incomplete repertoire" of elements associated with some genre other than the one which dominates the text and informs its external structure. A modulation thus draws upon "a selection only of the corresponding kind's features, and one from which overall external structure is absent" (107). For example, Shakespeare's *King Lear* belongs to the genre tragedy, but when Kent asks, after Lear's first speech over the dead Cordelia, "Is this the promised end?" (5.3.265), the play undergoes a brief apocalyptic modulation, since this momentary contemplation of the End introduces a key element of the corresponding genre's (i.e., apocalypse's) repertoire. The tragedy, then, operates here in an apocalyptic mode. Fowler dismisses the idea of modes "capable of existing on their own" (108) and criticizes the "inventing of new 'modes' that have no relation to any antecedent kind" (108).[1] Fowler's understanding of the term seems useful for its terminological consistency, and its linking of mode exclusively to genre offers a high degree of descriptive precision. It also offers considerable flexibility for determining when a modulation has occurred, allowing a wide range of textual events to fall into the category of "modulation"—events ranging from the most elusive and minimal of generic signals to the border of wholesale genre-mixing:

> Locally, modes may amount to no more than fugitive admixtures, tinges of generic color. All the same, they are more than vague intimations of "mood." . . . [A] mode announces itself by distinct

signals, even if these are abbreviated, unobtrusive, or below the threshold of modern attention. The signals may be of a wide variety: a characteristic motif, perhaps; a formula; a rhetorical proportion or quality. . . . Alternatively, the modulation may pervade much or all of the work. Then the latter may be said to belong as a whole to two genres, a kind and a mode. (107–8)

Yet this account also stakes out a very carefully circumscribed territory. A phrase like "tinges of generic color," vague and metaphorical though it is, reminds us, along with the references to "moti[ves]," "formula[e]," "theoretical proportion[s]," and "qualit[ies]," of the limits of the concept: the modulatory signals must be toward general features abstracted from a wide range of texts, and not merely allusions to a single text. This, of course, is precisely the sort of exclusion one would expect to operate in discussions of genre and mode.

Yet it is not clear that this exclusion is necessary or logical. Is it possible to fix a precise boundary between modulatory signals on the one hand and such devices as echo and allusion on the other? Gérard Genette's *Palimpsests: Literature in the Second Degree* insists even more explicitly than Fowler's work on the qualitative difference between allusion and mode. In his systematization of the five types of transtextuality, he places allusion in the first category, "intertextuality," which encompasses relations between individual texts (2); he considers mode and genre as aspects of the more general (and more properly "generic") phenomenon of "architextuality" (4–5). Somewhere between these two categories is that of the "hypertext," the category which *Palimpsests* examines in detail and whose members each explicitly remake a single, earlier work (as, for example, Fielding's *Shamela* remakes *Pamela*). But Genette later blurs the boundaries between his five categories, insisting that "one must not view the five types of transtextuality as separate and absolute categories without any reciprocal contact or overlapping" (7), and mentions, as one example of such overlapping, that a hypertext (a work that parodies another individual text) often "makes use of textual allusions" (8) in order to signal or even constitute its hypertextuality. One wonders, then, if there might be a homologous blurring between allusion and modulation: if an allusion to or echo of another text incorporates strong and clear repertoire elements from the genre to which the source text belongs, there seems no reason to presume that such an allusion could not carry a modulatory force. This is the very possibility considered by John Frow in *Marxism and Literary History* when he asks "whether one can speak of an intertextual relation to a genre" (156). Frow finds one answer to this question in the work of Laurent Jenny, for whom "any rigid distinction between the levels of code and text is not tenable" (Jenny, cited in Frow 156). To Jenny's insistence that "genre archetypes, however abstract, still constitute textual structures" (cited in Frow 156), Frow adds the following corollary: "reference to a text implicitly evokes reference to the full set of potential meanings stored in the codes of a genre" (157). This statement may go too far in claiming that an allusion may represent "the full set" of what Fowler calls a genre's "repertoire," and it would be safer to suggest merely that an allusion may evoke those elements of a genre's repertoire that are relevant to the content of the allusion. Many of Stevens's apocalyptic modulations will work in precisely this manner—alluding to previous apocalyptic texts, often by means of precise verbal echoes, and thereby modulating toward apocalypse and engaging with the history of that genre.

At the very least, Fowler's approach facilitates a considerable clarification of the precise textual and literary issues involved in any consideration of apocalyptic elements in fictional narrative texts and in lyric poetry—even in biblical texts. The sections of the Bible that make partial use of the machinery of apocalypse—Matt. 24–25 and Mark 13, Zech. 1–6, Isa. 65 and 66, 1 Thess. 4:13–18, and 2 Pet. 3, and so on—can be understood as apocalyptic modulations within the dominant genre of the text to which they belong: gospel (Matthew and Mark), prophecy (Zechariah and Isaiah), and epistle (1 Thessalonians and 2 Peter). The fact that Fowler's only references to apocalypse in *Kinds of Literature* occur in relation to an apocalyptic mode may serve as an index of a similar or even greater disproportion between the relative frequency of apocalypses and apocalyptic modulations in secular imaginative literature: "And some nonliterary— or no longer literary—kinds are usually recognized as having generated literary modes (topographical; mythological; apocalyptic)" (108); "Moreover, the verisimilar novel, presupposing an ordered society, has values incompatible with those of certain satiric subgenres, particularly apocalyptic satire" (189). The vast majority of the texts studied in such critical works as Abrams's "Apocalypse: Theme and Romantic Variations," Banta's "American Apocalypses: Excrement and

Ennui," Zbigniew Lewicki's *The Bang and the Whimper: Apocalypse and Entropy in American Literature*, John R. May's *Toward a New Earth: Apocalypse in the American Novel*, or Douglas Robinson's *American Apocalypses* are, I would say, apocalyptic in mode rather than genre. And if one wished to apply Derrida's "Of an Apocalyptic Tone Recently Adopted in Philosophy" to the discussion of apocalypse and apocalyptic modes, one might read (somewhat against the grain of Derrida's own writing) his comments on the constant "going-one-better in eschatological eloquence," the "untransgressible contract among discourses of the end" (80) that, in his reading, has been an inescapable feature of Western philosophy since Immanuel Kant, as an indication that much post-Kantian philosophy has been modally apocalyptic. This certainly is the suggestion of Lee Quinby's *Anti-Apocalypse*, though this work goes much further than Derrida in insisting that not just *all* Western culture from the Greeks to the present has been largely apocalyptic, but that even popular culture phenomena such as blue jeans advertisements participate in this dominant discursive mode. But Quinby's reading fails to respect the profound differences between ancient Greek and Jewish thought (something Derrida and Oscar Cullmann are careful to do in "Violence and Metaphysics" and *Christ and Time*, respectively), particularly in matters of purpose and pattern in history, and it relies on an understanding of apocalypse so broad that it loses all historical and textual specificity—in fact, it becomes somewhat apocalyptic itself in its gestures toward totalization. Above all, Quinby repeats, in a purely textual realm, the apocalyptic gesture she most strenuously opposes—the final division of all humanity into the damned and the saved—by appearing to divide all discourse into the categories of apocalyptic (damned) and antiapocalyptic (saved). This repetition of an apocalyptic tendency in Quinby's antiapocalyptic work touches, in fact, on a central problematic in the relationship between apocalyptic and antiapocalyptic modes that will be one of the crucial matters dealt with in this study.

First, however, I will turn to one of the most immediate and important implications of the concepts of genre and mode—namely, that to deal with a specific genre or mode is to deal with a history of texts, and that to claim even that a work incorporates "a selection only of the corresponding kind's features" is to place that work in relation to a whole history of the genre and mode in question. And apocalypse, as Stevens's reference to "past apocalypse" suggests, has a long and complex history. The sheer volume of work on apocalypse in recent years, together with the more limited scope of this study, militate against a complete recapitulation of that history here. My aim in what follows is merely to trace the course of those particular elements of the genre of "apocalypse" that seem to be most important to Stevens and that will figure most frequently in my analysis of individual poems. One general theme I wish to raise first, however, is the possibility that what Derrida describes as "an untransgressible contract among discourses of the end" ("Apocalyptic" 80) in post-Kantian philosophy might have existed in a different form in the times when the prophetic eschatologies and apocalypses of the Old Testament, the intertestamental apocrypha and pseudepigrapha, and the New Testament were written—a "contract" that manifests itself in "the form of a going-one-better in eschatological eloquence, each newcomer, more lucid than the other, more vigilant and more prodigal too than the other, coming to add more to it: I tell you this in truth: this is not only the end of this here but also and first of that there, the end of history" (80).

One example of such "going-one-better" emerges in the different ways that eschatological prophecy and apocalypse figure the relationships between the pre- and posteschatological worlds—a difference often considered crucial to an understanding of the two genres. R. H. Charles notes, for instance, that "in OT the hopes of Israel were in the main confined *to this world and to the well-being of the nation*," and that "the scene of this [messianic] kingdom was to be the earth purged from all violence and sin. But in the later period the gulf between the present and future begins to widen, and this process goes on till the last resemblances vanish, and the present appears a moral chaos under the rule of Satan and his angels, and the future is conceived as an unending kingdom of blessedness under the immediate sway of God or the Messiah" ("Eschatology" 1:742). Although this passage does not posit an absolute difference between prophecy and apocalypse—it acknowledges a gulf between present and future in prophecy—its emphasis on a difference in the degree and kind of separation between present and future in the two genres points to one of the ways in which apocalypse offers a "going-one-better in eschatological eloquence" over eschatological prophecy. Charles's account remains a classic, and recent work on eschatological prophecy offers little more than an increase in historical or textual detail, or a complication of the sources of apocalypse "proper." Paul D. Hanson's *The Dawn of Apocalyptic*, for instance, explores more thoroughly the social and religious tensions that produced Isaiah's occasional apocalyptic "going-one-better" on eschatological prophecy, whereas Norman Cohn's *Cosmos, Chaos, and the World to Come* emphasizes the influence of Babylonian myth in the emergence of apocalypse.

The Christian appropriation of eschatological prophecy and apocalypse could be understood as a third stage in the process of apocalyptic one-upmanship. Here, the going-one-better emerges in a rhetoric that grants peculiar importance and urgency to the present moment—as, for example, in the first words uttered by Jesus in Mark: "The time is fulfilled, and the kingdom of God is at hand" (Mark 1:15). The position of these words in Mark emphasizes the essentially apocalyptic nature of Jesus's mission, and, though we cannot be certain in what form Paul encountered such sayings, they are certainly among the many apocalyptic elements that provide authority for his claim that "now is the accepted time; behold, now is the day of salvation" (2 Cor. 6:2). Above all, the going-one-better of Christian apocalypse is effected by the incarnation—the "birth pangs of the Messiah" (Scholem 10) do not lie in some indefinite future but, as Gershom Scholem, John Ashton, and Karl Löwith point out, are happening *now* and, by the time of Paul, have become part of the historical past. The result is a double reorientation of the temporal structure of apocalypse, since the present now bears the burden of an especially intense double significance. Christopher Rowland investigates one aspect of this burden, writing that for Paul, "the present has become the moment to which all the Scriptures have been pointing" (48). And Oscar Cullmann, in *Christ and Time*, provides one of the most succinct accounts of Christian apocalypse's reorientation of the futural dimension of eschatological thinking: "What the Jews expected of the future is still expected of the future; but the future event is no longer the center of the redemptive history; rather, that center lies now in a historical event. The center has been reached but the end is still to come" (84). Thus, according to Ashton, Christians living after the crucifixion have lived with the knowledge that "the decisive event, the divine intervention that occupies the gap between 'before' and 'after' has already taken place. The point of rupture along the line of human history has been displaced, shifted back to the time occupied by the Gospel narratives" (225). The futural dimension of apocalyptic thinking does not disappear in Christian apocalyptic, but takes its meaning from the dominant central item of Christian belief. This heightened emphasis on the present as a moment of crisis continues even in the spiritual or internalized interpretations of the apocalyptic kingdom promoted by Augustine in chapters 6 and 7 of *The City of God*, and founded on Luke 17:21 ("behold, the kingdom of God is within you"). Every present moment becomes charged with significance as it holds the possibility of spiritual resurrection through faith.

To conceive of the history of apocalypse as a going-one-better is to read in it a struggle among eschatological and apocalyptic prophets for the greatest possible textual authority and power, and this struggle emerges in many other aspects of apocalypse. The very claim that an utterance comes directly from divine authority gives that utterance an unquestionable authenticity and power—at least for those who believe the initial claim as to its source. But the power struggle inscribed in apocalyptic literature, however, has a more than purely intertextual dimension, as Charles implies when he locates the distinction between apocalypse and eschatological prophecy in the former's hyperbolic account of the present as "a moral chaos under the rule of Satan and his angels" ("Eschatology" 1:742). Apocalypses also respond to a writer's actual social and political context, and to his/her perception of the history that has produced that context. Throughout the first chapter of *The Dawn of Apocalyptic* (1–31) Hanson emphasizes the role of a growing disillusionment with the historical realm in the development of apocalypse: the apocalyptic going-one-better also registers a greater level of oppression and marginalization being endured by the apocalyptic seers. The world has become so corrupt that only divine intervention can save it. And, in its horrific and bloody imaginings of the end of the world and the punishment of the wicked—the elements that lead Bloom to describe Revelation as "lurid and inhumane" (Introduction 4)—apocalypse challenges the existing power structure of the society that produces the discourse and permits a proleptic triumph, to paraphrase Patricia Parker (77), over oppressors. And apocalypse's peculiar discursive power derives not just from its claim to give shape and meaning to history, but from its promise of a final shape that will correct all the injustices inflicted during that history. It promises an inversion of the apparent (wrong) meaning of history thus far. Abrams, for example, touches on this aspect of apocalypse when he writes of "a coming end (the abrupt Second Advent of Christ as King, followed by the replacement of the old world by 'a new heaven and a new earth') which will convert the tragedy of human history into a cosmic comedy" ("Apocalypse" 9); and Theodore Bozeman, in his study of American Puritanism, notes that in Thomas Brightman's influential *Apocalyps* (Amsterdam, 1611), "the story to be told about the earth's last days [was] transformed from tragedy to full-scale 'Comedy'" (209). These discussions of apocalypse's capacity to interpret or reinterpret have a somewhat different context from the preceding ones, since they take the Fall as their main point of reference; here, apocalypse's reversal is primarily a reversal of the original Fall into sin, rather than of the current state of moral chaos. But clearly that state must still be understood as the last earthly result of original sin, and its existence is a sign that the end must be near. Northrop Frye, too, reads the Bible as comic in this sense, but notes that the "rises and falls of heathen kingdoms" do not appear as "tragic but simply as ironic" (*Code* 176): discussing the idea of hell, Frye notes that "the Bible's vision of misery is ironic rather than tragic" (73). One source of such irony is the ignorance of the wicked and powerful as to their final punishment at the last judgment. And an effect of ironic distancing emerges in Revelation's presentation of this judgment—for example, in the lament of the inhabitants of "Babylon the great" (Rev. 18:2) in Rev. 18:16–19, where the narrative framework and final command to "Rejoice" (18:20) prevents anything other than the most distantly ironic stance toward such pain.

Yet the designation of this aspect of apocalypse as "more than intertextual" needs some qualification, since even in these instances the locus of this power remains textual and imaginary rather than political and social. Adela Yarbro Collins sees Revelation's response to a situation of political powerlessness and religious marginalization as "an act of creative imagination which, like that of the schizophrenic, withdraws from empirical reality, from real experience in the everyday world" ("Power" 87). And Robert Alter complains, in "The Apocalyptic Temper," that apocalyptic thinking encourages an attitude of despair toward the present state of things, and thereby discourages individuals from participation in political process and social activism. Clearly, this is the aspect of apocalypse that underlies Longenbach's interpretation of Stevens's antiapocalyptic stance, and my purpose in looking at some of Stevens's responses to a situation of moral chaos and physical violence will not challenge Longenbach's reading but expose a second locus of resistance in Stevens's poetry.

If apocalypse thus deals with actual political and social disenfranchisement by transferring the hope for redress to an entirely imaginative or textual realm, it can be understood in the most general terms as a means of gaining power or mastery over the facts of history by constructing the eschatological position as the sole point at which the meaning of history becomes manifest; it brings together, as Malcolm Bull's introduction to *Apocalypse Theory and the Ends of the World* notes, the different senses of the word "end" (Bull 2–6). In fact, it has long been a commonplace to associate the idea that history has an end with the belief that it has a meaning, and to claim that this relationship first emerges in the prophetic writings of the Old Testament. In *Meaning in History*, Karl Löwith emphasizes the importance of history in prophecy, and the importance of prophecy *to* history and historical thinking. He "aims to show that philosophy of history originates with the Hebrew and Christian faith in a fulfilment" (2): "Within the biblical tradition, the Jewish prophets alone were radical 'philosophers of history' because they had, instead of a philosophy, an unshakable faith in God's providential purpose for his chosen people" (194). According to Löwith, then, meaning and teleology are inseparable, at least in relation to history, and he notes that "a statement about the meaning of historical events is possible only when their *telos* becomes apparent" (5).[2] Of course, such concepts are Derrida's target in "White Mythology," "Force and Signification," "From Restricted to General Economy," and "Violence and Metaphysics." Part of the power of apocalypse, then, is the power to create meaning, and to create the meaning of meaning.

To think of apocalypse in terms of such discursive mastery is also to think of it as a means of encoding an excessive desire. Geoffrey Hartman delineates this aspect of apocalypse in his discussion of Wordsworth's antiapocalypticism: "The term ['apocalyptic imagination'] may also describe a mind which actively desires the inauguration of a totally new epoch, whether preceding or following the end of days. And since what stands between us and the end of the (old) world is the world, I sometimes use 'apocalyptic' to characterize any strong desire to cast out nature and to achieve an unmediated contact with the principle of things" (x). A more purely textual approach to this issue emerges in Douglas Robinson's Derridean observation that "the predictive apocalyptic imagination attempts to rush across the gap of differance" (49), and in "the apocalyptic desire to precipitate 'arrival,' the impulse of the 'self-consuming artefact'" (226) that Patricia Parker describes in romance narrative. Robinson, of course, understands this desire as an impossible and ever-ungratified one, and one can thus consider apocalypse as a means of inscribing a wholly excessive desire, a desire that exceeds all possible fulfillments. Parker's comments, in fact, suggest that this desire poses a threat to textuality itself, or at least to the apparent integrity of a certain kind of textuality—an apocalyptic text would constantly desire its own destruction, since, to paraphrase Hartman, what stands between the text and the state of being it desires is the text itself.

These observations, however, do not do justice to the often tragic ways in which apocalyptic beliefs have become the site of actual political and social power struggles. Revelation itself proved very slow to gain acceptance into the canon, and persons and groups holding apocalyptic, millennial, and messianic beliefs have long been subject to oppression, both from government authorities—as the Waco disaster demonstrates—and from the Church itself. Thus, apocalyptic discourses—or at least different versions or interpretations of apocalyptic discourse—can appear to be both marginal and central to certain aspects of our culture. Marginalization stems to some extent from the sheer disruptive potential of apocalyptic ideas, their insistence that the present order of things is inherently evil and must be brought to an end. Here, Norman Cohn's *The Pursuit of the Millennium* not only offers insight into the sometimes violent methods by which those obsessed with the apocalyptic vision have sought to prepare for its fulfillment, or even to hasten its arrival, but tells of the violence with which the authorities have often greeted such beliefs in their efforts to eradicate them. Gershom Scholem, writing of the "explosive" nature of apocalyptic knowledge—knowledge which "could be reported only in a whisper" (7)—explores the tension between "the world of bonds and laws" (19), or Halakhah, and messianism: medieval Judaism, he tells us, "was deeply suspicious of that anarchic element which I discussed earlier—perhaps on account of a fear of the eruption of antinomian trains of thought, which apocalypticism, in fact, could easily produce" (26).[3] Philip F. Gura, in *A Glimpse of Sion's Glory*, also describes the wary reaction of Puritan authorities in New England to millenarian stirrings: "Because such a heightened excitement about the last days could readily degenerate into violence against those unwilling to accept an immediate rule by the saints, Massachusetts's magistrates and ministers were careful to control such beliefs, particularly so that the colony would not become another Münster, where a century earlier government by another group of 'saints' had resulted in ecclesiastical and moral anarchy" (128).[4] Furthermore, Augustine's spiritual and figurative interpretation of Revelation, which has for centuries exerted great influence on the understanding of apocalypse, owes its adoption as official church doctrine and, to some extent, its very existence, to its potential to neutralize any possible revolutionary force in apocalyptic discourse. If the dominance of the Catholic Church fulfills Revelation's prophecies concerning Christ's millennial reign on earth, then there is no reason to expect or desire the overthrow of that world order.[5] Control over the interpretation of apocalypse helps maintain ecclesiastical power.

The preceding, then, is not intended as the last word on the genre of apocalypse, nor as a definitive account of its history. My main purpose has been to highlight aspects of the genre that seem most relevant to Stevens's complex engagement with apocalypse, and to the account of an "antiapocalyptic mode" that constitutes the last part of this chapter. The bulk of this study will examine how these aspects of apocalypse emerge in Stevens's poetry, and will attempt to answer a series of crucial questions about their function in his work: What do they reveal about Stevens's response to the apocalyptic desire to end an old era and inaugurate a new one? How does Stevens situate himself in relation to apocalypse's figurations of supreme discursive power? What stance does he take toward the eschatological position's power to give meaning to history and the present? How might his poetry deal with apocalypse's excessive desire, a desire that exceeds all possibility of fulfilment? And, finally, what do the answers to these questions tell us about Stevens's place in relation to the two major epochs of twentieth-century literary history—modernism and postmodernism?

Some consideration of the term "antiapocalyptic" is in order here, not simply for the sake of clarification, but to give a more theoretical context for the possibility that an antiapocalyptic discourse may engage in its own kind of "going-one-better." These two issues emerge in Patricia Parker's discussion, in *Inescapable Romance*, of apocalyptic modulations (a term she does not herself use but which accurately describes the phenomenon in question) in romance narratives. Parker contrasts romance's desire to defer closure with apocalypse's desire for finality and closure. One might wonder, upon reading Parker, whether the writers of apocalypses were driven not only by a desire to discover a narrative in history, but also by an impatience with the history to be played out before that end, an impatience with the play of narrative and with their own place in an imagined narrative of history. They desire to arrive at least at knowledge of the end before the end itself arrives; apocalypse, in this reading, would be the genre that leaps to conclusions. In fact, Parker suggests that terminal apocalyptic modulations in romance narratives move us beyond the text, or beyond textuality itself, since the narrative content of these modulations often depicts the destruction of the narrated world and reveals the timeless truth toward which the narrative signs have been gesturing or progressing: "A poem may lead to 'revelation,' as evening leads to morning, or shadowy type to truth, but the moment of revelation is by definition discontinuous, beyond signs" (132). The work thus serves "as mere scaffolding, part of a discursive mode of knowing to be superseded, and obliterated, by the immediacy of revelation" (153). But this apocalyptic moment does not only occur at the end of the text; Parker also writes of an apocalyptic desire that seeks an immediate rather than a deferred fulfilment.[6] Thus, she contrasts, in *Paradise Lost*, "the lesson of patience, of submission to the discipline of time or temperance . . . to the apocalyptic impulse in its Satanic form" (11–12). She also notes, in her discussion of Spenser, that "the traditional function of Apocalypse is to portray the enemy as already defeated, in a vision of the end which places us outside the monsters we are still inside—as Job at the end of his trial is shown the externalized forms of behemoth and leviathan—and, by this act of identifying or naming, proleptically overcomes them" (77). Apocalypse, then, "can be a premature or preemptive end" (99) founded in "the apocalyptic desire to precipitate 'arrival,' the impulse of the 'self-consuming artefact'" (226), "the desire to penetrate the veil of meaning or to hasten the narrative's gradual striptease" (221). And if apocalypse thus disrupts or destroys the romance narrative, romance could similarly be seen as a site of resistance to apocalyptic desires:

> "Romance" is characterized primarily as a form which simultaneously quests for and postpones a particular end, objective, or object, a description which Fredric Jameson approaches from a somewhat different direction when he notes that romance, from the twelfth century, necessitates the projection of an Other, a *projet* which comes to an end when that Other reveals his identity or "name." . . . When the "end" is defined typologically, as a Promised Land or Apocalypse, "romance" is that mode or tendency which remains on the threshold before the promised end, still in the wilderness of wandering, "error," or "trial." (4)

As long as we remain in the romance world, the world of error, of doubt, twilight, and anticipation, we resist apocalypse—or the text does so and asks us to do the same. But Parker does not propose a straightforward opposition between romance (or narrative in general) and apocalypse. She suggests that romance might be considered an antiapocalyptic mode *only* in texts where "the 'end' is defined typologically, as a Promised Land or Apocalypse"—in other words in texts whose symbols, metaphors, allusions, rhetoric, or plain narrative content already gesture toward apocalypse. Parker thus touches on the complex ways in which the apocalyptic and antiapocalyptic may be intertwined; a text or a mode within a text does not begin to register as "antiapocalyptic" unless it is already "apocalyptic."

In "Of an Apocalyptic Tone Recently Adopted in Philosophy," Derrida offers, as does Parker, an understanding both of apocalyptic and antiapocalyptic modes, and while his reading of apocalypse bears certain similarities to Parker's, his sense of the paradoxes involved in the adoption of an antiapocalyptic mode proves especially enlightening. In his interpretation of "the genre of writings called 'apocalyptic' in the strict sense" (87),[7] Derrida asks us to adopt the fiction of a "fundamental scene" (83) of apocalypse. In this "fundamental scene," apocalypse is the discourse which reveals that "truth itself is the end, the destination, and that truth unveils itself is the advent of the end. Truth is the end and the instance of the Last Judgment. The structure of truth here would be apocalyptic. And that is why there would not be any truth of the apocalypse that is not the truth of truth" (84). As Derrida indicates, this "fundamental scene" is still "a philosophical, onto-eschato-teleological interpretation" (83). In this hypothetical scene, both apocalyptic mystagogue—the one who adopts the apocalyptic tone—and his critic, the rationalist *Aufklärer*, are united around some "exclusion," "some *inadmissible*" (79) which would emasculate or castrate the discourse of truth. It is because they both would speak the truth, and be the only true guardians of the truth, that mystagogue and *Aufklärer* remain within the same apocalyptic fold—in spite of the disruptiveness of the former's discourse, a disruptiveness which Derrida, in his reading of Kant's attack on the mystagogues, emphasizes through a rhetoric of leaping, derailment, and so on.[8]

But this "fundamental scene" of apocalypse, Derrida suggests, is sustainable only within the space of that "fundamental scene" itself, in which "*the* apocalyptic tone is not the effect of a generalized derailment, of a *Verstimmung* multiplying the voices and making the tones shift [*sauter*], opening each word to the haunting memory [*hantise*] of the other in an uncontrollable polytonality" (83). The fundamental scene is made both possible and impossible by a more generalized apocalypse which opens and is opened *in* Revelation. Derrida gives particular attention to how Revelation figures its own origins through the epistle(s) which begin(s) it. It opens with an "interlacing of voices and *envois*" (87), "so many sendings, *envois*, so many voices" (86), with lines that announce "the apocalypse as sending, as *envoi*, and . . . the *envoi* as apocalypse, the apocalypse that sends itself" (86): "By its very tone, the mixing of voices, genres, and codes, and the breakdown [*le détraquement*] of destinations, apocalyptic discourse can also dismantle the dominant contract or concordat. It is a challenge to the established admissibility of messages and to the enforcement or the maintenance of order [*la police*] of the destination, in short to the postal regulations [*la police postale*] or to the monopoly of the posts" (89). One might say, then, that the way in which this apocalyptic discourse figures its own openness to and "origin" in an absolute and irreducible *différance* gives it the peculiar status described in the preceding quotation; this opening of the genre of apocalypse to a *generalized* apocalypse challenges "the established admissibility of messages" because it opens onto a "place" outside the order of knowing. Derrida makes this point when he discusses the repeated citations of the word "come" in the final chapters of Revelation: "That 'Come,' I do not know what *it is*, not because I yield to obscurantism, but because the question 'what is' belongs to a space (ontology, and from it the learnings of grammar, linguistics, semantics, and so on) opened by a 'come' come from the other" (93–94). Derrida finds in this revelatory opening—and closing—of Revelation, then, a generalized apocalypse which itself opens the space within which the more specific philosophical and theological understanding of apocalypse as revelation comes into play, a generalized apocalypse which therefore can never become an object of either revelatory intuition (the imaginative leap of the apocalyptic mystagogue) or philosophical discourse (the work of the rationalist *Aufklärer*). And here Derrida turns to the question of writing: "Isn't this completely angelic structure, that of the Johannine Apocalypse, isn't it also the structure of every scene of writing in general? . . . Wouldn't the apocalyptic be a transcendental condition of all discourse, of all experience itself, of every mark or every trace? And the genre of writings called 'apocalyptic' in the strict sense, then, would be only an example, an exemplary revelation of this transcendental structure" (87). This apocalyptic sending thus locates a generalized apocalypse outside of the restricted economy of meaning, of philosophy, of history, of work. And not just apocalyptic writing, but all writing would belong within this space.

What remains to be made explicit in the foregoing discussion is Derrida's concern with the possibility or impossibility of moving beyond the discourse of the end (which is also the discourse of truth), of writing a purely "antiapocalyptic" discourse. According to Christopher Norris, "Of an Apocalyptic Tone Recently Adopted in Philosophy" continues a discourse of ends begun in "The Ends of Man" and "Cogito and the History of Madness," essays that "show that what is in question is *not* some ultimate, decisive leap beyond humanism, 'Western metaphysics' or the principle of reason. In fact they insist that no such leap is possible, that even the most seemingly radical statements of intent—like Foucault's desire to speak the very language of madness—must always at some point rejoin the tradition whose embrace they so fiercely reject" (239).[9] Derrida ends his essay by placing himself both inside and outside this discourse of the end at one and the same time. He wishes to put an end to the discourse of the end, yet he must simultaneously question whether this gesture can truly escape the eschatological program of apocalypse, "a powerful program that was also an untransgressible contract among discourses of the end" ("Apocalyptic" 80). The characteristically complex, punning prose in which the essay unfolds and which is announced in the untranslatable double "D'" of its original French title (*parler* "D'un Ton Apocalyptique" is to speak both *of* and *with* such a tone)—this prose both stands outside and continues the discourse of the end and of truth. It ends apocalypse and, therefore, is apocalyptic. Even his own announcement of "an internal and external catastrophe of the apocalypse, an overturning of sense [*sens*] that does not merge with the catastrophe announced or described in the apocalyptic writings without however being foreign to them" (95)—even this generalized apocalypse as absolute outside of the genre of apocalypse and its philosophical *Aufklärung* becomes one more party to that untransgressible contract: "But then what is someone doing who tells you: I tell you this, I have come to tell you this, there is not, there never has been, there never will be an apocalypse, the apocalypse deceives, disappoints? There is the apocalypse *without* apocalypse" (94–95).

When Stevens comes to apocalypse, it is to apocalypse as that onto-eschato-teleological fold within the generalized apocalypse described above—though of course Stevens himself employs no such terminology. But Stevens's desire to turn away from that "fundamental scene," to come to the end of the end, to imagine an end that comes without revelation, without teleology, without fulfilment, without final meaning, clearly raises similar questions about the possibility of escaping the discourse of the end. In his chapter on modern apocalypse (*Sense* 93–124), Frank Kermode claims that the modern sense of the present moment as crisis stems from the shift from imminence to immanence in apocalyptic thinking, and he associates current understandings of apocalypse with the idea of "a break with the past" (114). The apocalyptic crisis of "the new modernism" (114)—presumably what we now call postmodernism—resides in the very absence of apocalyptic beliefs, in its own break with the past and the discourse of the end, as Kermode claims in the following comment on Beckett: "It is a world crying out for forms and stations, and for apocalypse; all it gets is vain temporality, mad, multiform antithetical influx" (115). For Kermode, the very absence of apocalypse, the break with the fiction of the end, leads to or *is* this new apocalypse.

Again, Fowler provides a more specifically literary model for dealing with the problematical relationship between apocalyptic and antiapocalyptic modes in his treatment of the relationships between genres and antigenres: "We may think of certain new genres or 'antigenres' as antitheses to existing genres. Their repertoires are in contrast throughout. In smaller genres, this contrast may take the form of rhetorical inversion, whereby dispraise is modeled on inverted praise, malediction on valediction, and so forth" (175). Fowler's reference to rhetorical inversion will prove helpful, since Stevens sometimes employs such techniques ("There will never be an end / To this droning of the surf" [*CP* 23]) to take up an antiapocalyptic stance. But of greater interest is Fowler's sense of the complexities involved in the relations between the members of such oppositional pairs. In this vein, he writes of "the ambivalent bond of antigenres" (251), and notes, for example, that "the antinovel continually depends on evocations of the novelistic forms it avoids, so that if the novel were to become obsolete, so would it" (252). Obviously, Fowler is not practicing deconstruction, but the notion set forth in these last statements— namely, that a deliberate resistance to a particular genre would still rely on the characteristics of the resisted genre—provides a specifically literary analogue to some of the issues touched upon in Derrida's writings on apocalypse. The antinovel does not put an end to the genre of novel, but rather continues its development and expands its possibilities. Will an antiapocalyptic mode always continue and expand an apocalyptic one?

Answers to this question might finally be differentiated by their treatment of a crucial but perhaps undecidable issue, an issue crucial to apocalypse proper: desire. To what extent are these doubled relationships to the apocalyptic past marked by a desire to remain *within* an apocalyptic teleology of meaning, always with an eye on a certain discursive power? Derrida makes one function of this desire abundantly clear in "Of an Apocalyptic Tone":

> We cannot and we must not—this is a law and a destiny—forgo the *Aufklärung*. In other words, we cannot and we must not forgo what compels recognition as the enigmatic desire for vigilance, for the lucid vigil [*veille*], for clarification, for critique and truth, but for a truth that at the same time keeps within itself enough apocalyptic desire, this time as desire for clarity and revelation, to demystify, or if you prefer, to deconstruct the apocalyptic discourse itself and with it everything that speculates on vision, the imminence of the end, theophany, the parousia, the Last Judgment, and so on. (82)

There is a world of difference—or *différance*—between Derrida and Stevens, and I have no intention of eliding the gaps between the respective historical periods and textual genres to which these two writers belong, no matter how strongly Derrida himself might compel us to question the boundaries of genre. Nor do I wish to suggest that the retention of an "apocalyptic desire" in Stevens's most anti-apocalyptic moments has quite the same function within a deliberate strategy of demystification as it does for Derrida. I simply wish, at this point, to keep in mind a vestigial "apocalyptic desire" while holding open the difference between two formulations of such doubled textual relationships with the past: Eleanor Cook's statement that Stevens "decreates" his sources and then moves "beyond, in order to retrieve what, after much testing, will hold" ("King James" 241), and Linda Hutcheon's more general account of a postmodern form of parody—parody not as "ridiculing imitation" but as "repetition with critical distance that allows ironic signalling of difference at the very heart of similarity" (*Poetics* 26), parody as a range of textual practices that "at once use and abuse, install and then destabilize convention" (23). What needs to be heard here is the difference in purpose and temporal sequence. For Cook, Stevens's purpose lies in "finding what will hold," and he progresses from an emptying of the past to a replenishing of the space left by that initial act, even if it be filled by something "different in kind, not just in degree, from what has preceded it" ("King James" 241). For Hutcheon, postmodern parody works with the opposite emphasis and sequence, using in order to abuse, installing "and then" destabilizing—a doubled and paradoxical method that is itself destabilizing. Should Stevens be read as Cook suggests, or should we read his doubled relationship to the past as Hutcheon reads postmodern parody? Might there be other configurations, in which neither force gains precedence, or in which the balance remains undecidable? Stevens's engagement with apocalypse, I hope to show, facilitates a particularly rich exploration of these questions.

chapter two

An Ever-Enlarging Incoherence

War, Modernisms, and Masculinities

Stevens's responses to the war in his poetry, essays, and letters bear witness to a remarkable complex of anxieties: anxieties about the near-apocalyptic scale of physical destruction; anxieties about the concomitant emergence of a new cultural and imaginative dispensation, one that threatened Stevens's strongest beliefs about the imagination and its works; and, finally, anxieties about the possibility of constructing or reconstructing a masculine subject-position that would facilitate a certain poetic resistance to both of these disruptions. The need for such resistance is made clear in the following three samples from Stevens's letters; they give a sense of just how the war sometimes impinged upon the inner space the poet attempted to reserve for his creative activity.

> I make no reference in this letter to the war. It goes without saying that our minds are full of it. (*LWS* 356, May 24, 1940)

> I am afraid that what is going on now may be nothing to what will be going on three or four months from now, and that the situation that will then exist may even involve us all, at least in the sense of occupying our thoughts and feelings to the exclusion of anything except the actual and the necessary. (*LWS* 365, August 23, 1940)

> At the moment, the war is shifting from Europe to Asia, and why one should be writing about poetry at all is hard to understand. (*LWS* 501, May 16, 1945)

This configuration of creative and political anxieties appears with particular force and clarity in the 1942 essay "The Noble Rider and the Sound of Words," in which Stevens uses an apocalyptic rhetoric to describe not just the physical violence and sociopolitical disorder of the war years, but also the profound anomie and upheaval being experienced in the imaginative and cultural realms. More particularly, the essay's apocalyptic rhetoric—and especially the way Stevens applies it to the cultural realm—often sounds like a ghostly pre-echo of the language of postmodernism that was to emerge after the war in the writings of practitioners of this discourse and of more "detached" observers. As I indicated in my introduction, my purpose here is not to claim that Stevens's writing is in any sense postmodern or even that it offers premonitions of the postmodern that render it unique among the aesthetic products of that time. I hope to demonstrate instead that Stevens's simultaneous use of and resistance to an apocalyptic rhetoric functions, at the same time, as a resistance to this emergent cultural dispensation, a dispensation which Stevens can register only as a threat to his most cherished poetic values. Stevens's resistance to apocalypse, in other words, also figures a profound discomfort with the disintegration and delegitimation of modernism and modernist aesthetics.

Stevens's response to this situation is irreducibly gendered: his twofold resistance to the "more or less universal disaster" (*LWS* 353) involves a search for a masculine subject-position that might offer a locus of stability in the midst of such political and cultural upheaval. This search provides Stevens with the starting point for his essay: a historical survey of different equestrian heroes as figures of "nobility." I will defer a discussion of Stevens's survey to the end of this chapter, since its status as a strategy of resistance demands a prior articulation of the object or force that it resists. Here I wish only to note the specific complications I will introduce in relation to previous work on gender and masculinity in Stevens, most particularly that of James Longenbach and, more recently, Lee M. Jenkins. Two chapters ("It Must Be Masculine," 222–36, and "The Heart of the Debacle," 237–48) of Longenbach's excellent study focus on this issue, and investigate both Stevens's development of a "masculine" aesthetic during the war years, and his fascination with the figure of the hero as a poetic subject. Longenbach's account, for all its historical particularity in detailing the construction of military heroism as the hegemonic form of wartime masculinity, nevertheless places Stevens's concerns about gender within a polar opposition between a monolithic masculinity and monolithic femininity, so that, for example, when "Stevens's idea of masculinity tends to unravel," it does so by "reincorporating the idea of femininity he has rejected" (230).

Rather than following Longenbach's suggestion that for Stevens "the hero must be masculine" (232), I will suggest that Stevens explores and questions the notion that "the masculine" must be "heroic" and can be nothing else. Stevens's poetry presents many ways of being masculine, and there is often considerable tension among the different versions of masculinity that emerge in his texts. It is a question, in other words, of "masculinities" rather than of a monolithic "masculinity." This approach to gender is not without its own limitations, of course. The current tendency to pluralize concepts like "masculinity" or "feminism" is part of a project to question, undermine, and dismantle the apparent solidity of the hegemonic discourses and social structures implicated in those concepts. Yet such pluralization cannot quite eliminate the implied existence of an underlying "unity" that connects the multiple and often contradictory "masculinities," "feminisms," and so on. And it is not within the scope of this study, in fact, to dismantle the concept of gender itself and undermine the role it plays in our cultures. I am not interested in using Stevens's texts to produce a sociocultural critique, but rather in finding out whether the exploration of "masculinities" can help to get a grip on some aspects of Stevens's poetry. But before investigating how Stevens's different figurations of masculinity function as sites of resistance to apocalyptic fears, it is necessary to establish the relationship between Stevens's antiapocalyptic stance and his resistance to the radical cultural upheaval—the first harbingers of the death of modernism—he began to feel with the onset of the war.

The intensity of Stevens's resistance to a "new world" first emerges in "the idiom of apocalypse" (Jenkins 68) that Stevens sometimes adopts in his essay—as when, to borrow Jenkins's example, Stevens proclaims that "only the prophecies are true. The present is an opportunity to repent" (*NA* 21). In this passage, Stevens appears to adopt an almost wholly conventional apocalyptic stance—the stance of the Christian apocalyptists, including Jesus ("The time is fulfilled, and the kingdom of God is at hand" [Mark 1:15], "Behold, now is the accepted time; behold, now *is* the day of salvation" [2 Cor. 6:2]). Stevens does not simply assume the mantle of prophet but, more specifically, that of a latecomer prophet who now reflects on a whole history of prophecies and proclaims that the present moment is the unique moment of fulfillment, the arrival, at last, of a long-deferred truth. To insist on the necessity of repentance is to situate this negative moment of crisis in relationship to a possibility of future redemption, whether within or outside of history; it is to inscribe the act of repentance within a teleology of hope. Yet it seems necessary to ask whether there might be a note of irony here; the context of this passage suggests that Stevens is not so much making his own pronouncement on the situation as offering a summary of other voices speaking around him. Certainly, the fact that even secularized versions of repentance are far from Stevens's usual stance should arouse suspicions. Such irony clearly marks the speaker's distance from the rhetoric being used, though the ironic doubleness is of a fairly straightforward kind: there is little affective attachment to this rhetoric and there is little if anything in it that remains untouched by the ironic context.

A very different apocalyptic strain emerges at several other points in the essay, a strain that helps define Stevens's emergent sense of the social and cultural implications of the war *and* his resistance to those implications. In such apocalyptic passages, Stevens positions himself as witness to the inception of "a new world" (*NA* 20) and describes "the end of one era in the history of the imagination and . . . the beginning of another" (*NA* 22):

> The spirit of negation has been so active, so confident and so intolerant that the commonplaces about the romantic provoke us to wonder if our salvation, if the way out, is not the romantic. All the great things have been denied and we live in an intricacy of new and local mythologies, political, economic, poetic, which are asserted with an ever-enlarging incoherence. This is accompanied by an absence of any authority except force, operative or imminent. (*NA* 17)

> For more than ten years now, there has been an extraordinary pressure of news—let us say, news incomparably more pretentious than any description of it, news, at first, of the collapse of our system, or, call it, of life; then of news of a new world, but of a new world so uncertain that one did not know anything whatever of its nature, and does not know now, and could not tell whether it was to be all-English, all-German, all-Russian, all-Japanese, or all-American, and cannot tell now; and finally news of a war, which was a renewal of what, if it was not the greatest war, became such by this continuation. (*NA* 20)

Here, Stevens identifies that "radical break" so characteristic of eschatological writings as an event that has already occurred or is presently occurring, and identifies it specifically as a radical break with(in) aesthetic and cultural history, a radical reorganization of thought and perception like the one Abrams refers to as the "apocalypse of imagination" ("English" 53).

What emerges here is a far more complex stance toward apocalyptic rhetoric than the one marked in Stevens's call to repentance, a stance more ambivalent, too, than most of Stevens's critics have allowed. Stevens announces the end; but it is an end that has none of the closural and consolatory force of traditional versions of the end. Here, Stevens is no prophet, or at least no conventional apocalyptic prophet: there is no call to "Rejoice," no sense of the power of the eschatological position to rewrite history or project a release from moral chaos and physical suffering, no marks of a desire for the end. The passages stand in stark contrast to other moments of prophecy in Stevens, such as the prediction that "The sky will be much friendlier then than now" (*CP* 68), or the celebrated disappearance of the gods in "Two or Three Ideas" (1951)—a text that, for Longenbach, reveals "an apocalyptic urge" in Stevens's work "inasmuch as Stevens is interested in change" (88). But the changes described in "The Noble Rider" cannot be absorbed into a thematics of the desire for change: in the essay Stevens resists change, and the differences between the essay and the earlier poem are primarily the differences between a force that founds Stevens's poetry and one that threatens to end it— namely World War II and the cultural upheaval that resulted from it.

The apocalyptic modulations of "The Noble Rider," then, refuse one aspect of apocalypse's power. Stevens's pronouncements usher in an age when, lost "in an intricacy of new and local mythologies," we can no longer invest belief in any grand historical narrative. There may be powerful emotional reasons to resist apocalyptic interpretations of the war, and yet the person who rejects the consolatory and order-giving aspects of apocalyptic discourse might at the very least feel some ambivalence about the losses incurred upon entering the era *after* the era of the end. This loss certainly has consequences for a writer in search of an "idea of order." If, as Kermode and Robinson suggest, belief in "the End" makes aesthetic unity and closure possible—apocalypse "ends, transforms, and is concordant" (*Sense* 5)[1]— then the era *after* the end might well be one that no longer invests

belief in unity and closure; it would be an era of radical provisionality and relativism, "a period of perpetual transition" (*Sense* 28), to
borrow Kermode's phrase. A text that confronts such a situation might
well bear the marks of both desire and fear; the possible break with
the past promises a heightened freedom, but does so at the cost of a
certain kind of discursive power and poetic authority. Lee M. Jenkins illustrates just such a doubleness in Stevens's writings, but, oddly
enough, reduces it in the very act of describing it: "Stevens may have
been attracted, intellectually, to relativism and to the provisional, but
temperamentally he was drawn to unity, to closure, to the sealed world
of the poem where the poet himself calls all the shots" (54). Jenkins
relegates Stevens's provisionality and relativism to an "intellectual"
level, thereby reserving for the more conservative aspects of Stevens's
oeuvre the presumably deeper or more affective level of "temperament." The intellectual interest in "relativism" and "the provisional"
is thus subsumed within a teleology of Stevens's career in which the
conservative elements will have the last word. John Lynen makes a
similar distinction in *The Design of the Present*. Lynen, describing the
relationship between time and eternity in Stevens's poetry, writes that
"[Stevens's] primary assumptions make incarnation [of the Eternal]
both *emotionally* necessary and *logically* absurd" (15, my emphasis).[2]
It is puzzling that a radically skeptical critic like Jenkins should adopt
a classical opposition between emotion and intellect, an opposition
relied on by so conservative a critic as Lynen; this opposition could
not survive any strict poststructuralist analysis. Even if one were to
bracket out poststructuralism, one would still need to ask whether
each of these two opposing elements in Stevens's texts might belong
equally to the intellectual and affective realms (and any other "realms"
our minds may contain). A desire for complete relativism and openness *and* a desire to resist such values operate with equal force in
Stevens's oeuvre, and an exploration of this tension reveals his relationship to a particularly complex moment in literary history.

The significance of that moment emerges in Stevens's account of
the contemporaneous political turmoil and its cultural effects, an
account that might well pass for a summary of "la condition postmoderne."[3] In using this phrase, I do not want to suggest that Stevens's
language refers to precisely the same phenomenon as Lyotard's discussion of the *de*legitimation of the "grand narratives of legitimation—
the life of the spirit and/or the emancipation of humanity" (Lyotard

51); *The Postmodern Condition* is, after all, primarily concerned with the state of scientific knowledge, and Stevens's references to the "great things" and the "local mythologies" that replace them have none of the specificity of Lyotard's two "grand narratives" and "little narrative [*petit récit*]" (60). Nevertheless, when Stevens announces "the collapse of our system" and its replacement by an "intricacy of new and local mythologies, political, economic, poetic," an "ever-enlarging incoherence," "a new world so uncertain that one did not know anything whatever of its nature, and does not know now," he describes an experience of anomie and radically decentered relativism that Lyotard's much later account resembles in its general outline: "We may form a pessimistic impression of this splintering: nobody speaks all of those languages, they have no universal metalanguage, the project of the system-subject is a failure, the goal of emancipation has nothing to do with science, we are all stuck in the positivism of this or that discipline of learning, the learned scholars have turned into scientists, the diminished tasks of research have become compartmentalized and no one can master them all" (41). Lyotard's language is not apocalyptic here, but it nevertheless describes the same cultural and historical situation that others have described in specifically apocalyptic terms. Fredric Jameson, for example, refers to postmodernism as an "inverted millenarianism" (*Postmodernism* 1) that posits a break between present and past, and, adopting a rather Foucauldian rhetoric, writes that "the case for [postmodernism's] existence depends on the hypothesis of some radical break or *coupure*, generally traced back to the end of the 1950s or the early 1960s" (1). And as was discussed in my first chapter, Frank Kermode, while feeling his way uncertainly toward an understanding of "the new modernism," associates contemporaneous understandings of apocalypse with the idea of "a break with the past" (*Sense* 114), and perceives his own era's lack of apocalyptic beliefs as a new kind of apocalypse—one that ushers in "a period of perpetual transition" and a literature of "vain temporality, mad, multiform antithetical influx" (115). Such applications of apocalyptic rhetoric to what we call postmodernism also shape Derrida's "Of an Apocalyptic Tone Recently Adopted in Philosophy," which identifies contemporary philosophical discourse as a discourse of ends, of "the end of the subject, the end of man, the end of the West, the end of Oedipus, the end of the earth, *Apocalypse now*, I tell you" ("Apocalyptic" 80). Clearly, Derrida has in mind such instances as the celebrated conclusion of Foucault's *The Order of Things*, though one would, of course, have to include Derrida's "own" "voice" (or "voices") in this apocalyptic "concert" ("Apocalyptic" 81)—not only the voice that one "hears" in the ironically self-deconstructing "apocalypse *without* apocalypse" ("Apocalyptic" 95) announced in "Of an Apocalyptic Tone," but also the one that offers a "slightly embarrassing messianic promise" (Spivak lxxxi) in the first part of *Of Grammatology*: "The future can only be anticipated in the form of an absolute danger. It is that which breaks absolutely with constituted normality and can only be proclaimed, *presented*, as a sort of monstrosity. For that future world and for that within it which will have put into question the values of sign, word, and writing, for that which guides our future anterior, there is as yet no exergue" (5).

What is finally at stake in relation to Stevens, however, is not simply the fact that it has proved possible to conceive of the shift—or break, or rupture—between modernism and postmodernism in apocalyptic terms, or, more generally, that the change from one dominant or hegemonic episteme (to borrow Foucault's term) can be articulated by means of an apocalyptic rhetoric; what matters, above all, is the stance these writers take toward their own involvement in this rhetoric and the extent to which this stance registers resistance to or participation in the apocalyptic celebration. There is a world of difference, or of *différance*, between Stevens, on the one hand, and Lyotard and Derrida on the other. Lyotard in particular does not lament his situation, and finally insists that we "wage a war on totality," "be witnesses to the unpresentable," and "activate the differences and save the honor of the name" (82). This more celebratory stance is found in Derrida's writing, too; his own work comes after the point at which "the joyous wandering of the *graphein* . . . became a wandering without return" ("Ellipsis" 294), and it is from within this wandering that he asks, "Can one not affirm the nonreferral to the center, rather than bemoan the absence of the center? Why would one mourn for the center?" (297). A "refusal to mourn" distinguishes postmodernist from modernist aesthetics for Lyotard; in his formulation, "modern aesthetics is an aesthetic of the sublime, though a nostalgic one," whereas postmodernism denies "the consensus of a taste which would make it possible to share collectively the nostalgia for the unattainable" (81). Lyotard sees the desire for coherence as the problem, since it always threatens to lead to totalitarian terror; Stevens, though opposed to political totalitarianisms, nevertheless laments the loss of coherence. Of course, Stevens is responding first and foremost to a world situation of unprecedented horror, a world "physically violent for millions of our friends and for still more millions of our enemies and spiritually violent, it may be said, for everyone alive" (*NA* 26–27). Few could have welcomed such violence, or, for that matter, gladly embraced the social and aesthetic changes that were inextricably linked to that violence. But Lyotard also writes with World War II, the Holocaust, and Stalinist terror as his historical reference points, and his different stance toward the desire for coherence and order indicates a profound political and cultural shift. Stevens's language in the essay often expresses his immense discomfort with the cultural and aesthetic implications of this "new world," thereby clarifying the emotional and imaginative cost of positioning himself *after* the era of the end, the era after the disappearance of the gods, at a time when one might need the consolations such beliefs could offer. If Stevens writes here *about* a condition that sounds like "la condition postmoderne," he does so with what Jameson calls "a properly modernist nostalgia" (*Postmodernism* 19), a nostalgia that remains modernist, as I shall suggest shortly, in its desire not just to recuperate one particular aesthetic or cultural moment but to contact a transhistorical imaginative force that makes any authentic style possible.[4]

Stevens's essay testifies to a more ambivalent attitude toward apocalyptic rhetoric than has been outlined above. Stevens follows his call to repentance ("Only the prophecies are true"), for example, with a phrase—"This is familiar enough" (*NA* 21)—that transforms the preceding words into a half-ironic summary of *other* peoples' responses to the war, or of a whole history of such prophetic calls. And when Stevens positions himself as witness to the emergence of "a new world" (*NA* 20), he claims, just two pages later, to have seen only "the end of one era in the history of the *imagination* and . . . the beginning of another" (*NA* 22, my emphasis) and then undermines the apocalyptic force of both statements with a further addendum: "It is one of the peculiarities of the imagination that it is always at the end of an era" (*NA* 22). Such shifts signify, perhaps, Stevens's simultaneous attraction to and suspicion of the power of apocalyptic rhetoric, though the latter stance does not result from his fears of a "bitter end" without any new world to follow, but rather, as was suggested, from the nature of that "new world" he confronts. Again, such a response is not surprising in relation to the world situation of the late 1930s and early 1940s, but Stevens's resistance to the cultural and aesthetic implications of this situation should make us hesitate before classifying him as a postmodernist avant la lettre.

A similar hesitancy is necessitated by the differences between the formal strategies characteristic of postmodern literature and Stevens's attitude toward formal conventions in poetry and toward formalism itself as an aesthetic theory and practice. Here, I wish to return to Kermode's discussion of "the new modernism" (*Sense* 114), which corresponds to what some critics have called an early version of post-modernism. Kermode is useful in this regard not because he analyzes the emergence of postmodernism with particular clarity, but because he highlights the relationship between a resistance to one kind of apocalyptic rhetoric and a resistance to a major cultural and aesthetic shift; above all, he pays attention to how this shift is marked in the *formal* aspects of literature. The French New Novel, for example, reveals that "there is an irreducible minimum of geometry . . . which finally limits our ability to accept the mimesis of pure contingency" (*Sense* 132). The works that are the objects of Kermode's critique of "the new modernism" demonstrate, for Kermode at least, an inability to invest belief in the narrative forms that allow literature to create order out of the disorder of temporal "experience," and, more particularly, demonstrate this inability through an absolute rejection or avoidance of *any* conventional literary forms and procedures—the kind of negation that Derrida finds in "that which breaks absolutely with constituted normality" and that Paul Ricoeur, in *Time and Narrative*, considers an impossibility: "I hold that the search for concordance is part of the unavoidable assumptions of discourse and of communication. Either discourse or violence, Eric Weil has said in his *Logique de la Philosophie*. The universal pragmatics of discourse says what amounts to the same thing. Intelligibility always precedes itself and justifies itself" (2:28). In this respect, Kermode's understanding of the "new modernism" sounds similar to Lyotard's description of postmodern aesthetics: "A postmodern artist or writer is in the position of a philosopher: the text he writes, the work he produces are not in principle governed by preestablished rules, and they cannot be judged according to a determining judgment, by applying familiar categories to the text or to the work. Those rules and categories are what the work of art itself is looking for. The artist and the writer, then, are working without rules in order to formulate the rules of what *will have been done*" (81). In modernism, "the form, because of its recognizable consistency, continues to offer to the reader or viewer matter for solace and pleasure" (81)—the latter effect being one of the three "musts" of Stevens's "supreme fiction"; postmodernism, on the other hand, "denies itself the solace of good forms" (81). And in a more recent work (1993), Marjorie Perloff describes an early, "utopian phase of postmodernism" in similar terms; this discourse "was presented as being open, antielitist, antiauthoritarian, participatory, anarchic, playful, improvisational, rebellious, discontinuous" (*Poetry* 7). As noted, Lyotard's dominant context and concern is the more general situation of postenlightenment scientific knowledge, but his own decision to embrace the aesthetics described above appears motivated by the experience of World War II, the Holocaust, and Stalinist terror. His call to "activate the differences" (82) comes in opposition to the "high enough price [paid] for the nostalgia of the whole and the one" (81) and to "the desire for a return of terror" (82). If an instigating historical event in this aesthetic shift is World War II, then Kermode and Lyotard appear concerned with how this event has been inscribed not just in the content of our discourse but in the *forms* of that discourse, and with the extent to which it has shaken our belief in those forms. The two writers, of course, adopt radically different stances toward this loss of belief, but their analyses still lead to the same question about Stevens: to what extent is his resistance to apocalyptic interpretations of World War II *also* a resistance to a possible radical break with literary history, with his own "genealogical" relationship to "the indispensable and relevant past" (Kermode, *Sense* 123)? What would such resistance tell us about Stevens's place in literary history? An answer might begin with the observation that the process Lyotard describes sounds similar to the one *portrayed* in Stevens's "Of Modern Poetry," but not to the process *of* that poem, which Stevens develops carefully around an extended theatrical metaphor—a thoroughly conventional trope.

But an answer more relevant to the immediate context would begin by suggesting "The Noble Rider and the Sound of Words" shows a poet at least as concerned with the war's impact on the aesthetic and imaginative domains as with its consequences in physical, world historical, and political terms; and such an answer would continue by suggesting that the essay shows a poet who seeks a theoretical basis for his own need to preserve some "irreducible minimum of geometry" without, however, locking himself into a rigid repetition of existing poetic modes. When Stevens, apparently classing himself as "one [who] believes that [what is happening to the imagination] is what matters most" (*NA* 20), quotes Benedetto Croce's definition of poetry as "the triumph of contemplation" (*NA* 16),[5] and goes on to describe the present in terms of "the pressure of an external event or events on the consciousness to the exclusion of any power of contemplation" (*NA* 20) and as "a set of events . . . beyond our power to tranquillize them in the mind, beyond our power to reduce them and metamorphose them" (*NA* 22), he does so in order to ask whether the war can be inscribed in poetry without making some radical break with the aesthetic principles of lyric poetry or even of literature in general, or indeed whether the war will not write off poetry altogether. Here, Stevens's query as to "why one should be writing about poetry at all" might refer to more than the brief discussion of poetics that precede it in the 1945 letter quoted at the beginning of this chapter, especially since for Stevens "writing about poetry" often meant "writing poetry." Stevens does not argue for the viability of specific literary forms, however, but instead addresses the vitality of the imaginative powers that bring poetic form into being. His use of "metamorphose" is crucial in relation to Kermode's and Perloff's versions of the formal differences between modernism and postmodernism (or "the new modernism" in Kermode's case). This word tropes poetry as a change of form, not an abandonment of form in the name of the "anarchic"; poetry becomes creation of an aesthetic form out of the matter of "reality" by means of the poet's powers of "abstraction." And Stevens's use of the words "tranquillize" and "contemplation" may have a double function in relation to these anxieties: they describe the imaginative powers Stevens wishes to protect and, by echoing Wordsworth's preface to the 1812 edition of *Lyrical Ballads*, they provide verbal and thematic continuity with the poetic tradition that seems threatened by the war. Such a gesture proves especially telling in light of Stevens's emphasis on the difference between his and Wordsworth's historical circumstances: in the face of historical discontinuity, he seeks continuity with a previous discourse of the imagination.[6] But the relationship proves still more complex and fraught with anxiety, since Stevens's essay actually *reverses* the roles of emotion and tranquil contemplation as they appear in Wordsworth. Stevens seeks to tranquillize violent events and emotions through contemplation; but for Wordsworth, poetry "takes its origin from emotion recollected in tranquillity: the emotion is contemplated till, by a species of re-action, the tranquillity gradually disappears, and an emotion, kindred to that which was before the subject of contemplation, is gradually produced, and does itself actually exist in the mind (*Selected* 460).

Stevens's far more defensive stance is a measure both of the pressure of "events that stir the emotions to violence" and of his own need to protect himself and his poetics from external disruption. Even when Stevens tropes the imagination as "a violence from within that protects us from a violence without" (*NA* 36), he does so to suggest how we might preserve such "good forms" as are involved in "the concepts and sanctions that are the order of our lives" (*NA* 22).

In fact, that "within/without" figuration itself is crucial to Stevens's desire to preserve the "concepts and sanctions that are the order of our lives," since it is in terms of this basic opposition and, above all, in terms of the mode of creative selfhood that it sustains and validates that Stevens makes his case for any continued capacity to create and preserve aesthetic forms. For Lee M. Jenkins, Stevens's allegiance to modernist formalism emerges when his tentativeness, his "provisional vocabulary . . . is countered by his 'supreme fiction,' his desire for a heroic, unified and self-enclosed poetic 'world'" (54), or when, in "The Noble Rider," "instead of trying . . . to 'engage' or deal creatively with 'pressure' he simply resists it, cancels it" (69), thereby attempting to do "two things at once—to engage the present *and* withdraw from it" (71).[7] Stevens, in fact, does not require that the poet "withdraw *from*" reality (my emphasis), but that he "withdraw *with* him into his abstraction the reality on which the lovers of truth insist" (*NA* 23, my emphasis); withdrawal always assumes an initial *engagement* as its starting point and does not entirely negate that initial engagement. More significantly, the aesthetic and ideological tensions that Jenkins describes share a common foundation in Stevens's dedication to the concept of an autonomous self capable of *either* withdrawing "with" or engaging with reality, a self that understands itself as distinct and autonomous in relation to a reality defined as "external." In other words, Stevens's essential conservatism, or, at least, his essentially modernist and formalist intellectual profile, has more to do with the way both withdrawal and engagement are inscribed within a figuration that opposes self and world as inside and outside, a trope that cannot be sustained in a poststructuralist or postmodern context.

Here, Charles Altieri's discussion of lyric poetry's capacity to salvage a version of subjectivity and agency from postmodernism's endless ironies—or rather *within* those ironies—helps clarify the role of this inside/outside distinction in relation to Stevens's strategy of resistance, as does Altieri's distinction between a distinctively postmodern "aspectual self" and the modernist concept of a still autonomous selfhood. For Altieri, this "aspectual self" constitutes itself as an "I" that "is inseparable from the 'as,' inseparable from the rush of metaphor that follows upon the need to take account of the specific intentional position that the agent occupies": "The metaphoric 'as' sustains elaborate chains of identification that simultaneously compose and reveal the relational structures that are our primary signs of subjective interests. There is no possibility of hypothesizing any single relation as fundamental or any one metaphor as the substance term. We deal continually in aspects . . . there is no independent ground on which to prefer one or the other. Each has its function, and there are only functions" (*Postmodernisms* 78). Altieri does not merely offer a celebratory description of this postmodern mode of selfhood, but *proposes* that his readers adopt this postmodern reconceptualization of their own selfhood as the only viable alternative to the dead ends of both "Kantian ideals of self-possession and autonomy" (289) and a reductive postmodern version of subjectivity as "a fiction induced by social forces" (75). Especially pertinent to my purposes is the way Altieri contrasts this version of an aspectual self with a "modernist version of the aspectual, purified of all excrescences so that its fundamental structural principles will command attention" (80). The logic of this modernist self resembles Altieri's interpretation of what Stevens calls "abstraction," which, according to Altieri, "posits the possibility . . . of something deeply enough embedded in our lives and our metaphors to take form despite the demise of particular beliefs" ("Why" 89). Those possibilities of purification, of abstraction, of an "independent ground" of an "I" that is *separable* from particular contexts and engagements—those possibilities are inextricably linked to the capacity to mark off inside from outside that Stevens's essay takes as one of its basic assumptions. Stevens, at least at this point in his poetic career, understands the possible collapse of the inside/outside distinction as a catastrophe that happens *after the fact* to an opposition between self and world perceived as a given, whereas the postmodernist would view the opposition itself as "a fiction induced by social forces" (*Postmodernisms* 75), to borrow Altieri's phrase. This opposition thus performs a complex and paradoxical function in Stevens's essay: it is one of the fictions Stevens wishes to defend from "the pressure of reality" (*NA* 13); it actually *performs* that defensive function; and it paradoxically creates the necessity of such a defense. Such paradoxes remain internal to Stevens's figurations of withdrawal *and* of engagement.

In fact, the inside/outside figuration that seems so crucial to Stevens's defense of the imagination and the imagination's defense of itself proves difficult to sustain, as the following passage suggests: "Reality is life and life is society and the imagination and reality; that is to say, the imagination and society are inseparable" (*NA* 28). The main purpose of this sentence is to establish a basis for the social and political autonomy of the creative act; according to Stevens's logic, reality is equivalent to life but also merely a part of life and, therefore, part of itself; and, more significantly, the imagination exists both as a part of reality and as an independent adjunct to it—or, to put it differently, reality both does and does not include or contain the imagination. Does the mind's "violence from within" press back against a *containing* reality or a *contiguous* reality? Must it exert itself against both? The essay does not answer these questions; nor does it indicate whether these shifts in figuration are another of Stevens's deliberate paradoxes or mere symptoms of an unconscious anxiety over the validity of the boundaries implied by each of the two figurations. Yet although the figurations offer very different degrees of autonomy to the imagination, both assume the existence of a clear boundary between imagination and reality, a liminal surface at which the imagination feels the pressure of reality and presses back against it. As such, each figuration contradicts Stevens's usual epistemological skepticism over the possibility of distinguishing between imagination and reality. If reality is "a total double-thing" in which "We do not know what is real and what is not" (*CP* 472), it is difficult to understand how Stevens's metaphors of pressure and counterpressure, inside and outside, could be maintained. And, in fact, the two figurations presented in the essay cannot coexist: if one is true, the other must be false. The way Stevens thus simultaneously establishes and erases a boundary between reality and imagination suggests the extent to which the essay is driven by two competing needs. This contradiction may be shaped by a tension between Stevens's epistemology and his desire to maintain an essentialist foundation for both his understanding of the imagination's unique powers and the self's capacity to give meaning and order to experience on its own terms, both through writing and through action.

The preceding paragraphs give some sense of how "The Noble Rider" sets up points of resistance to any break with an "irreducible minimum of geometry" and with the version of creative selfhood required for such preservation of aesthetic forms. But it seems equally important to ask where Stevens belongs in relation to the all-leveling and bottomless irony described by Hutcheon, Jameson, and Altieri as one of the identifying markers of a uniquely postmodern textuality or consciousness. Linda Hutcheon's emphasis on this aspect of postmodernism actually undermines any definition of early postmodernism as an abandonment of all aesthetic forms or principles, as a "non mimetic, ultra-autonomous, anti-referential" discourse (*Poetics* 52)—such as occurs in Perloff's and Kermode's studies. For Hutcheon, postmodernism instead emerges with a specifically political and paradoxical version of irony and parody—a bottomless irony in which neither past nor present nor any imagined future offer an unquestioned ground for belief or ideological commitment; postmodernism is only that discourse which is "fundamentally critical in its ironic relation to the past and the *present*" (41), and "doubly parodic" (30) in the way "its art forms (and its theory) at once use and abuse, install and then destabilize convention in parodic ways" (23). In Frederic Jameson's more pessimistic formulation, the characteristic aesthetic method of postmodern texts is not parody, but "pastiche," which he describes as "parody . . . without a vocation" (17):

> But it is a neutral practice of such mimicry, without any of parody's ulterior motives, amputated of the satiric impulse, devoid of laughter and of any conviction that alongside the abnormal tongue you have momentarily borrowed, some healthy linguistic normality still exists. Pastiche is thus blank parody, a statue with blind eyeballs: it is to parody what that other interesting and historically original modern thing, the practice of a kind of blank irony, is to what Wayne Booth calls the 'stable ironies' of the eighteenth century. (17)

Jameson's and Hutcheon's emphases on parody and pastiche, despite the profound differences between the two writers, offer another way of figuring the break with(in) modernism—this time, not as the avoidance of all inherited literary forms but as the creation of multivalent parodies of previous forms in which *no* form or mode is left unironized, including this peculiarly postmodern version of parody itself. One might suggest that the "new modernism" and postmodernism described by Kermode, Lyotard, and Perloff, and the postmodernism described by Hutcheon, share an inability or refusal to invest belief in inherited literary forms and conventions, but articulate this stance by means of different formal procedures; Hutcheon, of course, would insist that only the "doubly parodic" mode constitutes a postmodern mode of textuality.

Here, Stevens's treatment of "nobility" in "The Noble Rider" reveals most clearly the difficulties involved in reading him as a postmodernist in these terms, or even as modernist unique for his anticipation of a postmodern poetics. The temptation to produce such a reading does not emerge from the essay's use of any formal procedures of parody or pastiche—despite the possibility of some faint irony in Stevens's call to repentance—but rather from the way Stevens emphasizes the impossibility, for himself and his contemporaneous audience, of investing belief in any of the four examples of nobility described in the essay, or, indeed, in *any* concrete historical version of "nobility": "There is no element more conspicuously absent from contemporary poetry than nobility. . . . The nobility of rhetoric is, of course, a lifeless nobility. Pareto's epigram that history is a cemetery of aristocracies easily becomes another: that poetry is a cemetery of nobilities. . . . It is hard to think of a thing more out of time than nobility. Looked at plainly it seems false and dead and ugly" (*NA* 35). Stevens's borrowed metaphor of poetry as "a cemetery of nobilities," though not an instance of parody or pastiche, nevertheless describes a historical situation in which parody and pastiche would become the only possible modes through which topoi of nobility could be included within a new literary work, especially since Stevens admits that "the disclosures of the impermanence of the past suggested, and suggest, an impermanence of the future" (*NA* 20–21). Even Stevens's own fictions must prove impermanent, but here Stevens does not celebrate, as he often does elsewhere, the fact that the waning of old fictions makes space for new fictions. Something greater than the disconfirmation of an individual fiction is at stake here, something greater, for Stevens, at least, than the affect or quality we would ordinarily understand "nobility" to involve; since Stevens insists that "the imagination gives to everything that it touches a peculiarity" and that "the peculiarity of the imagination is nobility" (*NA* 33), the vitality and viability of the imagination itself appear threatened by the current "episode . . . of our diffidence" toward nobility (*NA* 6). Thus, the poetry produced by such an age of "diffidence" would only offer a "critical or ironic re-reading of the art of the past" (Hutcheon, *Poetics* 23), and would prove incapable of producing any new version of nobility or of the kind of imaginative powers that make nobility possible. Any surviving imagination would be reduced to ironically surveying its own ironic position in relation to an already ironized past and present. To borrow the language of Jameson and Altieri, respectively, it would face "a field of stylistic and discursive heterogeneity without a norm" (*Postmodernism* 17), in which "there is no independent ground on which to prefer one of the other" (*Postmodernisms* 78).

Stevens's "cemetery of nobilities" may trope such a situation, but Stevens is not willing to rest there. Before and after his discussion of the "cemetery of nobilities," he insists on the viability of an

> inherent nobility [that] is the natural source of another, which our extremely headstrong generation regards as false and decadent. I mean that nobility which is our spiritual height and depth; and while I know how difficult it is to express it, nevertheless I am bound to give a sense of it. Nothing could be more evasive and inaccessible. Nothing distorts itself and seeks disguise more quickly. There is a shame of disclosing it and in its definite presentations a horror of it. . . . To fix it is to put an end to it. (*NA* 33–34)

> But as a wave is a force and not the water of which it is composed, which is never the same, so nobility is a force and not the manifestations of which it is composed, which are never the same. Possibly this description of it as a force will do more than anything else I can have said about it to reconcile you to it. (*NA* 35–36)

David R. Jarraway uses this passage to support his interpretation of Stevens as a postmodern or poststructuralist poet,[8] though this reading depends on the assumption that Stevens means by "force" the very thing that Derrida means by its French cognate in "Force et Signification"—a curious assumption, since the effects of *différance* should make any such identification questionable. More to the point, though, is the *function* of the "wave" simile, which is rhetorical and persuasive rather than descriptive or ontological. It serves as ancillary to Stevens's primary concern with "reconcil[ing]" (*NA* 36) his audience to the imagination's "nobility," helping to break down their culturally conditioned resistances to that affect—ironic defenses built up through successive revelations of the moral and intellectual emptiness of all previous "nobilities." Stevens, then, would like to occupy a non-ironic position *outside* this "new world" and its "intricacy of new and local mythologies, political, economic, poetic," its "ever-enlarging incoherence," and he would argue from that position for a transhistorical "nobility" impervious to any ironizing. Stevens's elaborate elusiveness thus defends "nobility" *against* the inevitable effects of time and change, against any "impermanence of the future." In this regard, the "wave" simile answers to Charles Altieri's understanding of the essentially modernist logic of Stevens's concern with "abstraction" and the construction of selfhood. It has more in common with, for example, Wyndham Lewis's rhetoric of energy, life, and vitality, his belief that the art of his time needed to remain in "direct contact with these intuitive waves of power" (40), "to get deeply enough immersed in material life to experience the shaping power amongst its vibrations" (40); it has more in common with Pound's concern at the same time (1915, in the essay "*Affirmations*: As for Imagisme") with the "energy [that] creates pattern" (374). If Stevens's movement away from the entanglements and distractions of "the noise of the world" and toward the security of a "fundamental structural principle"—the wave-force known through its disturbance of a body of water—is not enough to differentiate his textual world from that normless postmodern realm described by Jameson and others, then the fact that his final point of resistance to this "new world" replicates the discourse of early modernism might suffice to clinch this point. At any rate, the logic of the essay seems similar to that of the roughly contemporaneous poem "Gigantomachia," which posits heroism not in any heroic individual but in "the mass" (*CP* 289) that is both a synchronic and diachronic totality, "The life that never would end, no matter / Who died, the being that was an abstraction" (*CP* 289). And, finally, these passages are not undermined by any ironic or parodic contextualization, either serious or playful or both, and are themselves "voiced" in a *tone* that remains free of any sort of irony. Jenkins has complained that the "titular promise of a large and fluent disquisition in 'The Noble Rider' is countered by a language 'under blockage'" (67); but Stevens's final perorations on "nobility" are marked by an unswerving and even passionate sincerity and nobility, and nowhere does Stevens signal any ironic awareness that this discourse, too, will someday be interred in the "cemetery of nobilities." Indeed, the consistency of tone could be taken as proof of the continued vitality of nobility's wave-force. And even apart from the question of tone, the mere fact that Stevens nominates "nobility" as the imagination's defining feature should testify to his distance from postmodernism.

That elevated tone, in fact, is an appropriate one for Stevens to adopt when uttering this simile, since the wave also functions as a synecdoche for what Bloom identifies as the central topos of sublime self-recognition in American poetry—namely, the oceanic topos one encounters in Whitman, in Hart Crane, in some Williams (W. C.), and, of course, in Stevens. It is strikingly similar to the dominant trope of the transfiguration of "MacCullough" in the roughly contemporaneous *Notes* I, viii, a transformation sprung "from wave or phrase, // Or power of the wave, or deepened speech, / Or a leaner being, moving in on him" (*CP* 387). Stevens's recuperation of this trope as a means of persuading his audience of the nobility of the imagination and of the continued viability and validity of that nobility marks the ego's triumph over all the forces that have threatened it throughout the essay; considered in terms of the quasi-Kantian understanding of the sublime, it marks the imagination's recovery from a negative moment in which ungovernable external forces blocked its creative capacities. Even though Stevens himself does not exactly "s[i]ng beyond the genius of the sea" (*CP* 128) in this essay, and even though he does not openly proclaim that "the mighty imagination triumphs" over "a vacant sea declaiming with wide throat" (*CP* 456), he nevertheless demonstrates the imagination's capacity to internalize a trope of an uncontrollable external force and offer that trope as a figure of the imagination's *own* powers. There may be a certain doubleness to Stevens's gesture here, since while this act of interiorization figures the imagination's powers in terms derived from the external forces it seeks to defeat or annul, such interiorization itself provides one more instance of the imagination's superior force, or, at least, its capacity to believe in its own superior force.

This problem of the ceaseless historical disconfirmation of "nobilities" or, indeed, of fictions and tropes of any kind, appears repeatedly in Stevens's poetry of the 1930s and 1940s. One example occurs in the opening gesture and words of "Extracts from Addresses to the Academy of Fine Ideas":

A crinkled paper makes a brilliant sound.
The wrinkled roses tinkle, the paper ones,
And the ear is glass, in which the noises pelt,
The false roses (*CP* 252)

Yet as in "The Noble Rider," there is more at stake here than Stevens's habitual skepticism and imaginative restlessness. In writing, in 1940, that "Rain is an unbearable tyranny" and that "Sun is / A monster-maker, an eye, only an eye, / A shapener of shapes for only the eye" (*CP* 252–53), Stevens is either rewriting two of his favorite tropes of "reality" so that the reality they trope now includes the political situation of his own time (is such a sun a reminder of Japanese imperial emblems?), or he is presenting a speaker who cannot observe natural objects or processes without reading the political situation into them. In either interpretation, these tropes do not just tell us something about "reality," about the "blood-world" (*CP* 256) in which the "blood-rose," the "rainy rose" (*CP* 252) exist; they also demonstrate that the current state of reality—a state in which it is necessary to "[resist] each past apocalypse" (*CP* 257)—has robbed these tropes of any affirmative force they might have once had, or of any capacity to give comfort or pleasure. Stevens, I suspect, is concerned here with the way "total war" (*CP* 258) shakes the very foundations of aesthetics, but in conflating "false and true" he makes no "confident assertion[s]" against such a threat, as Longenbach suggests (*Plain* 218); rather, he tropes the ways fiction and reality are, in a time of war, alike delegitimized or invalidated as loci of positive values, of affirmation or satisfaction. The crisis in this instance does not result from the normal historical disconfirmation of old fictions, but from the impossibility of making aesthetic objects out of reality when reality presents the speaker with "ten thousand deaths" (*CP* 253). "False and true are one" because they now empty each other; neither provides access to a realm of satisfaction that Stevens presents through a highly idealized and conventional pastoral trope, the trope of a "summer warm enough to walk / Among the lascivious poisons, clean of them" (*CP* 252). The poem portrays, then, a consciousness unable to escape or evade the political realities of the time, unable to trope in a way that does not deprive both reality and poetry of comfort or consolation: reality has changed the tropes, and the changed tropes change reality.

The problem Stevens confronts in the poem's second canto, then, could be construed as analogous to the "cemetery of nobilities" in "The Noble Rider"—the problem of an infinite ironization of all possible aesthetic products or forms. The poem's crisis, in fact, has the structure of an ironic double bind: Stevens can neither complacently ignore the evidence presented by or to the eye in a time of war nor complacently aestheticize it or create easy fictions of consolation, as a "Secretary for Porcelain" (*CP* 253) might. And Stevens does not only locate the evil of this situation in the horror of "ten thousand deaths" (*CP* 253) and in aesthetic products that turn those deaths into a "catastrophe, / . . . neatly glazed." (Stevens surely wants us to hear this kind of evil infecting the "overturning" that moves tragic drama toward its conclusion, and infecting, too, the "well-tempered apricot" [*CP* 253] that pre-echoes evil's sneering "fugues" [*CP* 253] of laughter.) Stevens's description of "the laughter of evil" also identifies evil as a process of infinite ironization, an ironization that goes beyond "the spirit['s] laught[ter]" (*CP* 253) at the eye's complacent "communion" (*CP* 253); the laughter of evil convinces us that "The good is evil's last invention" and, therefore, renders us "Incapable of belief" (*CP* 258) in "the good," unable to compose "stanzas" (*CP* 258) or "chants of final peace" (*CP* 259). Evil's laughter seems related to the concerns that Stevens identified in a November 18, 1940, letter to Oscar Williams as "what this poem grows out of"—namely, "the Lightness with which ideas are asserted, held, abandoned, etc." (*LWS* 380). This "Lightness" sounds like a less threatening trope for the "ever-enlarging incoherence" of "The Noble Rider," but the poem implies more specifically that when we allow an ironic sensibility to disconfirm all possible values, when infinite irony leads us to lightly adopt and abandon ideas, we are to some extent complicit with the operations of evil. And the apparent predominance of evil in the world provides another motive for the poem's resistance to apocalyptic discourses; as was noted in my first chapter, apocalyptic desires often originate from a perception that the world is so dominated by moral evil that only divine intervention and a thorough (and destructive)

housecleaning can rectify the situation. Stevens's resistance to an apocalyptic reading of this situation involves a search for a value resistant
to the all-ironizing force of evil's laughter, the search for a capacity
to make an emotional investment in "a single thought" (*CP* 254), in
"chants of final peace"—to no longer be "Incapable of belief." In a
sense, then, the goal of the sequence is to triumph over irony, to
ironize infinite irony, to believe, as in canto ii's counter-catastrophic
overturning of evil's all-ironizing force, that "It is good death / That
puts an end to evil death and dies" (*CP* 253) and to find the "chants"
that might result from this ironization of evil's ironies. If the poem
"Resists each past apocalypse" (*CP* 257), it also seeks a position beyond
the incoherence of the present in its own rhetoric of finality and peace;
such a search for a position beyond irony seems, again, incompatible with the location of a postmodern irony in Stevens's work.

The poem's speaker needs, then, to move beyond the eye's naïveté
and complacent belief and to still the spirit's laughter at that naïveté
in order to create poetry, whose most durable form, at least in this
poem, has nothing to do with the eye and everything to do with the
living voice, with "preaching" (*CP* 254), with the "song / Of the assassin" (*CP* 256), with "The chants of final peace" (*CP* 259). He also
needs to abandon the impossible search for a "land beyond the mind"
(*CP* 252), though the poem's last two sections offer two different re-
placements for this idealized pastoral trope. If, in canto vii, "What /
One believes is what matters" (*CP* 258), and if what one believes is
"one's element" (*CP* 258), then Stevens's solution is one that straddles
or unites the inner and outer realms, one that involves not just the
purely inward capacity to believe but the investment of that belief in
an appropriate locus. Stevens's concern in canto vii is with the capacity to "[resist] each past apocalypse," and the source of that resistance
lies not just in what one "sees" in the present but in an always-present
inner ability to believe in "one's element" and in its capacity to provide "the deepest inhalation" (CP 258)—the sustenance of both life
and poetic voice. And yet canto viii offers a more inward solution; if,
in a time of war, all humanity comes to "live in a camp" (*CP* 258),
then the capacity for continued poetic creation can lie only in "the
heart's residuum" (*CP* 258), in the last traces of the will to believe that
have survived the militarization of "one's element." This movement
suggests that Stevens's final interest, as in the essay, is not in finding
one particular poetic formulation, one "right sound," but in finding

the force that makes any formulation possible, the muselike force of "music" that can produce "a single line" (*CP* 259).

Both "The Noble Rider" and "Extracts," then, show Stevens reading the war and the cultural upheaval that resulted from it in apocalyptic terms, and at the same time resisting the rhetoric of apocalypse. Above all, these works show Stevens taking up a somewhat protective or defensive stance against the possible "collapse of our system," seeking to establish points at which he can establish a valid and durable form of resistance to forces threatening to shatter or utterly disconfirm the aesthetic modes, ideals, and forms upon which his own work depends. The preceding analysis has demonstrated, I hope, that the essential conservatism—a term I do not use with any pejorative sense here—of Stevens's antiapocalyptic maneuvers makes it difficult to read his work, at least at this stage in his career, as being in any way postmodern. On the assumption that this point may be granted, the remainder of this chapter shall deal with the particularly gendered forms this resistance takes in "The Noble Rider," "The Figure of the Youth as Virile Poet," and "Repetitions of a Young Captain."

The wave simile discussed toward the end of the preceding section provides a link to the present section's concern with the configuration of gender in Stevens's essay, and not only because Stevens offers this simile after having abandoned the project of rescuing the male rider as a viable figure of the imagination's nobility. The wave appears at first to displace these obviously gendered figures with a gender-neutral concept of nobility and imagination, though one could argue that the understanding of waves that underwrites it has been produced by a scientific and hence masculine discourse. But such concerns are not the only ways in which gender haunts the wave simile. It is worth remembering Barbara Freeman's discussion of the distinctively masculine character of the Kantian sublime, so that the appearance of the wave simile marks the recovery of a specifically masculine ego while simultaneously masking that ego's concerns with the continued viability of a *masculine* creative capacity. Furthermore, Stevens's appropriation of the wave simile places him within a masculine literary tradition, and does so by interiorizing a force that is so often troped as feminine—whether as Whitman's "savage" (*Complete Poetry* 392) or "fierce old mother" (394), or, in Stevens's more comic phrasing, as "The Woman That Had More Babies Than That" (*OP* 104). Here again, Stevens's figuration betrays a certain doubleness: the nomination of the wave as a still valid figure of nobility may signal a masculine triumph-through-appropriation over the feminine other, yet this gesture still identifies the masculine creative capacity with the very element it defines as its opposite.

The preceding discussion repeats the terms I wish to move beyond in this chapter—namely, those that construct gender in Stevens as a monolithic binary of masculinity and femininity; Stevens's initial grave-robbing expedition through the "cemetery of nobilities" demands a more nuanced consideration of masculinity, since the essay's varying stances toward these figures are articulated not in terms of varying *degrees* of masculinity (and hence of possible effeminacy) but in terms of varying *types* of masculinity. Current theoretical discussions of "masculinities" suggest, at least, that one should not be surprised to discover different kinds of masculine identities in Stevens's poetry. Here, Judith Butler's *Gender Trouble* offers what may be the most radical theoretical basis for such accounts of masculinity, arguing, as it does, that gendered subjects find themselves confronting a "fluidity of identities" (176)—a fluidity and concomitant multiplicity made possible because the hegemonic discourses and practices that construct normative gender positions always inadvertently produce forms of subjectivity that are multiple, conflicting, and self-contradictory. In Butler's view, then, "The injunction *to be* a given gender produces necessary failures, a variety of incoherent configurations that in their multiplicity exceed and defy the injunction by which they are generated" (185). Butler's work, of course, is not concerned specifically with "masculinities," nor with such masculinities as might have been available in Stevens's time, but her application of a thoroughgoing and characteristically postmodern skepticism to the issue of gender has inevitable implications for any empirical or theoretical investigation of the construction of masculinity.[9] These implications are articulated with great clarity and concision in R. W. Connell's *Masculinities*:

> Yet [men's interest in maintaining power], formidable as it may be, is fissured by all the complexities in the social construction of masculinity mapped in this book. There are differences and tensions between hegemonic and complicit masculinities; oppositions between hegemonic masculinity and subordinated and marginalized

masculinities. Each of these configurations of practice is internally divided, not least by the layering of personality described by psychoanalysis, the contradictions in gender at the level of personality. Their realization in social life differs, as we have seen again and again, according to the interplay of gender with class relations, race relations and the forces of globalization. (242)

This tendency in recent theorizing suggests, then, a different set of questions that might be asked of Stevens's figures of "nobility," questions as to whether these figures might be marked by significant tensions or contradictions among different "masculinities," and whether these tensions and contradictions might, in turn, illuminate Stevens's poetic response to the crisis of the late 1930s and early 1940s.

What versions of masculinity are involved in Stevens's presentation of nobility? The two equestrian figures—Plato's and Verrocchio's—that Stevens unreservedly nominates as examples of nobility and hence, according to Stevens's definition, as instances of imaginative power, are both solitary heroes, apparently undistracted by any particular social constraints or sexual (at least, heterosexual) interests. Of these figures, Stevens sees only Verrocchio's as having any continuing relevance or validity, and it is significant that he presents this figure not only *as* the embodiment of military heroism, but *as though* it could be posited without any reference to a feminine "other":

> I have selected him because there, on the edge of the world in which we live today, he established a form of such nobility that it has never ceased to magnify us in our own eyes. It is like the form of an invincible man, who has come, slowly and boldly, through every warlike opposition of the past and who moves in our midst without dropping the bridle of the powerful horse from his hand, without taking off his helmet and without relaxing the attitude of a warrior of noble origin. What man on whose side the horseman fought could ever be anything but fearless, anything but indomitable? (*NA* 8)

Clearly, Stevens writes here with an eye on the war already raging in Europe and Asia and which the United States seemed ever more likely to enter; he seeks a definition of masculinity appropriate or sufficient to such a situation. Stevens admires the artifice of the sculptor *and* of the subject himself, who never relinquishes mastery over a "horse all will" (*CP* 249) or over his own "attitude" of heroic isolation and self-sufficiency. More significantly, Stevens constructs this self-sufficiency through the exclusion of any relation to "femininity": this emblem of heroic masculinity defines itself through its isolation and its potential relationship to other men and other forms of masculinity. Stevens's reference, for example, to the "attitude of a warrior of noble origin" reminds us not only that Colleoni was *literally* "noble"—that is, noble by virtue of his social class and family history—but that such constructions of nobility generally involve a privileging of paternal rather than maternal lines of descent (a privileging that one finds in Stevens's genealogical tropes and which, ironically enough, frustrated his efforts to gain admittance to the Holland Society). Furthermore, Stevens's sense of the contemporary relevance of this figure depends on a relationship among men, in which Colleoni not only serves as a figure of heroic strength but also confers such strength upon other men: no "man on whose side the horseman fought could ever be anything but fearless, anything but indomitable." Whether conceived as camaraderie among heroic compatriots or agonistic struggle against enemies, the version of masculinity presented here defines itself through an impossible fantasy of masculine self-sufficiency and self-enclosure.

On the other hand, in discussing Clark Mills's statue of Andrew Jackson, which the poet denigrates as a mere "work of fancy" (*NA* 10) "in which neither the imagination nor reality is present" (*NA* 11), Stevens emphasizes the way the warrior has relaxed his attitude and directed his attention toward a feminine presence: "There is in Washington, in Lafayette Square, which is the square on which the White House faces, a statue of Andrew Jackson, riding a horse with one of the most beautiful tails in the world. General Jackson is raising his hat in a gay gesture, saluting the ladies of his generation" (*NA* 10). It would be going too far to suggest that Stevens's dislike of Mills's statue has something to do with his fears of an imaginative emasculation at the hands—so to speak—of an assumed feminine presence, or even that his preference for Verrocchio might not be an instance of sound aesthetic judgment. In fact, rather than describing a demasculinization of masculinity-as-heroism, Stevens marks a shift from one masculine subject-position to another—from that of military hero to that of chivalric lover or, at least, a potential chivalric lover. This "gay gesture" suggests a certain theatrical self-consciousness, a consciousness of audience rather than of a "noble origin," and of a specifically female audience above all. Something of Colleoni's heroic isolation has been lost through a relationship to the feminine other, and this loss brings about a shift in masculine subject-position. This is not to say, of course, that Colleoni's "attitude"—Stevens's use of this ambiguous term must be deliberate—might not itself constitute a deliberate "performance," a masculine subject-position enacted with a self-conscious eye on its effect; but even according to this interpretation, the essay would still distinguish between two ways of positioning the self in relation to an audience, and to prefer the performance of heroic isolation that makes no direct acknowledgment of audience through a "gay gesture."

In Stevens's last example from the visual arts, an apparently contemporaneous painting by Reginald Marsh entitled *Wooden Horses*,[10] the physical presence of women and the still more deliberate theatricality of the rider register an uneasy but complete shift away from Colleoni's heroic masculinity and toward a very different gendered position:

> The horse in the center of the picture, painted yellow, has two riders, one a man, dressed in a carnival costume, who is seated in the saddle, the other a blonde, who is seated well up the horse's neck. The man has his arms under the girl's arms. He holds himself stiffly in order to keep his cigar out of the girl's hair. Her feet are in a second and shorter set of stirrups. She has the legs of a hammer-thrower. It is clear that the couple are accustomed to wooden horses and like them. A little behind them is a younger girl riding alone. She has a strong body and streaming hair. She wears a short-sleeved, red waist, a white skirt and an emphatic bracelet of pink coral. She has her eyes on the man's arms. Still farther behind, there is another girl. One does not see much more of her than her head. Her lips are painted bright red. It seems that it would be better if someone were to hold her on her horse. We, here, are not interested in any aspect of this picture except that it is a picture of ribald and hilarious reality. It is a picture wholly favorable to what is real. It is not without imagination and it is far from being without aesthetic theory. (*NA* 11–12)

Apparently, Stevens intends his audience to view this picture as an ironic and perhaps grotesque parody of the equestrian figures described earlier; even though the work "is not without imagination," it serves as a visual corollary or adjunct to his claim that "there is no element more conspicuously absent from contemporary poetry than nobility" (*NA* 35). Stevens is, no doubt, being deliberately playful, almost in the manner of the painting itself (or of some of his own more exuberantly comic *Harmonium* poems) in offering this painting as an example of the noble rider's contemporary fate and of the state of contemporary art in general. But he devotes most of his attention not to the grotesque reduction of "the powerful horse" to wooden, mechanical ones, nor to the supplanting of the hero's military outfit by "a carnival costume," but to the sexual element marked by the presence of female figures within the frame. Stevens points out the man's obviously phallic cigar—the man is a smoker, if not a "roller," of "big cigars" (*CP* 64); comments on the intense physicality of his partner, who has "the legs of a hammer-thrower"; notes the lips of the last solitary girl, which are "painted bright red"; and observes the "strong body" of the "younger girl" who "has her eyes on the man's arms"— a gaze suggestive of an adolescent's first sexual stirrings. Heterosexual desire flows in both directions in Stevens's account of the painting, even as the women are somewhat masculinized (a transgression in keeping, perhaps, with the carnival atmosphere). Finally, to further underscore the painting's erotic atmosphere, Stevens sums up the entire scene as "a picture of *ribald* and hilarious reality" (my emphasis). Stevens appears to enjoy the picture, but nevertheless finds it symptomatic of a certain absence. It would, again, be too easy to suggest that the absence of nobility in the picture stems entirely from a feminine sexual presence that robs the male figure of heroic isolation or of masculinity itself—the painting's parodic elements are too numerous and too richly overdetermined. Instead, the differences among Stevens's three ekphrases point to a tension between two different masculinities, two different demands made on those who would construct a masculine identity: be a heroic individual; be heterosexual.

This last consideration, however, only raises further questions: Why should Stevens posit such a tension between the heroic and the heterosexual? What is the precise significance of Stevens's focus on a specifically carnivalesque heterosexuality, and of the tension between this and Colleoni's heroic masculinity? Should Stevens's account of the masquerading man of *Wooden Horses* be viewed as a celebratory, destabilizing parody of Bartolomeo Colleoni and all that he represents?

The man's "carnival costume" calls to mind Bakhtin's concept of the "carnivalesque," or Butler's notion of the performative aspect of gender (i.e., as theater and as speech act) and, more specifically, of the subversive potential of any deliberate "parodic recontextualization" (176) of gendered subject-positions. But rather than casting the carnivalesque rider as what Lentricchia terms "the potential subverter of his official role as the young American male" (146), Stevens appears more concerned with a profound and perhaps unbridgeable gap between this figure and any "noble origin." In fact, Stevens, in a time of crisis, seems especially burdened not just with the demand to be heroic, but with the sense that this new demand cannot be reconciled with the masculine subject-position he had often occupied in his earlier poetry—the carnivalesque masculine heterosexuality embodied by the comedian, Crispin, Peter Quince, the lover or the clownish lover of so many of the Florida poems, the self-mocking speaker of "Le Monocle de Mon Oncle," the clown/poet of "The Man with the Blue Guitar" xxv, all those Stevensian speakers of a deliberately carnivalesque and often erotic language. Stevens's evident enjoyment of the picture might thus indicate some nostalgia for that earlier poetic self. But the shift from the first masculine subject-position to the second one also involves a critique of such nostalgia; in a time of war, Stevens reminds himself that he cannot turn back to *Harmonium*'s speakers and cannot waste time feeling nostalgia for those figures. Yet he cannot be Colleoni either. The ironic energy Stevens directed toward a "Monsieur . . . on horseback" (*CP* 123) or toward the statue of *Owl's Clover* emerges, too, in "The great statue of the General Du Puy" (*CP* 391), a poem written around the same time as the essay. The rigidity of the statuesque invariably represents an aesthetic risk for Stevens. Stevens seems stranded between these different versions of masculinity, while desiring a position that cannot be undermined by irony. One might wonder, then, if the more straightforward opposition between a univocal masculinity and femininity that also appears in Stevens's writing functions as a retreat from this uncertainty, a means of calming anxieties by investing in a comforting fiction of absolute gender difference.

Finally, though, "The Noble Rider" does not invest belief in a stable subject-position. Some of the equestrian heroes cited by Stevens may have once offered models, but over time Plato's charioteer "becomes antiquated and rustic" (*NA* 4), and even Verrocchio's statue seems "too favorable to the imagination" (*NA* 8) in Stevens's time. Instead of revitalizing these models of heroic masculine isolation, or overcoming the gap between the demand to be heroic and the demand to be heterosexual, the essay instead enacts one final tropic shift away from gendered figurations of nobility and into the apparently gender-neutral and scientific simile of the wave-force. This shift may solve Stevens's problem on a figurative level insofar as it claims to offer a still viable *simile* for "nobility," but this trope itself, in turning away from *human* figures of nobility, does not construct a subject position for the performance of nobility. A few questions still remain: Which kinds of poetic speakers can identify themselves with or internalize and thus harness this force for themselves? What particular subject positions can be constructed from this wave-energy? One might wonder whether the subject position *from* which Stevens offers this trope constitutes the noble selfhood whose appropriate figure he seeks; if this is the case, the essay differs from itself in enacting a subject position which it cannot figuratively represent. It is a puzzling retreat from the figure Stevens posits in the last poem ("Sombre Figuration") of *Owl's Clover* (1936), the "subman" (*OP* 96), who, as a "man whom rhapsodies of change, / Of which he is the cause, have never changed" (*OP* 96), seems to offer a masculine figure of the imagination's wavelike force. Most of the poem's critics, in fact, have remarked that "Sombre Figuration" itself retreats from or abandons the subman,[11] and it may be that Stevens found the subman to retain too much of the desire for permanence and especially for permanent political utopias that is the object of the sequence's critique. "The Noble Rider," perhaps, offers a compromise between the competing demands that lead to the puzzling conclusion of *Owl's Clover*.

I want to conclude this chapter by moving ahead to two works written after "The Noble Rider": "The Figure of the Youth as Virile Poet," an essay written for *Les Entretiens de Pontigny* in the summer of 1943, and "Repetitions of a Young Captain" (1944), one of Stevens's later, longer, but relatively neglected wartime sequences. Both these works seem to solve the problems left unresolved at the end of "The Noble Rider," constructing specifically gendered strategies of resistance to the possibility of cultural collapse, strategies that again help to situate Stevens in relation to the literary history of the last century. In both works, Stevens's points of resistance are constructed not just in

opposition to the war, but in opposition to a more threateningly doubled and subversive construction of gender that the works simultaneously expose and resist.

"The Noble Rider" almost looks like a prelude to "The Figure of
the Youth as Virile Poet"; it clears away the historical encrustations
that conceal the wavelike force of "nobility," so that "Figure of the
Youth" might continue and expand the essentially modernist project
of the earlier work, taking that "force" as its starting point, elabo-
rating upon it, and, most importantly, redefining it in specifically
gendered terms and appropriating it as or for the masculine subject-
position of "virile poet." Jenkins sees in the later essay a continuation
of the tension in "The Noble Rider" "between interior and exterior,"
a tension "heightened in 'The Figure of the Youth as Virile Poet' by
the context in which the paper was delivered" (76).[12] But one of the
two passages Jenkins offers as an example of this tension does not
offer strong support for this reading: "There is a life apart from politics. It is this life that the youth as virile poet lives, in a kind of radiant and productive atmosphere. It is the life of that atmosphere. There
the philosopher is an alien" (NA 57). Along with the apparent absence
of anxiety, the passage replaces the earlier essay's figuration of mutual,
agonistic "pressure" with a trope of mere contiguity, an "apartness"
that nevertheless involves some sort of side-by-side existence. The
later essay, in fact, figures the relationships between imagination and
reality or "fact" almost entirely as an inescapable interdependence—
"the world is a compact of real things so like the unreal things of the
imagination that they are indistinguishable from one another" (NA
65). This shift in figuration reflects a far greater level of imaginative
confidence, or, to offer a more critical formulation, a greater capacity to negate or repress consciousness of the actual world situation, a
capacity marked by the far more expansive elaboration in "Figure of
the Youth" of the specific function of imagination's "force" and its
structural relationship to historical change. The context differs in the
later essay, of course: here, Stevens seeks a definition of *poetry* rather
than examples of "nobility"—or rather, since even Coleridge produced
only "definitions that are valid enough but which no longer impress
us primarily by their validity" (NA 41), Stevens seeks out "a center of
poetry, a *vis* or *noeud vital,* to which, in the absence of a definition, all
the variations of definition are peripheral" (NA 44–45). The relationship between this "center" and the peripheral definitions resembles

the relationship between the wave-force of nobility and the individual examples of defunct nobility explored in "The Noble Rider." And the motivation behind this refusal to define resembles, too, the one that lies behind the earlier essay's rejection of any individual figure of nobility: Stevens needs to find a concept of poetry and a source of poetry that will resist both history's disconfirmations and his own ironic sensibility, a sensibility that needs to invalidate each achieved embodiment or product of this "force," and that knows "the poet may come to nothing because he succeeds" (*NA* 45). This search seems characteristic of that essentially modernist desire to recover something that "will hold" from the ruins of "actual" and literary history, to find, in a phrase remarkably similar to the conclusion of "The Noble Rider," "the element, the force, that keeps poetry a living thing, the modernizing and ever-modern influence" (*NA* 45). For Stevens, contact with this force involves a process of "purification" (*NA* 51, 60) to which, if I may adapt John Ashbery's phrase, impurists will object (*Selected Poems* 310), a process that leads to "the establishing of a self" (*NA* 50) conceived as a separable and autonomous entity—again, an essential modernist rather than postmodern version of subjectivity. Above all, this self is a masculine self, and Stevens's only references to the political climate in which he wrote the essay highlights the importance, for him, of the essay's location of the noble rider's "force" within such a self. Reminding his audience "of the crisis through which we are passing today" (*NA* 64), pointing out that they live *"in a leaden time and in a world that does not move for the weight of its own heaviness"* (*NA* 63), Stevens affirms the value of the poet's "virility": "he feels his own power to lift, or help to lift, that heaviness away" (*NA* 63).

An obvious enough question emerges here: exactly what does Stevens mean by "virile"? The terms "virile" and "virility" are not, for Stevens, merely synonymous with "masculine" and "masculinity," since, as has already been suggested, there are versions of masculinity that Stevens might not consider to be "virile." Here, it may prove helpful to situate the essay in relation to some poems that deal with similar issues. For example, "Country Words," a poem written in 1937, some six years before "The Figure of the Youth," offers a number of more immediately complex and contradictory figurations of the relations between politics and poetry, as well as of their respective claims of access to "virility." When read in conjunction with "The Figure of the Youth," the poem not only seems less certain than the essay about the possibility of discovering "a life apart from politics," a life in which "the youth as virile poet lives, in a kind of radiant and productive atmosphere" (*NA* 57), but demonstrates considerable ambivalence in assessing the relative values of sociopolitical power and poetic power, and in determining what relationship between those two forms of power would best serve the interests of poetry. And the essay emerges as an effort to disentangle the poetic and the political, though there are, as I shall later suggest, reasons to question the extent to which the essay escapes ambivalence.

Contextualization seems essential, in fact, since a comparison of "Country Words" with some earlier Stevens poems does not reveal a consistent definition of or stance toward virility, but a series of shifting positions. "Virility," in "Country Words," appears initially at least to have a simple enough physiological basis—namely, the possession of a penis and the ability to use that instrument for sexual purposes. The poem, of course, does not celebrate the speaker's virility; if what the speaker desires above all is "words virile with [Belshazzar's] breath" (*CP* 207), then virility is precisely the quality he lacks. A "cuckoo cock" would be, according to folklore, a cuckolded and therefore psychologically (if not physically) emasculated lover/poet, and, in a pun for which Stevens seems to have had a particular fondness (witness *Harmonium*'s "universal cock" [*CP* 75] and "perfect cock" [*CP* 82], or the "Cock bugler" [*CP* 405] of *Notes* III, ix and the "cock bright" [*CP* 377] of "Credences of Summer"), it is the portion of the male anatomy most directly affected by cuckolding. The nonvirile "cuckoo," then, has the appropriate equipment but is prevented from using it by his chosen partner's unfaithfulness; he is the poet deserted by his muse and thus left singing only of a desire for greater creative power. Here, the "cuckoo" of "Country Words" differs from *Harmonium*'s cocks in his apparent stance toward virility: "Bantams in Pine-Woods" and "The Bird with the Coppery, Keen Claws" direct their satirical energies toward the grandeur and expansiveness of a "universal cock" and the "perfect cock" of a "parakeet of para[Keats]"; the former poem in particular confidently asserts the superiority of the "inchling" to the "ten-foot poet" (*CP* 76)—in poetry, at least, size doesn't count, or, if it does count, it counts only to the extent that less is more. The poem's stance toward sexuality also differs from that of the comically frustrated speakers of such poems as "Last Looks at the Lilacs," "Two Figures in Dense Violet Night," "Depression before Spring," and "Disillusionment of Ten O'Clock." The sense of sexual and creative diminishment can be treated in "Country Words" with neither the confident unconcern of "Bantams" nor the distancing irony of "Last Looks" and other similar poems. If the criticism of "universal cock[s]" in "Bantams" is directed not just toward other poets but toward a transcendental tendency within Stevens's own creative personality, and if the earlier poem's stated preference for an "inchling"'s "Appalachian tangs" (*CP* 76) promotes a more diminished set of poetic ambitions without exactly silencing some more expansive ones, then "Country Words" seems marked by a desire for the very qualities that the earlier poems criticized. Of course, the question of *why* the later poem should differ in this way remains to be answered.

Like many other Stevens poems from the 1930s, "Country Words" is marked by a heightened awareness of the social pressures placed upon the poet in a time of particular social and political upheaval, and it may be these pressures that influenced the reconceptualization of virility that one finds in this poem. In desiring "words virile with [Belshazzar's] breath," the speaker indicates that virility is no longer just a matter of sexual and poetic potency, but of political potency as well. A virile poet here would be one whose words can unite "the luminous pages . . . / Of being" (*CP* 207) with larger political concerns; and his poetry would gain a particular kind of sociopolitical relevance and authority from that union. To move from "an old rebellious song" (*CP* 207) to "words virile with [Belshazzar's] breath" would be to move poetry from a marginal to a central position, from disenfranchisement to authority. If one thinks of the poem's two figures as aspects of Stevens's own personality—the man of lyric interiority on the one hand and the man of the world, of business, and of law on the other—then the poem would seem to desire a mutually beneficial cooperation between these two aspects of the poet's life. Yet the poem develops a characteristically complex and ambivalent stance toward this understanding of virility. We know, after all, from Daniel, that Belshazzar is a lesser king than his predecessors, and that the central incident of his reign, or at least of his great feast, is the revelation of the fragility and ephemerality of his power. Even as Stevens redefines poetry's virility in terms of its capacity to engage in the larger concerns of political and social reality, "Country Words" allows an ironic counterforce—another "old rebellious song," perhaps—to undermine that definition.

In "The Figure of the Youth as Virile Poet," the understanding of virility shifts again. Stevens playfully reminds us of the physical and sexual component when he includes William James's insistence that, since he is a metaphysician, he is therefore an "invalid" and *"can't do anything that befits a man"* (*NA* 58–59, italics in original). Yet if the sexual element remains a constant, the means of proving one's virility in relation to the social and political sphere has changed radically, as is suggested in the essay's claim, cited above, that the "life that the youth as virile poet lives" is "a life apart from politics" where "the philosopher is an alien" (*NA* 57). Here, poetry's "virility" is linked not to its capacity to expand its range of concerns to include the political and social, but rather to its ability to resist the pressures placed upon it to undertake any such expansion. Virility becomes a matter of creative autonomy, rather than political engagement—autonomy from the political realm rather than autonomy within the political realm becomes the touchstone of the virile. The countercurrent that flowed through "Country Words" with its ironic and skeptical questions about poetry's expansion into the political arena would appear to become the dominant force in "The Figure of the Youth." In this regard, the poet's capacity "to lift, or help to lift . . away" (*NA* 63) the "heaviness" of "a leaden time" is founded on an association not only between masculine sexual potency and physical strength, but between that potency and a certain kind of creative autonomy. Such conceptual linkages appear often enough in early modernist accounts of creativity. Pound, for example, elaborates upon the notion of the artist's *virtù* in "I Gather the Limbs of Osiris," and *"virtù"* shares, of course, the etymon *vir* with "virility." *Virtù*, for Pound, includes the "donative" artist's ability "to draw down into the art something which was not in the art of his predecessors" (Pound, *Selected Prose* 25); to use one of Pound's later formulations, such an artist has the capacity to "start his machinery going" ("*Affirmations*" 376), unlike the merely passive artist who has "no emotional energy, no impulse" (376). The key point in Stevens's essay is that this kind of autonomy, this capacity to resist the cultural and political situation that Stevens formerly figured in such apocalyptic terms, now has a viable *masculine* identity, image, and name: "virile poet."

But in thus constructing the position of "virile poet" the essay reveals a new set of anxieties about the relationship of virile poet to other masculine subject-positions. "Figure of the Youth" replaces the earlier essay's imagination/reality boundary with a boundary between philosophy and poetry, conceived of, respectively, as "the official view of being" and "an unofficial view of being" (*NA* 40), as two discourses "pursuing two different parts of a whole" (*NA* 54). But the great peculiarity of "Figure of the Youth" is Stevens's disinclination to stop at a distinction based on philosophy's and poetry's respectively rational and imaginative approaches to truth (*NA* 42); he goes on to translate this difference into a difference between "logical and empirical knowledge" (*NA* 54), between logical consistency and "agreement with reality" (*NA* 54), between "*les idées*" and "*la vie*" (*NA* 56), and, finally, between "the gaunt world of reason" (*NA* 58) and "a kind of radiant and productive atmosphere" (*NA* 57). Stevens's concern is to assert the greater discursive power of poetry and to define this power as a productive, virile engagement with life: the poet is an Aeneas, an embodiment of heroic masculinity (*NA* 53). Metaphysicians, in the passage from William James already quoted in part above, are "*invalids. I am one, can't sleep, can't make a decision, can't buy a horse, can't do anything that befits a man; and yet you say from my photograph that I must be a second General Sherman, only greater and better! All right! I love you for the fond delusion*" (*NA* 58–59, italics in original). Stevens, no doubt, shows much playful humor in citing this passage and adding that "we do not want to be metaphysicians" (*NA* 59)—at least as much humor as James shows in loving his addressee for his or her "fond delusion." But a little humor may conceal a considerable anxiety, and Stevens takes peculiar pains throughout the essay to define poetic virility in opposition to another form of masculinity that seems, in comparison, lifeless, irrelevant, emasculated.

But the question remains as to why Stevens finds it necessary to establish the validity of a virile, poetic/heroic masculinity by contrasting it to a diminished and emasculated philosophic masculinity. One possible reason emerges from Paul Weiss's comments to Peter Brazeau on Stevens's essay; Weiss complains that Stevens failed to deal with any "real, full-sized philosopher who's making a great contribution, one of the great historic figures" (cited in Jenkins, 75). This observation may betray a philosopher's pique, and in fact does not quite address the essay's real shortcomings—"Figure of the Youth" does not just fail to engage with "full-sized philosophers," but fails to fully engage with the ideas of any of the figures it discusses in its argument for poetry's greater virility. Stevens was more than intelligent and knowledgeable enough to say, when speaking on "A Collect of Philosophy" in 1951, that he was "not a philosopher" (*OP* 275), and it may well be that he needed to evade or bracket out this awareness—an awareness that he could not meet "full-sized philosophers" on their own terms—in order to assert the superior discursive power of poetry. The essay operates almost entirely on the level of rhetoric, metaphor, symbol, poetic "flash," and this strategy, conscious or not, has its costs, since in making things rather too easy for himself Stevens paradoxically undermines his claim for poetry's greater discursive power.

But Stevens may also be working out a more important conflict within himself, or a conflict that is for him internal to poetry in general. His rhetoric most resembles the agonistic mode of "The Noble Rider" not when he argues that poetry "may be [philosophy's] superior" (*NA* 43), or when he imagines poetry's ability to "[cancel] the borrowing and [obliterate] the confusion" (*NA* 57) of its "borrowed and confused" philosophical commonplaces; the agonistic mode emerges at full pitch when the essay details a struggle between different *kinds* of poetry: "In the most propitious climate and in the midst of life's virtues, the simple figure of the youth as virile poet is always surrounded by a cloud of double characters, against whose thought and speech it is imperative that he should remain on constant guard. These are the poetic philosophers and the philosophical poets" (*NA* 54–55). Was Stevens in danger of being a "philosophical poet," of not being sufficiently "on guard" against a "double character" within himself, or at least of being read as such? The issue could be framed in broader terms: the war puts a premium on being a "man," on a certain capacity to resist catastrophic upheaval in the name of both social and aesthetic survival; but the same pressure reveals masculinity to be multiple, variable, shifting, always open to question. How can one be certain of being man enough? By constructing the figure of the virile poet in contradistinction to the "invalid" metaphysician, Stevens simultaneously reveals and triumphs over a point of considerable poetic anxiety. He constructs an "other" masculinity against which he can measure poetry's greater power, but simultaneously reveals the possibility of failure. In fact, Stevens's illustration of poetry's triumph over philosophy and philosophical poetry—Sarah Bernhardt's performance of Hamlet's act III soliloquy (*NA* 56–57)—involves a curious mixing of genders. Masculinity here is pure performance, a woman "performing" as a fictional hero who must "himself" learn to "perform" the role of hero, to face "the slings and arrows of outrageous fortune" (*Hamlet* 3.1.58). Stevens offers a glimpse of a more complex and unsettling version of masculine identity, an irreducible impurity in the establishing of a self, and then resists its implications. But since to write thus is to imply a teleology in the conceptualization of gender that posits performativity as its end, it seems preferable to say that the performative aspects of Stevens's example simply do not register on any level for him; they are not part of the intellectual framework within which he constructs gender. Yet it is suggestive that the rhetoric of vigilance is strongest when Stevens distinguishes between "simple" and "double" discourses, between the pure and the mixed or impure. The essay's main goals may not just be a disentangling of poetry from philosophy, of virile from invalid masculinity, but a disentangling of "simple" from "double" discourses. Here, Stevens's privileging of the "single" over the "double" again suggests his profound difference from a poststructuralist or postmodern construction of the issue, particularly since his spatial metaphor—a central simplicity surrounded by dangerous doubles—so clearly belongs to classical formulations of the relation between center and periphery.

"Repetitions of a Young Captain" provides a suitable terminus for this part of my study, since it clarifies the relationship between Stevens's masculinization of the "force" of imagination and his sense of the catastrophic political and cultural upheaval of the war. "Repetitions" has received less commentary than any of Stevens's longer war lyrics, and the fact that it recapitulates many aspects of *both* of Stevens's wartime essays may account for its obscurities and consequent critical neglect. The poem works through "The Noble Rider"'s figuration of the "pressure of reality" and the effect of this pressure on the imagination, but also partakes of "The Figure of the Youth"'s more expansive and masculinized elaboration of the imaginative powers that counter that destructive force. The poem begins with a figure of sudden and irreversible political upheaval and cultural change:

A tempest cracked on the theatre. Quickly,
The wind beat in the roof and half the walls.
The ruin stood still in an external world.

It had been real. It was something overseas
That I remembered, something that I remembered
Overseas, that stood in an external world.

It had been real. It was not now. The rip
Of the wind and the glittering were real now,
In the spectacle of a new reality. (*CP* 306)

Jarraway (220) rightly associates the things repeated by the "young
captain" with Stevens's own version of the imagination-as-theater trope
in "Of Modern Poetry." Stevens seems here to reject that trope or at
least to admit to its fragility, and to suggest further that the very distinction between inside and outside or the desire to remain in a protected inner realm of imagination comes into question in a time of war,
a time when "everything moves in the direction of reality" (*OP* 242).

But the poem's energies are directed largely toward repairing the
theater's ruined walls, or, perhaps, toward forgetting the ruin; it re-
constructs figures of interiority that emphasize, again, a power capable
of surviving the destruction of any individual fiction. The speaker
realizes in canto iii that the route to the external world "lies through
an image in [my] mind" (*CP* 307), and, in canto iv, that when the
soldier departs to that world "There is no change of place // Nor of
time" (*CP* 308). Stevens's language in the latter instance offers a hyperbolic response to "The Man with the Blue Guitar" vi, where the audience desires to find itself "in the tune as if in space, / Yet nothing
changed, except the place // Of things as they are" (*CP* 167). It is a
rhetoric of interiority that Stevens continues in "Analysis of a Theme"
(1945), where the realm of "ugly, subconscious time" contains "no
subconscious place, / Only Indyterranean / Resemblances // Of place"
(*CP* 348), and again in "The Owl in the Sarcophagus," whose title
figure dwells in a time "Less time than place, less place than thought
of place" (*CP* 433). The passage from "Repetitions" has a double function, completely interiorizing the disruptive movement to an "external world" enforced by the theater's destruction, but also troping this
recuperation as a new contact with reality. And if the poem rejects
any nostalgia for "The finikin spectres in the memory" (*CP* 307), it
nevertheless asserts the value of "a memorandum voluble / Of the
giant sense" (*CP* 308), suggesting the continued viability of memory's
process rather than of any particular contents of memory. Such an

elision of the mind's specific contents or products is characteristic of Stevens's thinking at this point in his career: he seeks to identify the cognitive powers, the actual "force" or "process" that will survive the disconfirmation of any individual content and product, and he celebrates the discovery of this force in the poem's climactic moment:

A few words, a memorandum voluble
Of the giant sense, the enormous harnesses
And writhing wheels of this world's business,

The drivers in the wind-blows cracking whips,
The pulling into the sky and the setting there
Of the expanses that are mountainous rock and sea;

And beyond the days, beyond the slow-foot litters
Of the nights, the actual, universal strength,
Without a word of rhetoric—there it is. (*CP* 308–9)

Stevens's "central [response]" (*CP* 308) to the destruction of the theater leads beyond the recuperation of individual tropes and beyond the temporal movement of days and nights that both create and invalidate them. While there is already something faintly theatrical about the "pulling into the sky and the setting there / Of the expanses that are mountainous rock and sea," and while Stevens fully recuperates the theatrical metaphor at the beginning of canto vi ("theatre for theatre"), his goal, finally, is a revelation of "the actual, universal strength, / Without a word of rhetoric" (*CP* 309). Stevens's language here is close to that of "The Figure of the Youth," whose poet hears only his "*own speech and the strength of it*" (*NA* 63, italics in original), "exercise[s] his power to the full and at its height" (*NA* 63), and "becomes his own master" (*NA* 63). Furthermore, the *function* of "the actual, universal strength" has at least as much in common with the wave-force simile that appeared at the end of "The Noble Rider": it is a means of asserting a subsisting and transhistorical imaginative power that will survive the destruction of each individual product of that power—such as the theater of canto i, or the rather Browning-esque "rainy arcs // And pathetic magnificences" (*CP* 310) celebrated in canto v and abandoned in canto vi. This function, I think, again raises a question for Jarraway's reading of Stevens as a poststructuralist; his account of the "nonoriginary 'strength'" of the "young captain" as a "force of absence" (220) seems to miss the desire for an *escape* from history's ironies inscribed in this figuration.

In a certain sense, then, "Repetitions," like "The Figure of the Youth as Virile Poet," resolves, or attempts to resolve, the problem that was left unresolved at the conclusion of "The Noble Rider"—namely the absence of a masculine subject-position capable of resisting the worst implications of the war for poetry and the imagination, the absence of a poetic speaker that would harness or embody the wave-force of nobility. Written a year after "Figure," "Repetitions" in a certain sense also goes beyond that essay insofar as it offers "Repetitions *of*" (my emphasis on Stevens's ambiguous preposition) words spoken from a position of masculine authority and strength, rather than merely describing that position. But as Longenbach (232–33, 235–36) notes, it achieves this confidence at the cost of an apparent reduction or rejection of the feminine and "personal," or, as I have suggested throughout this chapter, of masculinity understood as a capacity for heterosexual relationships; its primary difference from the essay, in fact, lies in the near absence of anything other than a single, heroic, homosocial conception of masculinity. But there is, of course, something irreducibly double about including the *ex*clusion of the feminine in the poem, both in the rejected "bride come jingling, kissed and cupped" (*CP* 308) and in the necessary choice between "Her vague 'Secrete me from reality,' / His 'That reality secrete itself'" (*CP* 309). To hear the woman's "vague" request as a statement of desire is to hear it as an appeal from and *to* one part of Stevens's creative self, and to hear the somewhat hyperbolic and strangely incomplete alternative as an exaggerated homosocial masculine stance set up in resistance to this temptation. In fact, if Jarraway is correct to read Stevens's "choice as one 'of' rather than 'between'" (223), it becomes necessary to ask about the gender of the "us" in Stevens's statement of his final choice: "Secrete us in reality" (*CP* 310). The purely homosocial construction of masculinity may remain an impossibility.

If this discussion has sometimes returned to the very position it sought to avoid—namely, a straightforward opposition between masculinity and femininity—I hope it has so complicated the concept of "masculinity" that this position now seems less secure and familiar than it might first have appeared. Perhaps one area for future exploration of Stevens's configurations of gender would be a possible tension between two different definitions of masculinity that are themselves structured around irresolvable tensions—first, one that involves tensions between masculinity and femininity, and, second, one that involves tensions among different kinds of masculinity. My next chapter will continue to focus on the second of these constructions. It will move back in time to a group of poems written from 1938 to 1942 in order to give a fuller account of the relationships between Stevens's resistance to apocalyptic interpretations of the war and the complexities of masculine subject-positions.

chapter three

What Could Not Be Shaken

Meditation in a Time of War

It should come as no surprise that Stevens's concern with apocalyptic interpretations of the war and with the possibility that the war might produce a "radical break" with(in) literary and cultural history also marks the poetry written shortly before and after "The Noble Rider and the Sound of Words." Here again, the poetry's figurations of gender do not just alternate between masculine and feminine positions, but explore, as the essay does, a wide range of different masculinities. Here, it is worth remembering that Stevens lived out several such masculine roles: son, lover, husband, father, businessman, poet, and so on. In the following pages, I shall investigate the ways Stevens tests their continued viability and relevance—in both social and poetic terms—in a time of war. And since poetic genres and modes also have inscribed within them particular conventions of gendered identity which their speakers must negotiate in order to produce the recognizable marks of those genres—the poet/lover of pastoral, the prophet of apocalyptic vision—the essay will also consider the role of specific poetic genres and modes in Stevens's resistance to the possibility of a "radical break" with(in) literary history.

The discussion that follows focuses on three short wartime lyrics—"Girl in a Nightgown" (1938) and "Martial Cadenza" (1940) from *Parts of a World* and "Dutch Graves in Bucks County" (1940) from *Transport to Summer*—and also explores the problems generated by these works in relation to a number of Stevens's other wartime lyrics. The first two of these poems in particular cannot be considered "major" texts in the Stevens canon and have not received a great deal of critical attention outside of studies, like that of Filreis's *Wallace Stevens and the Actual World*, that are explicitly concerned with the politics of Stevens's war poetry. All questions of aesthetic value or thematic "weight" aside—"Girl in a Nightgown" in particular does not strike me as one of Stevens's more successful "minor" works—these poems are useful precisely because of their marginality: they show us Stevens working through problems that often appear to have been resolved (or, as Marjorie Perloff suggests, elided) in the major achievements like *Notes toward a Supreme Fiction*. My purpose, then, is not to move these texts from margin to center, nor to construct a narrative of Stevens's poetic development during the war years around these texts. The unresolved and crisis-ridden "Contrary Theses (I)," for example, comes from the same year (1942) as the far more confident "Martial Cadenza," and appears at a much later point in *Parts of a World*, and the seaside idyll of "Variations on a Summer Day" appears between the more problematical "Girl in a Nightgown" and "Martial Cadenza." What one finds in the poems of this period is not so much a clear line of development as a sequence of shifts between two very different affective responses to the war. My purpose, then, is simply to explore three individual moments of crisis in Stevens's wartime poetic career, and, in particular, to demonstrate how a series of shifts in the masculine subject-positions embodied by the poems' speakers help clarify Stevens's response to the possibility of a "radical break" in or with the world historical and cultural/aesthetic continua.

In "Girl in a Nightgown," a war-haunted poem of 1938, Stevens tests three different masculine positions (father, prophet, pastoral poet) and two poetic modes (apocalyptic, pastoral) against "a violence from without" that threatens the speaker's lyric interiority and sense of connection to literary tradition. Alan Filreis insists that "Girl in a Nightgown" is not concerned with war at all, since it was written in 1938 (*Actual World* 63); but although the poem obviously cannot reflect upon a *world* war that has not yet begun, it nevertheless can respond to the *civil* war already brought about by Spanish fascism. It can also express fears that further war might be instigated by highly militaristic, expansionist, and racist fascist governments in other countries.[1] In other words, 1938 was as good (or bad) a year as any for worrying about war, and I hope to show that "Girl in a Nightgown" struggles with the problem of inscribing such public and political fears within the largely private and interior realm of lyric poetry.

It is possible to read "Girl" as an almost autobiographical meditation on the way world politics impinge upon domesticity, and such a reading could garner additional support from a similarity between the poem's basic situation and that of Yeats's "A Prayer for My Daughter." But Stevens's fondness for domestic settings and female figures as metaphors for the inner world of imagination and the source of poetic inspiration suggests that "Girl in a Nightgown" does not only deal with a political crisis, but with a *poetic* crisis instigated by an unstable political and social situation. Certainly, both the setting of "Girl in a Nightgown" (the "room" of the mind, and night, the time of visionary and imaginative experience), and its attire (a playful weave of nocturnal and textile tropes for imagination and poetry) suggest that the title figure functions as an early version of this interiorized muse, and a prefiguration, too, of the title figure of the much later "Puella Parvula." When the speaker describes "the repose of night" as "a place, strong place, in which to sleep" (*CP* 214), he inevitably evokes the specifically literary sense of "place" as topos, and especially night and sleep as topoi of imaginative and visionary activity. If this reading is justifiable, the poem marks an important shift in Stevens's representation of his source of poetic inspiration, a shift from the eroticized, external and sometimes powerful or even threatening Floridean muse to a more chaste, domesticated, and vulnerable version of this figure. The fact that such a shift occurs in a poem concerned with the possibility of war suggests that this situation has forced Stevens to confront some anxious questions about what place, if any, his imagination might have in a world on the brink of war; questions, too, about the kinds of poetic stanzas and genres he can inhabit or build at such a time; and questions about the necessity, possibility, or mere validity of protecting his own muse and poetic self from the violence of the external world. The poem thus somewhat tentatively prefigures Stevens's more detailed consideration, in "The Noble Rider and the Sound of Words," of a world situation that threatens the very possibility of poetic creativity itself, a world situation that may cause a radical break with or within imaginative history or at least within Stevens's own creative career.

As the preceding material suggests, Stevens develops these issues in "Girl in a Nightgown" by playing at the boundaries between a number of oppositional pairs—inside and outside, imaginative and actual, feminine and masculine, private and public, domestic and political. But if the purpose of this conceptual structure is to test the security of the conventional positions that can be assumed in relation to these pairs, the positions and the boundaries that separate or establish them prove less stable than might be supposed or desired. The speaker, much as he may wish to position himself inside a house of fiction, and to speak of and from the inner world of imagination, cannot sustain this gesture of lyric self-containment: it proves both necessary and inevitable that he speak of the possibility of war that dominates the exterior, public, political world. That inside/outside boundary, for example, is doubly established in the poem's first two lines, not only through the delineation of the interior location but through the clipped syntax and metrical abbreviation suggestive of a wary or guarded stance, a protective drawing in of imaginative energies. Yet this boundary is established in the name of "A look at the weather" (*CP* 214), an opening to an exterior world, which further broadens to a consideration of the political and social climate. The poem itself becomes a kind of counterfactual artifact, since in weaving both of these different worlds into its figurations, it interiorizes tropes of the outside world within its own poetic space and crosses boundaries as it establishes them. As was suggested in the preceding chapter, this boundary becomes crucial to Stevens's figurations of imaginative autonomy as a capacity to resist external pressures. But their simultaneous inscription and erasure in "Girl" proves difficult to interpret with any certainty. Does Stevens demonstrate the necessary dismantling of a fiction he can no longer sustain, or does he attempt to reinforce the boundary even as it disappears?

A poststructuralist reading of Stevens would have it that Stevens always consciously deconstructs the inside/outside opposition which plays such a crucial role in the conventional metaphysics of subject and object, imagination and reality, in Western philosophy and literature. And much as we might expect Stevens's restlessly questioning temperament to draw him toward the poststructuralist position, he seems, during the war years at least, to have been strongly motivated to desire a greater degree of certainty about that boundary. A number of other poems from the war period deal with this problem of *how* to inscribe the war in poetry by self-consciously staging a confrontation between inside and outside, testing the boundaries and, at times, fearfully portraying their collapse. "Contrary Theses (I)" (1942), for example, contrasts a pastoral scene of present plenitude and fullness with the equally present violence of war, and does not resolve the tension between its contraries:

Now grapes are plush upon the vines.
A soldier walks before my door.

The hives are heavy with the combs.
Before, before, before my door.

And seraphs cluster on the domes,
And saints are brilliant in fresh cloaks.

Before, before, before my door.
The shadows lessen on the walls.

The bareness of the house returns.
An acid sunlight fills the halls.

Before, before. Blood smears the oaks.
A soldier stalks before my door. (*CP* 266–67)

Stevens's obsessive repetitions disrupt the peaceful world portrayed in the other lines and finally leave their mark on the inner world when "The bareness of the house returns. / An acid sunlight fills the halls." Stevens's benign pastoral tropes of natural plenitude turn into malignant tropes of an interior corroded by contact with reality. In fact, the obsessiveness, the deliberate imaginative indigence, and the irregular placement—the speaker seems unable to maintain the ordered pattern of the first two couplets—of these refrains suggest the extent to which an ordering impulse has already been unsettled by external forces. They seem emblematic of the bareness of this particular house of fiction. Such inside/outside troping, of course, haunts much of "The Noble Rider and the Sound of Words," nowhere so famously as in the essay's final definition of the imagination: "It is a violence from within that protects us from a violence without" (*NA* 36). It has a crucial function in "Outside of Wedlock" from 1942's "Five Grotesque Pieces," in which "the moon above East Hartford / Wakes us to the emotion, grand fortissimo, / Of our sense of evil" (*OP* 112) and "The old woman that knocks at the door / Is not our grandiose destiny" (*OP* 112). At the beginning of "Esthétique du Mal," in a testing of the adequacy of literary conventions of the sublime in the face of war, the window of a café marks the boundary between an unnamed reader's "paragraphs / On the sublime" and the eruptions of Vesuvius, whose "sultriest fulgurations, flickering, / Cast corners in the glass" (*CP* 313–14). And, in "Repetitions of a Young Captain," some particularly complex, shifting, and contradictory versions of this figuration emerge when "The wind beat in the roof and half the walls" of Europe's theater (*CP* 306), as has already been suggested.

One approach to reading this inside/outside opposition in "Girl" is through the context provided by other contrasting conceptual pairs in the poem—above all, present and past, and apocalyptic and pastoral modes. The presence of an apocalyptic mode is marked not just in the poem's concern with terminations but in a recurrent rhetoric of "shaking":

> This is the silence of night,
> This is what could not be shaken,
> Full of stars and the images of stars—
> And that booming wintry and dull,
>
> Like a tottering, a falling and an end,
> Again and again, always there,
> Massive drums and leaden trumpets,
> Perceived by feeling instead of sense,
>
> A revolution of things colliding
>
> . . . .
>
> It is shaken now. It will burst into flames,
> Either now or tomorrow or the day after that. (*CP* 214)

The "day of the lord" of the Old Testament and the parousia in the New are also times when the peoples of the earth will be shaken by much shaking, as in the following passages from Isaiah, Haggai, and Hebrews:

> Therefore I will shake the heavens, and the earth shall remove out of her place, in the wrath of the Lord of hosts, and in the day of his fierce anger. (Isa. 13:13)

> For thus saith the Lord of hosts; Yet once, it is a little while, and I will shake the heavens, and the earth, and the sea, and the dry land; And I will shake all nations, and the desire of all nations shall come. (Hag. 2:6–7)

> Yet once more I shake not the earth only, but also heaven. And this word, Yet once more, signifieth the removing of those things

that are shaken, as of things that are made, that those things which cannot be shaken may remain. (Heb. 12:26–27)

The somewhat didactic tone of the third passage—evidently a gloss on Isa. 13:13 or Hag. 2:6–7—makes it less poetically appealing or rhetorically seductive than that of the others, but "Girl in a Nightgown" seems to follow St. Paul's variations on "shake" quite closely. In imagining such "a tottering, a falling and an end"—the end of both a world historical dispensation and a particular imaginative dispensation or tradition—Stevens's speaker "goes one better" on his forebears' apocalyptic intensity, due to the absence of any hope of future restoration and the concomitant inability to believe that anything might "remain" in place after such shaking. One element of that imaginative dispensation, in fact, would be the capacity to invest belief in an end that transforms and gives meaning to all that precedes it. And part of what precedes this new eschatology is a pastoral mode that appears only in a spectral form in the poem, as part of a lost past or an imagined world of "should"—realms in which "the repose of night, / *Was* a place, strong place, in which to sleep" (*CP* 214, my emphasis), and in which "The night *should* be warm and fluters' fortune / *Should* play in the trees when morning comes" (*CP* 214, my emphasis).

What requires interpretation here is not just this second pair of oppositions—present/past, apocalyptic/pastoral—but its relationship to the inside/outside figuration. The first two pairs could be described, respectively, as being essentially temporal and essentially spatial, so that the poem's dominant line of development involves the displacement of an initial spatial figuration by the temporal relationship between past and present; and the latter relationship is in turn figured as the displacement of one literary mode by another—pastoral by apocalyptic. Such a progression suggests that the poem's main purpose is to reinscribe the collapse of the inside/outside boundary as a concrete historical event, a catastrophe that has a particular location in time and a concrete historical referent. Such a positioning of this collapse seems markedly different from the poststructuralist analysis of the relationship between inside and outside, since there the distinction itself is reinscribed within a nonoriginary "invagination" that has no history but is, in fact, the "outside" that any conventional inscription of the inside/outside boundary will seek to exclude (and will unwittingly include). By giving this moment a specific historical location, and by presenting it through an apocalyptic modulation that has been emptied of all desire, Stevens would appear to offer resistance to that collapse, and to understand it as a historical accident that can be resisted. And by embodying the contrast between past and present in a contrast between these two poetic modes, Stevens also translates the opposition between lyric interiority and its "outside" into a tension between two literary modes, interiorizing that more problematical boundary between poetry and nonpoetry as an intrapoetic boundary. The results are not entirely comforting however, since the pastoral topoi are thus given a time (the past) but not an actual place.

A similarly irreducible dividedness appears in the poem's articulation of gender. As I have already suggested, "Girl in a Nightgown" domesticates Stevens's muse, and the poem's language and situation lead me to the conclusion that the speaker is not the titular figure but the father of that figure. By replacing the relationship between desiring lover and elusive beloved that appeared so frequently in *Harmonium* with one between father and daughter, Stevens shifts the balance of power toward the male speaker, who thus assumes the role of authoritarian and protective male. But since both these positions also represent different aspects of Stevens's creative personality, the poem still reflects a deep internal division in its response to the contemporaneous political world—a sense of vulnerability and a new sense of strength and authority; a desire or need to be protected and a desire or need to protect; a desire to turn inward and a desire to face the reality of the external situation. In fact, the father/speaker embodies two different speaking positions constructed within the pastoral world, as Annabel Patterson suggests in *Pastoral and Ideology.* "While the selfhood of Tityrus is associated with reflection (*meditaris*), with echoes, with song, with literary allusion, and especially with leisure and protection, the community to which Meliboeus belongs is connected to (at the moment of its severance from) the most value-laden word in Roman culture, the *patria,* subsuming the concepts of origin, national identity, and home" (2). In other words, while the inclusion of references to a hostile "outer" world is a common element of pastoral—the genre tends to self-consciously establish the pastoral retreat *as* a retreat from worldly troubles—the difficulty faced by Stevens's speaker in "Girl in a Nightgown" may reside in his straddling of two different subject positions available within the pastoral mode, the second being one that pastoral internalizes as a figuration of its own "outside." Stevens, in other words, is *both* Tityrus and Meliboeus, speaking from both inside and outside the pastoral realm, considering both the privacies of lyric, pastoral interiority and the public and sometimes apocalyptic discourse of political actuality. The question posed by the poem, then, would concern which of these subject positions might "suffice" in a time of war.

Finally, the poem's uncertainties emerge in their most concentrated form in a single punctuation mark. The dash in the seventh line seems syntactically unnecessary—its removal would in no way disturb the passage's grammaticality or intelligibility—but its silent interruption of "the silence of night" tells us much about Stevens's stance toward the violence it introduces. As an emotionally charged suspension, it speaks silently of a desire not to speak, of a hesitation before the pronouncement of a violent conclusion. Within the sentence in which it appears, it marks a boundary between, on the one hand, the protected pastoral "repose" of night, and, on the other, the political and apocalyptic realms that disrupt and supplant this space. Thus, the dash also bespeaks something of the disruptive force of the vision (or audition) that it introduces; it interrupts and breaks off from "what could not be shaken." In fact, Stevens echoes prophetic eschatology even when evoking the realm of pastoral innocence ("This is the silence of night, / This is what could not be shaken"). He thus further undermines the boundaries the poem appears to establish for itself, as though the apocalyptic rhetoric had rippled backward across the dash. Stevens's dash is thus both strangely weightless and overladen with significance: it marks, hesitates before, and rushes across the boundaries between interior and exterior, private and public, domestic and political, order and disorder, peace and war.[2] If, as I suggested earlier, the dominant direction of the poem's creative energies is toward the containment or neutralizing of a radically disruptive force, then this dash, in its irreducible doubleness, underlines the incompleteness of this project in "Girl in a Nightgown."

If "Girl in a Nightgown" seeks but does not achieve a satisfying resolution to the creative crisis figured both through the inside/outside figurations of poetry and war (or of different kinds of poetry) and through the tensions among different masculine subject-positions, "Martial Cadenza" figures a renewal of creative confidence by returning to one of the masculine subject-positions *not* explored in "Girl"—that of the heterosexual male lover—and attempting to establish its validity in a time of war. The poem thus functions as a poem of recovery—a recovery of poetic strength and also of continuity in Stevens's poetic career, since that erotic persona was one of the versions of masculinity adopted most frequently in *Harmonium.* And it also recovers a genre that seemed unsustainable in "Girl in a Nightgown"—namely the nocturnal-pastoral poem of erotic desire. Yet if the return to this speaker is a means of minimizing the effect of the war on the creative world and of resisting, again, that possibility of a "radical break" with the historical and literary past, the poem remains haunted by the very tensions this return seeks to overcome. Stevens seems divided about just what sort of aesthetic return he can make by returning to this poetic mode and uncertain about the political implications of such a gesture. The poem does not so much unfold in a pastoral mode as self-consciously reflect on the fact that it is doing so. For all its triumphant reiterations of "again," "Martial Cadenza" remains troubled by uncertainties about the validity of a rhetoric of return in such circumstances and about the possibility of maintaining a sense of historical and literary continuity in a time of war.

Stevens's complex sense of achieved continuity does not just extend to his own earlier works, but also to a particular masculine tradition in American poetry, since "Martial Cadenza" (1940) begins and ends with echoes of Whitman's great war elegy "When Lilacs Last in the Dooryard Bloom'd." Whitman begins "Lilacs" with a memory of mourning, of a time when "the great star early droop'd in the western sky in the night" (459), and later addresses the star as follows:

> O western orb sailing the heaven,
> Now I know what you must have meant as a month since I walk'd,
> As I walk'd in silence the transparent shadowy night,
> As I saw you had something to tell as you bent to me night after
>   night,
> As you droop'd from the sky low down as if to my side . . . (461)

Stevens, at a time of immense social upheaval, when the sheer scale of warfare brings forebodings of a disruptive conclusion to history, turns to the poetic past in order to achieve a sense of historical continuity, as the poem's opening and concluding lines indicate:

Only this evening I saw again low in the sky
The evening star, at the beginning of winter, the star
That in spring will crown every western horizon,
Again

. . . .

           Only this evening I saw it again,
At the beginning of winter, and I walked and talked
Again, and lived and was again, and breathed again
And moved again and flashed again, time flashed again.
   (*CP* 237–38)

But, significantly, Stevens finds his sense of continuity through a relationship to another time of upheaval, disruption, and loss as recorded
in one of the great war elegies of the nineteenth century, a poem
which commemorates Lincoln and "all the slain soldiers of the war"
(466). Stevens continues where Whitman ends, responding to the
earlier poet's initial forward-looking stance—Whitman "shall mourn
with ever-returning spring" (459)—as well as to his final valedictory
comments: "I cease from my song for thee, / From my gaze on thee
in the west, fronting the west, communing with thee, / O comrade
lustrous with silver face in the night" (466). Thus, Stevens's "again,"
a crucial word in "Martial Cadenza," marks a certain continuity with
the last time the poem's speaker saw the star and with the star's most
celebrated appearance in an American war lyric; Stevens sees the
star again, and he hears Whitman's words about the star again, and
gives them new poetic life. Stevens achieves this regeneration not by
merely repeating but by turning from or against Whitman's words
even as he turns back to them (or as they return to him). For Whitman, the star is a sign of mourning, a sign of loss; the planet of desire
and love returns only to mark the absence of the beloved, for whom
there can be no "again." Stevens's "again" turns this star in a new direction; it does not gesture toward a lost past, but rather *is* "The present close, the present realized, / Not the symbol but that for which
the symbol stands" (*CP* 238). Stevens returns to Whitman's marker
of memory and loss only to make a doubled gesture, to turn it, paradoxically, into a trope that turns away from the past and toward new
beginnings.

   That new beginning also establishes another kind of continuity for Stevens, since, as was mentioned, a previous poetic self also returns with the evening star—a self that also turns away from Whitman's interweaving of military/heroic homosociality and homoeroticism. What returns for Stevens in this poem is not just "The evening star," Venus, the planet of erotic desire, the planet that Stevens referred to in *Harmonium* as the "fantastic star" (*CP* 49), the "furious star" (*CP* 14), as "la belle étoile," "Good light for drunkards, poets, widows, / And ladies soon to be married" (*CP* 25); what returns is the position of the poet as (heterosexual) lover and the definition of masculinity as male heterosexuality, which Stevens assumed in writing those phrases and which were elided in "Girl in a Nightgown":

> Only this evening I saw again low in the sky
> The evening star, at the beginning of winter, the star
> That in spring will crown every western horizon,
> Again . . . as if it came back, as if life came back,
> Not in a later son, a different daughter, another place,
> But as if evening found us young, still young,
> Still walking in a present of our own. (*CP* 237)

In adopting the position of the poet/lover, Stevens also rejects both the father position adopted in "Girl in a Nightgown" and any deferred or vicarious fulfillment "in a later son, a different daughter." Since "the beginning of winter" symbolizes throughout Stevens's oeuvre a decline of both sexual desire and imaginative power, the star's return also suggests an unexpected restoration of both sexual proclivity and poetic creativity. In fact, the poem's own figurative shifts dramatize the process of creative rejuvenation as the poem unfolds. While the typically cautious "as if" in stanza 1 alerts us to the speaker's self-conscious awareness of the fictive or conjectural status of his rejuvenation, the disappearance of this tropic marker in the poem's final lines suggests that the conclusion, to adapt some Bloomian terminology, achieves a self-transumption. Here, Stevens, by removing this self-conscious distancing, triumphs over his initial caution and ambivalence toward the lover position and claims to become as young as, if not younger than, his earlier poetic self:

> Only this evening I saw it again,
> At the beginning of winter, and I walked and talked

Again, and lived and was again, and breathed again
And moved again and flashed again, time flashed again.
   (*CP* 237–38)

The sense of "return" and rejuvenation is marked with particular force
in the tropes of continuity and permanence (the vaguely theological
"ever-living and being, / The ever-breathing and moving," "the vivid
thing in the air that never changes" [*CP* 238]) that displace the poem's
formulation of a present "apart from any past" and that unfold in a
single long sentence that flows across the break between stanzas 3 and
4 with a new confidence, a confidence asserted in the face of the war.
At a first glance, then, the question of the viability of this earlier poetic
self in a time of war would seem to find an increasingly positive answer
in "Martial Cadenza."

   But "Martial Cadenza" does not simply speak the speech of an earlier poetic self; it self-consciously stages the return of that self in order
to problematize the very idea of repetition and, furthermore, to problematize that idea not merely in abstract philosophical or poetic terms
but in specifically historical, political, and gendered ones. Even at the
poem's conclusion, the repetitions of "again" mark the language as
the re-turning of an old trope, so that we are as much aware of the
presence of historical difference as we are of identity; and the precise
difference included *in* this repetition is the historical context—war
in Europe—that interrupts the speaker's meditation on the star in
the poem's central sections. And if the poem stages an increasingly
confident response to the possible rebirth of an earlier erotic poetic
sensibility as a means of resisting the war's infringement of the creative and aesthetic realm, this progression is counterbalanced at its
center by an unsettling question concerning the viability of such a
poetic self in a time of war:

   What had this star to do with the world it lit,
   With the blank skies over England, over France
   And above the German camps? It looked apart. (*CP* 238)

This question proves double-edged: the speaker wonders (as have a
number of the poem's critics) how he can become an erotic stargazer
in such a troubled time. How can the planet of love lead him to think
of the distant war? The experience that feels "like sudden time in a

world without time," in a world "of what there was" (*CP* 237), the experience that opens the possibility of fresh poetic speech after "the silence before the armies" is a sudden consciousness of *both* erotic/ creative energy and martial violence. Another way of phrasing this problem would be to ask what place the planet of love has in a "Martial Cadenza" or, more simply, what Venus has to do with Mars. Greek mythology provides some answers, of course, in the illicit love between the goddess of love and the god of war. The answers provided, though, are neither straightforward nor necessarily comforting, especially if, as the article on Ares/Mars in the *Oxford Classical Dictionary* suggests, Aphrodite/Venus's "eroticism is at least as likely to subvert the *polis* order" (152) as is Ares/Mars's violence. If it is this association which allows the Venerean material to enter into a "Martial Cadenza," then Stevens would appear to be touching on an unsettling relationship between creative/erotic energies and destructive ones. He marks this possibility in the punning assertion that the "evening star" "looked apart" (*CP* 238): it is both "apart" from and "a part" *of* that war. Such a reading remains consistent with the Stevens who later describes the imagination as "a violence from within that protects us from a violence from without" (*NA* 36) and claims that "the war is only part of a war-like whole" (*NA* 21), or writes, in the different figuration of *Notes*, that the war depends on and runs parallel to "a war between the mind / And sky" (*CP* 407). Yet the relationship between Mars and Venus also creates a more positive place for Stevens's former poetic self, suggesting either that the earlier poetic mode can adapt itself to the demands of the time or that martial material can be adapted to or subsumed under the requirements of the lyric; at the very least, it points toward the possibility of some union between erotic and martial poetic *ethoi*. Perhaps, too, one needs to understand the martial and heroic as aspects of Stevens's creative personality, aspects with which he may not be entirely at ease. Here, the poem's title proves relevant. In music, a cadence or cadenza most often provides closure; but "Martial Cadenza" seems to be a poem *against* closure, against the stasis of "a world without time." The cadenza of the classical concerto, however, unfolds in a space left free for improvisation between two tutti chords, an interval suspended between two iterations of a dominant pedal.[3] It puts off closure through or in the name of improvisation. Does Stevens's adumbration of the myth of Venus and Mars create a place and time for lyric extemporization in the midst of war? Is it Mars himself who takes time off to improvise in this context? Perhaps the poem's speaker is not so much an old poetic self as a new, heroic one who now understands his relationship to a previous self.

The poem's uncertainties about establishing such continuity in spite of or as a result of an experience of profound discontinuity are marked with particular force and economy in its figurations of time and in another heavily overdetermined punctuation mark—another dash. As a purely syntactic sign, this dash *is* a moment of "blank time" (*CP* 342) in the poem, an interruption in which meaning is suspended; it creates syntactic discontinuity at the very moment when the speaker recognizes the relationship between erotic and martial energies, a relationship that grounds his sense of poetic continuity and his creation of a more stable masculine identity. The dash might indicate the speaker's hesitation before the disturbing revelations thus made about the nature and sources of creativity. It also marks a hesitation before the development of a characteristically Stevensian version of temporal continuity, one in which continuity proves to be grounded upon discontinuity, upon the reiterations of a pure present that exists "apart from any past, apart / From any future."[4] In fact, the dash appears at the precise moment of Stevens's strongest assertion of this paradoxical temporality ("Yet it is this that shall maintain—Itself / Is time"), as though he could not avoid an irreducible discontinuity at the heart of temporal movement. Stevens clearly proposes this version of continuity as a positive alternative to "the silence before the armies," troped elsewhere as "a world without time," as "that which is not . . . or is of what there was" (*CP* 237). But the hesitation marked by the dash may also indicate some level of discomfort with a continuity grounded on an irreducible discontinuity or with that discontinuity itself. And questions remain, of course, about the peculiar multiple splicing performed by this dash: it joins continuity and discontinuity in a metaphoric equation; it does the same for the two versions of masculinity; and, finally, it splices together these two concerns, so that the paradoxical nature of temporal continuity becomes linked to the problematic relationship between martial and erotic masculinities—or, to put it in more general terms, so that the rather abstract issue of temporal continuity is articulated in concretely gendered terms. The ever-subsisting wave-force of nobility and the "modernizing and ever-modern influence" (*NA* 45) of Stevens's two wartime essays may have some bearing on the problems articulated here. The "ever-living and breathing" star sounds like another version of the force that survives the disconfirmation of each individual imaginative construct, a force that is, perhaps, also part of what brings about each disconfirmation. In "Martial Cadenza," Stevens appears to make a suggestion nowhere present in the essays: namely, that this force may also facilitate the resurrection of a previously invalidated fiction from the "cemetery of nobilities" (*NA* 35)—here, the poet/lover of *Harmonium*.

The importance of "Martial Cadenza" as an unsettled and unsettling poem of recuperation becomes still clearer if one considers its position in *Parts of a World*, between "Yellow Afternoon" and "Man and Bottle." The relationships among these three poems has been obscured, perhaps, by the fact that "Man and Bottle" was originally published alongside the much more canonical "Of Modern Poetry" as one of "Two Theoretic Pieces" in 1940. But the three poems appear in their order of composition in *Parts of a World*, and when taken as a mini-sequence within that volume they adumbrate a micro-narrative of a crucial shift in Stevens's wartime poetics, a shift from one masculine subject-position (lover) to another (martial hero).

The speaker of "Yellow Afternoon," then, seems to lack a means of uniting different aspects of his creative personality, or of understanding just *how* an interior and erotic muse can be made a part of "the fatal unity of war." The poem, in other words, unfolds, as did "Girl in a Nightgown," along a gendered division and a division between interior and external realms; its male speaker initially defines his sense of selfhood in relation to an external reality defined as "the patriarch,"

> that which is the end
> And must be loved, as one loves that
> Of which one is a part as in a unity,
> A unity that is the life one loves,
> So that one lives all the lives that comprise it
> As the life of the fatal unity of war. (*CP* 236)

But for all its rhetoric of unity, the poem finally ends on a note of division between this external, patriarchal world and the interior space occupied by the lover and his beloved muse:

The thought that he had found all this
Among men, in a woman—she caught his breath—
But he came back as one comes back from the sun
To lie on one's bed in the dark, close to a face
Without eyes or mouth, that looks at one and speaks. (*CP* 237)

Stevens's odd and somewhat uncharacteristic syntactic distortions—
again marked by a dash that appears to inscribe the catching of breath
itself within the poem—indicate the difficulty of incorporating this
return to the figuration of the interior, lyric realm and the erotic muse
into a poem so concerned with the self's alignment with a patriarchal
reality. Stevens, in fact, offers a grotesque heightening of his muse's
essential interiority—not merely placing her in "one's bed in the dark"
but further denying her any means of visual contact with the external world or any avenue of verbal communication with that world
and its poet-representative. Stevens's muse here is remarkably similar
to the "Disquieting Muses" painted so often by Giorgio De Chirico.
This kind of surrealism is unusual in Stevens's poetry, and suggests a
stylistic distortion or self-mutilation in the very texture of the poem
as a concomitant to the disfiguration of his muse. The speaker seems
uncertain, then, of how to accommodate "The thought that he had
found all this / Among men, in a woman"—the fact, in other words,
that a creative sensibility troped as a relationship to the feminine and
interior has been the means of access to a reality troped as masculine
and external. The problem seems remarkably similar to the tension
between homosocial and heterosexual constructions of masculinity
in "The Noble Rider." The poem's imagery suggests a deliberate effort
to suppress one aspect of Stevens's creative personality, an uneasiness
with the way in which this inner muse draws him away from "the
fatal unity of war," and yet the very act of inclusion shows the impossibility of eliding the importance of this figure, just as the last line,
in which the disfigured muse "looks at one and speaks," figures the
necessary failure of any such attempt at suppression. This poem, then,
shows Stevens arriving at a certain impasse which the figuration of
Venus and Mars helps him to overcome in "Martial Cadenza."

If Stevens disfigures his feminine muse in "Yellow Afternoon," and
discovers a potentially unsettling relationship between the erotic muse
and a martial temperament in "Martial Cadenza," "Man and Bottle"
seems, by troping the imagination as all male, to go beyond or even

to abandon the latter work's attempt to create a space for the poet/
lover as a means of continuing the poetic career in a time of war:

> The mind is the great poem of winter, the man,
> Who, to find what will suffice,
> Destroys romantic tenements
> Of rose and ice
>
> In the land of war. More than the man, it is
> A man with the fury of a race of men,
> A light at the centre of many lights,
> A man at the centre of men. (*CP* 238–39)

Here, the position of poet/lover disappears, as does any tension between heterosexuality and military/heroic homosociality: Stevens
does not just trope the imagination as male, or define masculinity
exclusively in terms of relationships among men, but figures masculinity and intramasculine relationships as violent and destructive,
as though he had wholly internalized the martial character that was
approached more tentatively in "Martial Cadenza." "Man and Bottle" has received much criticism for this gesture; according to Jahan
Ramazani, the poem, in spite of admitting a complicity between artistic creation and military destruction, "approximates the more fright-
ening accommodations of war not only in Nietzsche but also in the
later Yeats" ("War Elegy" 33); and Longenbach tellingly pits against
the poem Kenneth Burke's critique of using war as a "constitutive
anecdote" (*Plain* 216).

There are, indeed, good reasons to criticize Stevens's thinking here,
but my immediate concern is simply to clarify the place of this gesture
in relation to the shape of his poetic career and perennial aesthetic
concerns. Stevens directs this internalized violence specifically against
the literary past—its run-down houses of fiction or "tenements"—so
that poetry becomes not "a war between the mind / And sky" (*CP* 407)
but a war between Stevens's mind and other minds (most of them
male). Stevens adapts the terminology of war to his career-long engagement with literary tradition and imaginative history, an engagement that has unfolded on the levels of both theme and, as such
critics as Bloom and Cook have shown, influence, allusion, and
echo; or, to put it another way, the internalization of war reduces the

violence of the present and its possible implication of a radical rupture with cultural tradition, aesthetic tradition, and history itself by subsuming such violence under one of Stevens's dominant thematic concerns. And it is not merely the internalization of war that serves as a means of resisting the radical cultural shift discussed in the preceding chapter, but also the way in which Stevens places the present disruption within a whole history of destruction, the mind's destruction of "romantic tenements / Of rose and ice," of "an old delusion, an old affair with the sun, / An impossible aberration with the moon" (*CP* 239), within a whole history of imaginative destruction undertaken by "A man with the fury of a race of men" (*CP* 239). The wholly characteristic language and symbolism of this passage underlines the process of incorporation or "accommodation" taking place therein, another means of asserting the continued viability of Stevens's established poetic modes in the face of war. More importantly, Stevens's term "race" is not just a synchronic hyperbole—part of that rhetoric of heroic magnification and synecdoche typical of much of Stevens's war poetry—but also a kind of diachronic metonymy; it opens a historical dimension to the poet's furious creative/destructive activity by reading that activity as one element in a racial history of creation and destruction.[5] This reading of the phrase is consistent, for example, with the later "Men Made Out of Words" (1946), in which Stevens writes that "The whole race is a poet that writes down / The eccentric propositions of its fate" (*CP* 356), or with his use of the myth of Aeneas and Anchises as a figure of poetic tradition in "The Figure of the Youth as Virile Poet" (*NA* 52–53) and "Recitation after Dinner" (1945). A number of apparently contradictory gestures come together, then, in this poem: Stevens registers the violent disruptiveness of the war in his own tropes of imaginative violence, and thereby asserts this poem's continuity with both his own poetic career and with literary tradition in general (or at least with his reading of literary history). Any radical break is reduced to a shift of gender roles *within* the various masculine possibilities open to a male poet: the military/heroic speaker supplants the heterosexual speaker.

In "Dutch Graves in Bucks County," a 1942 poem rooted both in his reaction to World War II and in his increasing interest in family history, Stevens adopts the position of neither lover nor father but rather of son, or, more generally, of the latest male descendant of a lengthy patriarchal line. This brief description of the poem makes it sound as though Stevens wholeheartedly aligns himself with this patriarchal lineage, but in fact the poem explores this position as a site of intensely conflicting desires. Critics have tended to narrativize this conflict, telling a tale of the speaker's progression from an initial perception of discontinuity between past and present to a final realization of continuity between the two—in other words, limiting each of the different stances toward the past to a specific part of the poem.[6] "Dutch Graves" may be haunted at *every* point by Stevens's continuing ambivalence toward positions of authority and toward the relationships between past and present which such positions maintain (and are maintained *by*). For Stevens, situating himself as male heir of this tradition opens a troubling relationship to the past: he thereby gains access to an established position of authority but also burdens himself with Christian prophetic and apocalyptic traditions that have shaped that position and which, through their claims to a unique relationship to truth, place particular ideological limits upon both the truth-seeking self and the definition of the truth it seeks. On the other hand, a radical break with this past opens the possibility of freedom but takes away the position of authority offered by alignment with the tradition—takes away, perhaps, even the possibility of a position from which one can deny the authority of the Christian past and enact a break with that past. Neither stance, in other words, offers a comfortable resting point for Stevens, and as a result the poem is always divided in its stance toward past and present and the relationships between them. Stevens's solution to this impasse lies not just in seeking a compromise between absolutes of either continuity or discontinuity, but in differentiating among various figurative *modes*—metonymic, synecdochal, metaphoric—for mapping the relationships between past and present, present and future, and fixing his own location in this nexus.

The full complexity of Stevens's stance toward the past and toward the position he occupies within it emerges most clearly when, yet again, a dash marks a moment of particular tension in the poem. This dash appears when Stevens names the one aspect of his cultural inheritance which he is, unsurprisingly, most reluctant to accept or pass on to another generation: his forefathers' Christianity and their prophetic and apocalyptic reading of the American topos and of history in general:

And you, my semblables, whose ecstasy
Was the glory of heaven in the wilderness—

Freedom is like a man who kills himself
Each night, an incessant butcher, whose knife
Grows sharp in blood. The armies kill themselves,
And in their blood an ancient evil dies—
The action of incorrigible tragedy.

And you, my semblables, behold in blindness
That a new glory of new men assembles. (*CP* 292)

Stevens's brief phrase—"the glory of heaven in the wilderness"—proves
difficult to interpret with any absolute certainty in this context; it may
refer either to the inner glory of Christ's spiritual kingdom in the life
of the individual believer, or to the interpretation of the American
topos as fulfillment of biblical prophecy—the Promised Land, the
place where the New Jerusalem shall descend to earth. Stevens finds
his own ecstasy, at any rate, by taking a position outside either of
these concepts, the position of the self-mutilating "freedom" found
in a present that rejects and is rejected by the past. Stevens's "semblables" are forced to exchange their vision of "the glory of heaven in
the wilderness" for another, paradoxical vision, in which they "behold
in blindness / That a new glory of new men assembles" (*CP* 292).
Stevens's ancestors may well turn in their graves when he turns their
plots into tropes of the absolute pastness of the past:

And you, my semblables, are crusts that lie
In the shrivellings of your time and place. (*CP* 291)

And you, my semblables, in the total
Of remembrance share nothing of ourselves. (*CP* 291)

And you, my semblables, know that this time
Is not an early time that has grown late. (*CP* 292)

Stevens's plot of history is one of a constant "divergence" (*CP* 293) in
which each moment follows a new inclination, turning away from the
past without having any absolute end (in both senses of that word) in
sight. Stevens's ancestors, of course, enacted their own "divergence,"
having departed, as emigrants, from the country whose "old flag" now

"flutters in tiny darkness" (*CP* 290), or, as Protestants (members of the Dutch Reform Church, to be specific), having broken with the Catholic Church. But Stevens's tropes of the present also insist on its own divergence from the past ("these are not those rusted armies" [*CP* 292], "The much too many disinherited" [*CP* 292], and so on). Stevens does not "follow down" the same "divergence" as his ancestors; rather, his different divergence informs his self-contradictory sense of continuity.

Other parts of the poem, however, suggest a certain discomfort with the cost of the freedom Stevens claims for himself and his present—a cost, perhaps, already inscribed in that simultaneously suicidal and phoenixlike freedom figured in the poem's tenth stanza. The poem contains a *mise-en-abîme* of ends, a sequence of substitutions that suggests, finally, that Stevens's attempt to step into the position of authority inscribed within or by the ancestral tradition must simultaneously undermine that position. The sixth of the longer stanzas, for example, coming roughly at the poem's midpoint, presents a vision of history as a teleological progression toward a final state of rest:

> An end must come in a merciless triumph,
> An end of evil in a profounder logic,
> In a peace that is more than a refuge,
> In the will of what is common to all men,
> Spelled from spent living and spent dying. (*CP* 291)

This earthly era of final and total peace sounds like a version of the millennium, though a thoroughly secularized one. Stevens's language also gives more emphasis to the struggle that leads to "a peace that is more than a refuge" than to the peace itself, and his uncomfortable paradoxes—"an end of evil" can come only through "merciless triumph"—certainly undercut any possible complacency one might feel about such a final peace. Yet the emotional urgency suggested by the modal "must" and the cumulative force of the appositions that occupy the three central lines of the stanza also suggest a desire or nostalgia for such a "triumph." Stevens writes here, after all, of an essentially consolatory concept of history in which all present expenditure will eventually be recouped in the form of peace, so that "spent" will mean more than merely "exhausted, worn out, used up" ("spent" II.6, *OED*). And yet the next stanza threatens to undo all this with a vision of an expenditure without compensation: "There were other soldiers, other people / . . . Year, year and year, defeated at last and lost / In an ignorance of sleep with nothing won" (*CP* 291). This realization, apparently forced upon Stevens by recollections of the futility of earlier wars, leads to the

> pit of torment that placid end
> Should be illusion, that the mobs of birth
> Avoid our stale perfections, seeking out
> Their own, waiting until we go
> To picnic in the ruins that we leave. (*CP* 292–93)

Stevens's adoption of the prophetic stance allows him to see an end to all ends, an end to the idea of a "placid end" determined by a "profounder logic." The fact that this prediction appears *after* Stevens's overwriting of his ancestor's "glory of heaven" suggests, first of all, the extent to which their Christian rhetoric remains legible beneath Stevens's palimpsest—after all, in the earlier passage he smuggled the word "glory" across stanzas and historical eras. Such an inscription situates Stevens between eras and between different attitudes toward ends. A certain anxiety emerges when Stevens, realizing that "placid end" is "illusion," places himself in the "pit of torment," since his vision of history undermines the very position of authority from which he would undermine and usurp his ancestors' authority. By the poem's end, when the opening stanza's "wheels [that] are too large for any noise" (*CP* 290) have been broken into arches by men who march "Under the arches, over the arches, in arcs / Of a chaos composed in more than order" (*CP* 293), it seems clear that the fate of Stevens's end of ends is to foresee even its own end. Stevens plays his rhetoric of "divergence"—a word whose etymology speaks of both inclinations and bends and turns—against a future generation that will "Avoid our stale perfections." One may "avoid" the past by turning away from it, but Stevens does not allow us to turn away from that word's etymology, which speaks not of turning away, but of a more radical and absolute emptying. In the portrait of the "violent marchers of the present" who "March toward a generation's *centre*" (*CP* 293, my emphasis), the spatial metaphor of the "centre" may offer some minimal compensation for this absence of narrative patterning on the temporal scale, without reinscribing that desire for pattern within a rhetoric of "ends."[7]

The two preceding paragraphs separate two different affective responses to the historical problematic Stevens encounters in this poem—his anxiety over the cost of continuity with the past and his anxiety over the cost of any radical discontinuity—responses which, in fact, are registered simultaneously throughout the poem. The peculiar formal procedures of "Dutch Graves" embody this duality, since they both separate and join the stanzas of the present and the refrains of the past, and the whole poem remains suspended in an irresolvable tension between these two tendencies. The dashes described earlier also demand a double reading. Are stanza 10 and its two surrounding refrains more successfully spliced together than any other such units in the poem, or do the dashes only underscore syntactic incompatibility of the stanza and refrains? Does Stevens hesitate before his vision of freedom, or does this vision rush in upon the refrain of the "semblables"? Even if the dash establishes a new syntactic connection between the two stanzas, it does so while the stanza and refrains insist semantically on the divergence of past and present. It joins in order to mark a separation. Everywhere, then, the past and present turn toward each other in their mutual divergences, and these double turnings collide in the poem's final refrain: "Time was not wasted in your subtle temples. / No: nor divergence made too steep to follow down" (*CP* 293). "Divergence," the act of turning away from the past, or even from the present, paradoxically unites the different epochs in their differences.[8] If these formal strategies record an affective ambivalence toward the figurations of historical relations—a peculiar combination of desire and anxiety—a similar overdetermination may lie behind Stevens's appellation of his ancestors as "semblables." As I have already suggested, these skeletal figures resemble Stevens in their apparent isolation from both past and future: they abandoned their past just as Stevens attempts to abandon his own (including his ancestors and their beliefs). Stevens, too, resembles them in his own isolation from the actual events of World War II—although he may think and write about the combat and sympathize with those who suffer in it, he remains on American soil and learns of the war largely through journalistic mediation. The Baudelairean echo, then, may also bear an element of self-reproach, with Stevens identifying himself—somewhat unreasonably, given his age and physical health—as another "hypocrite lecteur," reading and writing about the war but ultimately remaining as distant and inactive as his "doubly killed" ancestors. But another form of self-reproach, and one more relevant to the dominant tendency of my interpretation of "Dutch Graves," may emerge through a consideration of the doubleness of Stevens's stance toward the past: he turns away from his ancestors, yet positions himself as speaker in relation to that tradition, and, in a sense, claims his ancestors' plot as the ground that validates his own utterance. Stevens thus inscribes within his poem an uneasy nostalgia for the very possibility of such a ground.

Finally, though, the poem's primary tensions and most significant rhetorical shifts do not involve the opposing poles of continuity and discontinuity, but emerge instead in the different *modes* through which Stevens figures continuity *and* discontinuity. Here, in naming his ancestors not as ancestors but as "semblables"—a word that, ironically enough, lacks a good, idiomatic *semblable* in English—Stevens substitutes a relationship of similarity for the temporal/causal connection that the genealogical topos might lead us to expect. One might frame the problem in terms of the Jakobsonian figuration elaborated by David Lodge in *The Modes of Modern Writing* and suggest that Stevens understands his connection to his ancestors in metaphoric rather than metonymic terms (assuming that the assertion of similarity in "semblables" is a more tentative version of an essentially metaphoric statement of identity).[9] In fact, Stevens's metaphoric relationship to his ancestors appears concomitantly with tropes that attempt to sever any temporal or causal connection—tropes that deny, in other words, a relationship on the metonymic plane. In two of the refrains already quoted above in full, for example, Stevens insists on his ancestors' isolation from himself specifically on a temporal/metonymic plane (figured as "the total / Of remembrance" and "an early time that has [not] grown late"), and he further rejects such tropes elsewhere in the poem ("your children / Are not your children," "The much too many disinherited" [*CP* 292]) or translates this temporal figuration into an essentially spatial metaphor ("crusts that lie / In the shrivellings of your time and place"). What Stevens writes in these passages is, appropriately enough, a sequence of metaphors for the absence of a metonymic connection between past and present. It seems reasonable to claim, as other critics have done, that the poem's most notable rhetorical shift occurs in its final refrain; but if my reading of the tensions between the metonymic and metaphoric aspects of language in "Dutch Graves" is accurate, it is necessary to add that the poem does not shift from a perception of discontinuity

to one of continuity but rather from metaphoric to metonymic relation: "Time was not wasted in your subtle temples. / No: nor divergence made too steep to follow down" (*CP* 293). Here, Stevens raises
the possibility of "follow[ing] down" his ancestors' path, of establishing a kind of continuity that unfolds on a metonymic or narrative level.
But what is to be followed is "divergence," an act of turning away or
differing, so that Stevens follows his "semblables" only through that
act of divergence. The peculiarly dense tangle of metaphoric and metonymic forces in this passage finally suggests that the metaphoric relationship Stevens posits between himself and his "semblables" *depends*
on their metonymic distance in time and space, that the assimilating
drive of lyric metaphorizing *depends* on a prior fact of difference on
the metonymic plane which can never be erased by that metaphorizing tendency, so that the productive tension between the two is never
quite resolved.

Of course, these observations merely establish a framework for more
important questions: what, precisely, is at stake for Stevens when he
structures the poem around these two figurations for the relationship
between past and present? Why is there such an urgent need for him
to work out his debt to his ancestors in terms of this complex interplay of metonymic and metaphoric figurations? One possible answer
would be that Stevens claims for himself a certain freedom from any
causal or determining influence by the past while nevertheless, through
his tropes of similarity, denying the kind of absolute rupture that
would leave him adrift in the condition of "disinheritance" encountered in "Cuisine Bourgeoise" (1939), a poem in which the poetic voice
itself is figured as being silenced in "this present, this science, this un-
recognized, // This outpost, this douce, this dumb" (*CP* 228). A bitter
little poem from the same year as "Dutch Graves" (1942), "Outside
of Wedlock" (discussed in brief earlier in this chapter) offers another
more negative assessment of this sense of "disinheritance":

> The strong music of hard times,
> In a world forever without a plan
> For itself as a world,
> Must be played on the concertina.
>
> The poor piano forte
> Whimpers when the moon above East Hartford

Wakes us to the emotion, grand fortissimo,
Of our sense of evil,

Of our sense that time has been
Like water running in a gutter
Through an alley to nowhere,
Without beginning or the concept of an end.

The old woman that knocks at the door
Is not our grandiose destiny.
It is an old bitch, an old drunk,
That has been yelling in the dark.

Sing for her the seventy-fold Amen,
White February wind,
Through banks and banks of voices,
In the cathedral-shanty,

To the sound of the concertina,
Like the voice of all our ancestors,
The *père* Benjamin, the *mère* Blandenah,
Saying we have forgot them, they never lived. (*OP* 112)

Stevens finds himself stranded in a present separated from the past, since the hymns sung for the old woman by the "White February wind" will sound like "the voice of all our ancestors, / The *père* Benjamin, the *mère* Blandenah, / Saying we have forgot them, they never lived" (*OP* 112). Stevens's sense of the present's illegitimacy—it was born "outside of wedlock"—and of the artistic diminishment marked by the substitution of the concertina for the "poor piano forte" bespeak the poetic anxieties created by this sense of disenfranchisement. Clearly, part of Stevens's apprehension of evil resides in the fact that he has not inherited his ancestors' capacity to find order and meaning in the flux of history—the lost "beginning or the concept of an end" and "grandiose destiny" have not been replaced by any suitable new principle. Stevens's appellation of his ancestors as "semblables" in "Dutch Graves" may thus function as an attempt to reconcile two conflicting desires—one for freedom and another for the stability and order that can come from a relation to tradition.

What we might refer to, then, as a certain cautiousness on Stevens's part, a disinclination to purchase freedom by handing over the power that comes from tradition, can also help us to situate Stevens's way of figuring historical process in relation to both apocalyptic and postmodern figurations of history. There may be a strong temptation to see in this aspect of Stevens's work a prefiguration of some characteristic postmodern historiographical rhetoric. Certainly, according to my account, Stevens's poetics of history is very different from the "modernist poetics of history" of Pound and Eliot, for whom, according to James Longenbach, "the present is nothing more than the sum of the entire past—a palimpsest, a complex tissue of historical remnants" (*Modernist* 11). Stevens's version of history, and especially of imaginative history, as a series of apparently isolated, unrelated moments, is not unique to "Dutch Graves"; in "Description without Place" (1945), for example, Nietzsche's vision of "the much-mottled motion of blank time" (*CP* 342) reveals that the "eccentric souvenirs of human shapes" are "all first, / All final" (*CP* 342)—though Stevens playfully places "first" at the end of one line, and "final" at the beginning of the next. In addition, Stevens tends to view the past through a dominant metaphor of depth and discrete layering rather than one of linear continuity, as in that "deep pool / Of these discolorations" (*CP* 342) studied by Nietzsche, the "figures verdant with time's buried verdure" (*CP* 352) of "A Completely New Set of Objects," the "cemetery of nobilities" visited in "The Noble Rider and the Sound of Words," or the "tiny darkness" of Stevens's "doubly killed" (*CP* 290) ancestors six feet or so beneath the topsoil of Bucks County. Stevens's dual emphasis on the depth metaphor and on temporal discontinuity could readily seem emblematic of the midcentury shifts in historiography noted by Michel Foucault in *The Archaeology of Knowledge*: a shift from a linear metaphor to one of depth and stratification; and a shift from a concern with continuities to the study of "the phenomena of rupture, of discontinuity" (*Archaeology* 4). The discipline which Foucault no longer calls "history" but instead refers to as "archaeology" undertakes a "displacement of the discontinuous: its transference from the obstacle to the work itself; its integration into the discourse of the historian, where it no longer plays the role of an external condition that must be reduced, but that of a working concept" (9). To return to a formulation cited earlier, postmodern discourse and its critics tend to figure postmodernism as enacting "some radical break or *coupure*" (Jameson, *Postmodernism* 1), and the new procedures both described and put into action by Foucault would constitute one instance of just such a "radical break." Could one apply Foucault's description of "archaeology" as a discourse "willing . . . to speak of discontinuities, ruptures, gaps" (*Archaeology* 169) to Stevens's historicopoetic discourse? Here, "willing" may prove to be the crucial term— not because Stevens's poetry shows an unambiguous willingness or *un*willingness to situate itself within and speak from a time of "rupture," but rather because it remains so deeply divided in the stance it takes toward this historical situation. Stevens does not deny the actual physical violence of the war, its radical disruption of the social world and of everyday life, but his poetry does not register this violence as or through a radical rupture with all previous cultural and aesthetic forms; his poetry does not offer the "vain temporality, mad, multiform antithetical influx" that Kermode finds in the work of Beckett (*Sense* 115), or in later avant-garde fiction that attempts to make "a break with the past" (114), to "[destroy] the indispensable and relevant past" (123). It is worth considering here the language used by Joseph G. Kronick in his reading of genealogy in Stevens ("Of Parents, Children, and Rabbis: Wallace Stevens and the Question of the Book"). Kronick offers a largely postmodern reading of Stevens—that is, a reading of Stevens *as* postmodern or poststructuralist, a poet for whom "there is a lapse between parents and child, a gap that cannot be bridged by discourse. It is not, however, a rupture within a genealogical line; it is writing, a fragment that is 'neither a determined style nor a failure, but the form of that which is written'" (105–6).

In his reading of Stevens's late lyric of poetic lineage "The Role of the Idea in Poetry," Kronick notes that Stevens "transforms the diachronic descent of parentage into a synchronic pattern of relation— fathers do not breed sons; they bear the dream of patriarchal order" (110). Kronick reads the shift from genealogical continuity to shared dream as a shift toward or all the way *into* a poststructuralist mode of thinking, and, as is evident, his rhetoric finds its own "semblable" in that of Foucault, among others. Presumably, refiguring the father as the "bearer" of the "dream of patriarchal order" decenters the authority of each such bearer, inscribing him within an already fictive discourse and thereby inscribing that patriarchal order itself—the very order postmodernism seeks to undo—within that same discursive realm so that it no longer functions as a self-grounding truth. Yet putting aside counterarguments concerning the essential conservatism in Stevens's decision to align himself even with a self-consciously fictive patriarchal order, and bracketing the possibility that the gesture toward synchronicity could also involve a formalist freezing of historical process and difference, one would still need to note that Kronick's mode of analysis does not leave room, at least in this instance, for questions of affect, of desire and nostalgia for patriarchal fictions of order, or of fear in the face of genealogical "rupture." Neither does it leave room for a sense of Stevens's specific historical context and the ways in which this context is inscribed in his poetry. The affective complexity of Stevens's poetry and of "Dutch Graves" in particular suggests a desire to minimize the "rupture," to somehow protect the aesthetic, interior, imaginative realm from having inscribed within itself the absolute violence occurring in the "external" world. Stevens's designation of his ancestors as "semblables" may function as his point of resistance to this rupture and thereby allows us to situate him, first, as a poet living through a time that radically challenges the mind's capacity to find order, meaning, and continuity in its experience of history, and, second, as a poet still *searching* for and desiring something from that past that he may carry over into the present on his own terms.

It is my hope that these readings have introduced some important complications to the discussion of apocalypse and gender in Stevens's poetry of the war years. Stevens's attitude toward apocalyptic fictions may be more complex than has been previously suggested, not only because of the paradoxes involved in situating oneself after the era of the End, but because of the possibilities for consolation that are lost with the end of that era. Such a loss is especially significant if, as Ramazani has suggested, Stevens's response to the war was a predominantly elegiac one. These poems also show how Stevens's engagement with different poetic genres and modes, and with the different speakers associated with them, functions in relation to his engagement with apocalypse: to resist apocalypse is to resist writing in a specific genre or mode and to resist reproducing a particular type of poetic speech. Such resistance involves, therefore, an exploration of poetic modes that may make an antiapocalyptic stance possible. For Stevens, this resistance also involves the reassertion of the viability of the poetic modes and speakers he worked with prior to the war, as a means of denying the possibility of any "radical break" with(in) his own poetic career or history and literary history. And, finally, besides suggesting that Stevens's gendered figurations explore multiple versions of masculinity at least as much as they alternate between masculine and feminine figurations of poetry and imagination, this chapter has suggested that these explorations are not often free of anxieties and uncertainties, regardless of whether these affective elements result from tensions within or between different masculine subject-positions or from Stevens's ambivalent and troubled relationship to such versions of masculinity.

Part II: Stevens and the Genres of the End

chapter four

The Refuge That the End Creates

Pastoral and Apocalyptic Modes in
"Credences of Summer"

Given the relationship outlined thus far between Stevens's resistance
to apocalyptic rhetoric and the fears aroused by World War II, one
might expect the poems that emerged after the war to be relieved of
the apocalyptic burden. Yet this is not the case, at least not in "Credences of Summer" (1946). Even critics such as Huston and Berger,
who see the poem as a largely pastoral celebration of a state of peace,
have noted the presence of apocalyptic or, in the case of Berger, "counterapocalyptic" elements in the poem. Why should a poem of pastoral
peace employ either of these modes? One answer to this question
would be that "Credences" demonstrates an imagination still making adjustments to a new set of requirements after being accustomed
to working at a particular (apocalyptic) pitch or in a particular mode,
an imagination still negotiating a path between the old and the new
social and literary contexts. But the conflicting modal identifications
made by Huston and Berger—apocalyptic and "counterapocalyptic"
respectively—suggest a second possibility, particularly if one assumes
that the text legitimates both of these readings. If Stevens is still struggling to resist apocalyptic rhetoric and thinking in a postwar world,
it may be that the resistance to apocalypse encountered in his wartime
poems is not exclusively directed toward external sources of that rhetoric. In other words, "Credences" may lead us to ask whether Stevens's
wartime resistance to apocalypse is a struggle against a tendency within
himself, a struggle with his own apocalyptic desires and prophetic
ambitions; the presence of both apocalyptic and antiapocalyptic rhet-
orics in "Credences of Summer" may be a continuation of this *internal* struggle.

The presence of these two modes touches on a second critical
conflict, a conflict between those who read "Credences" as a highly
idealized version of pastoral, a poem of achieved or desired perfection, stability, and peace (Vendler, Huston, Berger, Carroll, the earlier

Riddel) and those who see it as an ironization of pastoral topoi (the later Riddel, Jarraway). My purpose is to explore as fully as possible the forces operating in the poem that have generated *both* the ironist and idealist readings and a few others as well. I hope to show that a desire for certainty, stability, or absolutes, and a mistrust of such desires—a mistrust that can be construed as an active desire for uncertainty, change, for the "half colors of quarter-things" (*CP* 288)— function as equal, positive forces in the poem, and that these forces are marked most clearly in the complex interplay of pastoral, apocalyptic, and antiapocalyptic modes. This interplay does not involve an ironization of the pastoral mode. Stevens seems to have been aware that a dismissive attitude toward pastoral poetry was common among both poets and critics: in distinguishing, for example, between "High poetry and low" (*CP* 490) in canto iii of "Things of August," he clearly aligns pastoral with the latter category. But rather than ironizing pastoral, "Credences" regularly heightens the pastoral mode by incorporating eschatological and apocalyptic modulations. Yet the poem is still more complex than that formulation indicates, since these modulations simultaneously become the objects of a cautionary ironization, of a desire for self-limitation, a desire to undermine or resist an excessive desire, as though Stevens both desired and mistrusted the sense of poetic power inscribed within the apocalyptic position. This double desire and mistrust again leads to the kind of reconsideration outlined above of Stevens's wartime engagement with apocalyptic rhetoric: his resistance to apocalypse may have as strong an internal source as it does an external one.

These considerations should remind us, too, that Stevens's engagement with apocalypse is an engagement with what we might now call a "master narrative"—in fact, with the master narrative of all master narratives, at least in Western thought—and that "mastery" and "master narrative" have come to be buzzwords in efforts to distinguish the modern from the postmodern. They are the fictions that postmodern art forms either abandon, according to critics like Ihab Hassan or Jean-François Lyotard, or both "use and abuse, install and then destabilize" in Linda Hutcheon's formulation (*Poetics* 23); for Hutcheon, postmodern art and theory are marked by their "masterful denials of mastery" (20). If apocalyptic language can thus be conceived as offering a maximum of discursive power and mastery, then Stevens's engagement with its "master narrative," along with the apocalypse-haunted masculine figures of discursive power that appear throughout "Credences," can help clarify the extent to which he remains or desires to remain within this tradition. The poem's masculine figures, which I shall examine in greater detail, remind us that the phrase "master narrative" is deliberately gendered, that "master narratives" belong within a tradition in which absolute or univocal truth is consistently associated with male speakers and a male deity. In "Credences," Stevens's engagement with this tradition and with the kinds of masculine subject-positions inscribed within it—as well as with a few subject-positions that offer alternatives to such masterful, masculine poetic speakers—is deeply ambivalent; the poem, in other words, constantly questions the positions of masculine discursive mastery that it also desires. This is not to suggest that Stevens's figures of "mastery" function as a conscious entry on his part into the postmodern problematizing of "mastery" and masculinity, but simply that his attitude toward these figures in "Credences" helps place him in relation to that discourse. They also have a place in the poem's complex engagements with pastoral and apocalyptic modes, and this chapter's main purposes will be not just to explore these issues on their own but to understand how they might be articulated together.

I begin my reading of "Credences" with some observations on the poem's masculine figures, and, in particular, with the one figure that does not belong to the apocalyptic cast list: the "bristling soldier" (*CP* 375) of canto v. And it may be helpful first to situate this figure in relation to the more general disengagement from heroic and military rhetoric—a sort of a demobilization of the imagination—under way in some of the shorter lyrics written before and after "Credences" and under way in that poem. Berger has already commented on this aspect of "Credences"; for him, it is "a poem of recovery even more than of peace" (84), one that deals with "the difficulty of believing that a *state* of peace has arrived, as opposed to an interval" (83–84). A number of poems written *after* "Credences" and published under the collective title "More Poems for Liadoff" in the fall of 1946 could be similarly described, since peace remains desired rather than fully achieved in each. In "Extraordinary References," for example, the speaker cannot ignore the difference made by war, despite the "peace" attained when "The mother ties the hair-ribbons of the child." That "peace" transforms the present into a time of elegiac speech, "compos[ing] us in a kind of eulogy" (*CP* 369) that places "These earlier dissipations of the blood"—a sheer wasteful expenditure—among its "extraordinary references" (*CP* 369). The articulation of the relationship between past and present in terms of gender seems particularly telling here: the present is characterized by the mother's and daughter's shared creation of order and peace; violence and "heroism" are the characteristics of men no longer present, perhaps of men who no longer *have* a place in the present—a great-grandfather who "*was an Indian fighter*" and a father who died in the war (*CP* 369). The sense that these female figures live "In the inherited garden, [where] a second-hand / Vertumnus creates an equilibrium" (*CP* 369), points to a shift in creative priorities in a time of peace that must always be marked as a *belated* peace, a peace that includes a new knowledge of war. Of course, the qualifiers "inherited" and "second-hand" suggest a still more complex relationship between bellicose past and peaceful present; both in the world historical and literary historical realms, the garden's pastoral peace is informed, if not entirely created, by the heroic expenditures of previous generations and "larger" genres. Postwar pastoral retains, then, an awareness of its relationship to or difference from the wartime genres. Sometimes, Stevens betrays an uncertainty as to the validity of pastoral peace in a postwar world: when the speaker who tells of "The Dove in the Belly" (fall 1946) asks "How [it is] that / The rivers shine and hold their mirrors up, / Like excellence collecting excellence" (*CP* 366–67), the need to pose this question may be underwritten by the lingering consciousness of the war, by an inability to believe in "War's miracle begetting that of peace" (as in "Mountains Covered with Cats"—*CP* 368). These lines may also mark a certain discomfort with the possibility that war might be forgotten in the enjoyment of pastoral peace—or perhaps with the idea that war makes peace possible. As early as 1942, Stevens seems to have had some sense that postwar poetry would not be able to forget the war and naively return to its prewar subjects, manners, and modes; he recognized, in "Repetitions of a Young Captain," that "the departing soldier . . . in [his prewar] form will not return" (*CP* 308). And in the early postwar poem (from the fall of 1946) "A Woman Sings a Song for a Soldier Come Home," his concern with the psychic wounds endured by returning soldiers dramatizes the difficulty of demobilizing his own imagination. If the "Woman" is Stevens's muse, or the feminine aspects of his imagination, and the "Soldier" that "violence from within that protects us from a violence without" in a "war between the mind / And sky" (*CP* 407), this poem shows Stevens openly questioning the possibility of poetic recovery, of domesticating or quieting that more heroic aspect of his imagination: "the walker speaks / And tells of his wound, // Without a word" (*CP* 360). Even when he manages to return to a favorite Stevensian trope and "Talk of the weather" (*CP* 361), the soldier remains an outsider, left "Just out of the village, at its edge, / In the quiet there" (*CP* 361), an alienated, marginalized, and yet irreducible presence.

This continuing demobilization of Stevens's own imagination may help make sense of one of the more troubling elements in "Credences": the "bristling soldier" who "looms" (*CP* 375) near the poem's geographical center in canto v. On a more literal level, the soldier may function as a return of the repressed historical fact, a reminder of Stevens's place in a history that includes recent slaughter, a slaughter that the troubled mind of canto i must, as I shall later detail, "lay by" before beginning its pastoral meditation. And soldiers were still a part of the European landscape, involved in the demilitarization of the Axis powers, the establishment and maintenance of new geopolitical boundaries, the reconstruction of infrastructures, the repatriation of prisoners of war, Holocaust survivors, displaced persons of all kinds and nationalities, and so on. As one of "the land's children, easily born, its flesh, / Not fustian" (375), the soldier is an inescapable part of the postwar scene, a reminder that the maintenance of peace—the very condition that makes "Credences of Summer" possible and is celebrated by the poem—may involve the continued expenditure of masculine, military energies.

More purely creative matters may be at stake here, too. Vendler objects to this section's "too avid logic" (238), but the most striking aspects of the canto are the internal tensions among its different figurations, tensions that have their source in the incommensurability of the canto's logical schemata to the force of its desire for a particular kind of poetic power. The three exempla Stevens contemplates at the beginning of the canto all deal with the sources of different types of power:

One day enriches a year. One woman makes
The rest look down. One man becomes a race,
Lofty like him, like him perpetual.

Or do the other days enrich the one?
And is the queen humble as she seems to be,

The charitable majesty of her whole kin? (*CP* 374–75)

The tensions among these figurations are especially problematical in
the two human exempla offered by Stevens. The relationship between
queen and "kin," "One woman" and "The rest," works in essentially
synchronic terms, and raises questions about the sources of power. It
asks whether an idealized concept gains its power from the particulars
from which it has been abstracted, or whether the particulars gain
their power from their relationship to that ideal. Stevens's statement
about the relationship between "One man" and "a race," however,
combines synchronic and diachronic figurations, since the "One man"
could be either an exemplar—a figure who embodies or sums up the
ideals of the culture to which he belongs—or an origin, a first progenitor, an Adam, a father of all succeeding fathers; he could also fill
both roles simultaneously. The shift toward this ambiguous figuration and to diachronic, genealogical relations among masculine figures
suggests that a particular anxiety about "lofty" and "perpetual" poetic
lineages is at stake for Stevens, and especially about masculine and
feminine figurations of imaginative power. This anxiety becomes especially clear when Stevens introduces "The bristling soldier, weather-
foxed, who looms / In the sunshine" (*CP* 375). The last eight lines of
the canto are dominated exclusively by masculine figurations; the
queen and her kin disappear; a possible progenitor is displaced by a
"filial form," thereby shifting the locus of power from male origin to
male latecomer, father to son; and the masculine genealogy is projected onto nature itself, onto the relationship between the pastoral
day's "more than casual blue" (*CP* 375) and year. This last projection
figures a desire that the relationship between past and present be "more
than casual," that it follow the causal logic of genealogy; and it suggests that a desire to think of poetry in a postwar situation in terms
of this kind of masculine energy and continuity is the dominant force
behind these figurations. MacCaffrey rightly identifies the "bristling
soldier" (*CP* 375) as "one of Stevens's 'giants,' a recurrent figure sig-
nifying imagination's power to transcend or make transparent the particular" (426), though this reading too readily absorbs the specifically
military element—an especially significant detail in 1946—into a

more general thematics of masculine imaginative power. This "bristling" figure presumably "looms" larger and more martially than the "inchling" poet who "bristles" in "Bantams in Pine-Woods" (*CP* 76), and his presence acknowledges Stevens's awareness of irreducible masculine, heroic energies in the poetic self that constructs these alternately pastoral and sublime landscapes, or at least indicates a lingering desire to conceive of his own poetic energies in such terms. There is still some sort of "violence from within" in the workings of the imagination.

And yet if the "bristling soldier" is one of Stevens's "giants" or tropes of imaginative power, he is not the only such figure in the poem, and one of the problems in reading "Credences" lies in the relationship of this distinctly military giant to the figures of prophetic power that otherwise dominate the poem's landscapes. The soldier draws attention, in other words, at the center of the sequence, to a certain problematic relationship between two of Stevens's dominant tropes of power from the war years—the soldier and the visionary/prophet (the latter represented by such figures as "Canon Aspirin" of *Notes* or the "plentifullest John" [*CP* 345] whose "Description is revelation" [*CP* 344] in "Description without Place"). In "Credences," Stevens never seems entirely at ease with the latter figures. The poem is not just divided in its figurations of poetic power, but divided in its stances toward one of those figurations in particular; the poem's prophetic figures seem marked by a desire for poetic power and a desire to limit that desire. It would be too simple to suggest that the soldier gives us a glimpse of what Stevens suppresses when he populates the poem with seers and visionaries—too simple, and difficult to support on the basis of the text. What may matter here, in other words, are not the continuities between the two kinds of figurations, but the differences, the gaps, the discontinuities. These gaps and discontinuities, I hope to show, may have something to do with pastoral's tendency throughout its history to situate itself in relation to both epic/political concerns and eschatological ones. But before I turn to the differences between these two figurations of masculinity, it is necessary to explore the relationships between apocalypse and pastoral and to situate the poem's prophets and seers in that context. First, then, comes a detailed consideration of the relationships between those modes, both within Stevens's poem and in the literary tradition.

At the very least, the history of the pastoral genre offers another way of understanding the soldier's presence in "Credences." When Stevens brings the soldier into his poem, or when he refers, in the poem's first line, to a recent past that left "all fools slaughtered" (*CP* 372), he marks a boundary between the world of pastoral peace and the world of historical/political conflicts. Here, I wish to return to Annabel Patterson's *Pastoral and Ideology: Virgil to Valéry*, which sees such boundary marking as one of the defining gestures of pastoral. This gesture appears, significantly enough, in the first of Virgil's *Eclogues*:

> the *we* represented by Meliboeus must exclude the *you* represented by Tityrus. And every other aspect of those first five lines explains and passionately justifies that exclusion. While the selfhood of Tityrus is associated with reflection (*meditaris*), with echoes, with song, with literary allusion, and especially with leisure and pro-tection, the community to which Meliboeus belongs is connected to (at the moment of its severance from) the most value-laden word in Roman culture, the *patria*, subsuming the concepts of ori-gin, national identity, and home. To which of these sets of values should Virgil's readers (by definition here, readers of poetry) be expected to affiliate themselves? (2)

This is one version of what Harold Toliver calls "the dialectical, ten-sive structure characteristic of all worthwhile pastoral" (Toliver 5). Toliver's "worthwhile" is particularly telling here: it is a reminder of the commonplace perception of pastoral as "low" or "minor" poetry, particularly when it lacks that "dialectical, tensive structure." Pas-toral, according to this view, needs to deal with something more than just rural contentment in order to be "worthwhile." Stevens's version of Virgil's gesture seems to involve the bracketing out of the imme-diate historical past (an element also present in Virgil through the fact of Meliboeus's exile), of violence and "slaughter," and one won-ders whether in Stevens this act indicates a need or desire to bracket out one of the poetic selves that lived in and responded to that his-torical situation, as well as the kind of poetry written in response to that context. But the gesture also brackets *in* the same elements, draws them into the poem and thereby relates the world of pastoral fulfillment and peace to something larger than itself. Such postwar poems as "Extraordinary References," "A Woman Sings a Song for a Soldier Come Home," and "Mountains Covered with Cats" could be understood to engage with pastoral convention in a similar fashion, and for similar reasons.

Yet in the opening canto of "Credences" Stevens also introduces another "dialectical, tensive structure," one that involves a complex of conventional relationships between pastoral and apocalypse. Canto i is set on "the last day of a certain year / Beyond which there is nothing left of time" (*CP* 372). These words initiate a rhetoric of terminations that reappears throughout the poem and culminates in what Berger calls the "counterapocalypse" (87) of canto viii.[1] In canto i, this mode is marked not only by the speaker's claim to speak from an eschatological position, but by the desire to leave behind "The fidgets of remembrance" (*CP* 372) and the troubling thoughts of slaughtered fools—a desire, perhaps, to forget the disasters of history in the pure present of a hypostatized "this." Stevens, by placing his pastoral vision on "the last day of a certain year / Beyond which there is nothing left of time," begins to revise a whole history of relationships between the pastoral and apocalyptic modes, a textual *history* in which the two constantly assume new configurations. The pastoral imagery one finds in such biblical eschatological writings as Isa. 11:6–9, 35, and 51:3, or Joel 3:18—sacred versions of what is sometimes referred to as "golden age" pastoral—describes a future state of perfected earthly existence and, more specifically, perfected existence within the holy land (other lands will not fare so well). The biblical prophets foretell a state of natural and of *super*natural blessedness, when the "earth shall be full of the knowledge of the Lord, as the waters cover the sea" (Isa. 11:9), when "the sun shall be no more thy light by day . . . but the Lord shall be unto thee an everlasting light" (60:19). The last chapter of Revelation, with its stream of life and two trees on either side of that stream in the midst of the New Jerusalem, unites two veins of imagery—the urban (or templar) and the pastoral—that appear throughout Old Testament prophetic eschatology and apocalypse.[2] This use of the pastoral topos to figure the postapocalyptic world reappears in much Christian poetry and above all in certain loci classici of pastoral elegy. In an apocalyptic modulation that offers consolation to the mourning shepherd of Spenser's "November" eclogue, Colin Clout speaks of a pastoral afterlife: "No daunger there the shepheard can astert: / Fayre fieldes and pleasaunt layes there bene, / The fieldes ay fresh, the grasse ay greene" (ll. 187–89). Milton, in a similar passage in "Lycidas," imagines the deceased shepherd risen "Where other groves, and other streams along, / With nectar pure his oozy locks he laves" (ll. 174–75). Here, however, the relationship between the two modes becomes double-edged, since in both works the elegist's world is already a pastoral one, and the transfigured pastoral vision has an essentially contrastive relationship to the earthly pastoral—a doubled relationship rather neatly articulated by Toliver: "In generic terms we notice that most renaissance Christian and Platonist poetry begins with the concrete body of Arcadian imagery, using it not only dialectically—as something to be discarded in the course of discovering paradise—but also substantially, as the body of paradise itself" (140). The final stage of this dialectic—the heavenly pastoral—ironically empties the first, earthly stage, or achieves what Harold Bloom might call a metaleptic triumph over earlier versions of the topos—just as the New Jerusalem of Revelation and the pastoral fulfillments envisioned in earlier prophetic books prove superior to any earthly version of such "places." Any configuration of apocalypse and pastoral that forgets or elides this relationship would still need to be read in terms of that omission, as Toliver again suggests when noting that Restoration pastoral is "no longer dominated by the Christian-Platonist view—though of course not unmindful of it" (206–7).

Two sets of questions emerge from these considerations. The first concerns the presence in the poem's first canto of two different "dialectical, tensive structures," both of which are thoroughly conventional and thoroughly embedded in the history of the pastoral genre. One of my purposes in the following paragraphs will be to make some sense of this modal and generic tug-of-war and to link these conflicting strains to the relationship between the soldier and the prophetic figures. The second set of questions concerns the relationships between pastoral and apocalypse in Stevens's poem, and more particularly the ways in which "Credences" rewrites previous relationships between these genres and to what end. It seems particularly difficult to decide whether "Credences" is a predominantly pastoral poem with apocalyptic modulations, or an apocalyptic poem with pastoral modulations. My purpose is not so much to make a final decision in this matter as to suggest why the decision remains so difficult to make. To this end, I will move on to the second of these two sets of questions.

How does Stevens rewrite the relations between pastoral and apocalypse? If canto i's fictive claim that "There is nothing more inscribed" (*CP* 372) means that the speaker is inscribing, in that very claim, the final version of the relationship between pastoral and apocalyptic modes, then that final version would appear to present a paradoxical and doubled relationship both between the two modes and between itself and the history of that relationship. The eschatological moment usually stands at the threshold of its own destruction or emptying—it occurs in "this" world but gestures toward the next one. But Stevens redefines or reinscribes it as a pure boundary or limit, an end with no "after," a surface with no depth, an inside with no outside; it is a thoroughly hollowed eschaton. In "Credences," this boundary casts all desire back upon the "this" which "must comfort the heart's core against / Its false disasters," the pastoral world in which the mind "lays by its trouble" and "lovers [wait] in the soft dry grass" (*CP* 372). If Douglas Robinson's account of the characteristic tendency of American apocalypse is accurate—he notes that American apocalypses do not explore whatever lies beyond the eschatological boundary but rather seize and explore that liminal territory itself (Robinson xii, 7)—then Stevens's text "goes one better" in this limiting of the eschatological limit; it explores what lies *before* the boundary. Certainly, this is the effect of canto iv, which develops the rhetoric of terminations more strenuously than any other part of the poem, but just as strenuously empties that rhetoric of any reference to a point beyond itself, and especially beyond the harvest metaphor, with its long history in Christian eschatology. The "[limit] of reality" (*CP* 374) is a limit that cannot be transcended. Stevens can be understood here as reversing an earlier reversal, ironizing an earlier irony in his reformulation of the relationship between apocalyptic and pastoral modes. It may be significant that canto iv is the only canto in which Stevens *names* the landscape he describes as the actual landscape of his childhood: it is here that the poem becomes most thoroughly "topographical" in mode. This gesture toward greater geographical and historical specificity may also function as a counterweight to that apocalyptic tendency, especially if one bears in mind Hartman's comments that "what stands between us and the end of the (old) world is the world" and that an apocalyptic desire involves a "strong desire to cast out nature" (x). To name and celebrate the particular is to establish resistances to that desire.

Desire, then, offers one way of understanding the relationships between pastoral and apocalyptic modes in "Credences of Summer." Throughout the poem, Stevens treats pastoral not just as a mode of desire but as a mode that facilitates a certain disciplining of desire. Pastoral offers fulfillment, but it offers a distinctly "lesser" sort of fulfillment than the kind imagined in apocalyptic discourse. Canto i insists that the mind "[lay] by its troubles" and find "comfort" in the pastoral "now" of "midsummer come," in the insistently repeated "this" (*CP* 372) that has been separated from the reality of the recently ended historical catastrophe ("all fools slaughtered" [*CP* 372]) and from any possible future ("autumnal inhalations," "there is nothing left of time" [*CP* 372]); in so doing, it presents a hyperbolic version of a characteristic Stevensian rhetoric against the idea that there is anything "more than" or "beyond" the "this." The first part of canto vii similarly develops pastoral as a site for the mastery of desire. When the pastoral singers of canto vii's first half sing "desiring an object that was near, / In face of which desire no longer moved, / Nor made of itself that which it could not find" (*CP* 376), they sing of a desire to discipline an irreducible desire and identify the desire to limit desire as the force that produces the pastoral song "of summer in the common fields" (*CP* 376). If this disciplining of desire has a positive value for Stevens, as Bloom suggests (*Climate* 250–51), then Stevens's attitude toward these singers cannot be as dismissive as Huston (269) claims. But then the second part of canto vii must also be less celebratory or tolerant of "unreal songs" than MacCaffrey (432–33) and Bloom insist. Although singing "of summer in the common fields" from "Far in the woods" involves a disciplining of desire by that which *could* be found, it still falls short of the more severe discipline of the "savage scrutiny" undertaken by the "thrice concentred self," a self that no longer "avert[s]" itself and instead sings "in face / Of the object" (*CP* 376). More importantly, Stevens puns on the desire that produces both: one is always in the woods/woulds when singing of "summer in the common fields"—a common pun in Stevens, as in "Bantams in Pine-Woods" or the "dogwoods" of the "dog [that] had to walk" (*CP* 229) in "Forces, the Will & the Weather." The song "of summer" remains distant from such a poetics or such a "concentring" of desire; it merely desires the mode of desire whose actualization Stevens describes in the latter portion of the canto. Even here, there is the possibility of some remainder of desire, since a "savage scrutiny" does not, at least etymologically, get one out of woods/woulds, whether these be "obscurer selvages" (*CP* 317) or not. "Concentring" may involve a disciplining of desire that cannot do away with desire.

It is not surprising that desire should be thus persistent in the work of a poet so enamored of desire, a poet for whom poetry and even perception itself are driven by "desire, set deep in the eye" (*CP* 467); but it is surprising to find in Stevens a desire to discipline or reduce desire, to find an object "In face of which desire no longer moved" (*CP* 376). But of course the desire to discipline desire may be the most intense and ungovernable desire of all, as is suggested not just by the implicit violence of a "savage scrutiny" but by the possibility that in undertaking such a scrutiny we are still in the woods/woulds. In other words, Stevens, even as he constructs pastoral as a mode that facilitates a disciplining of desire, leaves in his texts the marks of the intensity and irreducibility of the desire for such discipline. Even the absence of desire needs to be restlessly redescribed as "eternal foliage," "arrested peace," and "permanence," an "essential barrenness" (*CP* 373). Thus canto ii's desire to "see the very thing" (*CP* 373) rather than the desires (the punning "physical" or "metaphysical pine[s]" [*CP* 373]) that construct the objects of desire is nevertheless couched entirely in the imperative mode, a mode of desire rather than fulfillment, and the "hottest fire of sight" (*CP* 373) hovers ambiguously between a trope of purgation and a trope of desire. To see "the very thing" would be to see it without any such tropes. One also needs to ask why canto i echoes the "deep heart's core" (l. 12) from Yeats's "The Lake Isle of Innisfree," a pastoral of exile, desire, and nostalgia, particularly since "Credences" elsewhere seems to be, as Eleanor Cook points out, a poem of homecoming ("Stevens and Catullus" 73).

What, exactly, is the nature of this problematical desire, and why do attempts to reduce it only multiply the text's figurations of desire? Huston claims that in canto ii Stevens's "vision is momentarily apocalyptic" (265), and while this reading may seem at first to contradict my sense of the speaker's self-imposed disciplining, it should be clear that such self-discipline can only be necessary in the presence of an excessive desire. Such a desire, in fact, might be the "metaphysical pine" whose "anatomy" the speaker of canto ii would prefer to "postpone"—though postponement itself only prolongs desire. Might a "metaphysical pine" resemble what Derrida calls an "apocalyptic desire" ("Apocalyptic" 82)? Does another Stevensian version of apocalypse emerge in this canto, one that cannot quite be subsumed as a negative moment within a predominantly antiapocalyptic interpretation of "Credences" and of Stevens's oeuvre in general—and might it belong to an apocalyptic tendency that has always existed alongside Stevens's antiapocalyptic stance? I suggested earlier in this chapter that Stevens's antiapocalyptic rhetoric may always have been directed toward an apocalyptic tendency within himself, and not simply against an apocalyptic rhetoric that appeared in the political discourse of the war years and against the war itself. As I discussed in my first chapter, apocalyptic texts encode a desire not just "to cast out nature," as Hartman writes (x), but to break with "the indispensable and relevant past" (Kermode, *Sense* 123), to cast out a history, which, for an apocalyptic seer, only "deserves . . . to perish" (Scholem 10). Such desires begin with the conviction that nature and history cannot satisfy us in any lasting way, or that history itself and human action cannot right the wrongs of history. The very restlessness of Stevens's desire, its constant desire to move on to fresh satisfactions after each encounter with "what will suffice," its eventual dissatisfaction with and rejection of each achieved moment of satisfaction, may always harbor the danger of becoming an apocalyptic desire. Such an implication emerges, for example, in "Man and Bottle" (1940), which informs us that "the mind"

> has to persuade that war is part of itself,
> A manner of thinking, a mode
> Of destroying, as the mind destroys,
>
> An aversion, as the world is averted
> From an old delusion, an old affair with the sun,
> An impossible aberration with the moon,
> A grossness of peace. (*CP* 239)

Filreis is critical of the implicit politics of this passage, since they suggest an acquiescence to the idea that war is a normal part of political reality, but the poem is double-edged in realizing concurrently the violence of the imagination—here, the imagination does more than merely "[press] back against the pressure of reality" (*NA* 36) and actually initiates a violence against the past from its own desire for change. The poem registers, in other words, an awareness of the dangers of the imagination. "Man and Bottle" brings out the apocalyptic potential of two Stevensian topoi whose separate appearances elsewhere have less clearly eschatological implications for the poet: the poem reminds us of the earlier statement that "poetry is a destructive force" that "can kill a man" (*CP* 192–93); it reminds us of Stevens's frequent insistence that the imagination always knows (or should know) "that what it has is what is not / And throws it away like a thing of another time" (*CP* 382). Stevens's essentially self-protective and reactive figuration of the mind's violence in "The Noble Rider" reads as an attempt to tame the force described in the earlier "Man and Bottle," or perhaps articulates the increase in external pressure Stevens felt by the time he wrote the essay. "Man and Bottle" also bears a certain homology, in its figuration of the dangers of that otherwise positive and generative force, to Stevens's recognition of the unsettling relationship between erotic desire and martial energies in "Martial Cadenza." Canto ii of "Credences" seems also to respond to those problematical associations. It marks the presence of a potentially apocalyptic desire, a "desire / For what is not" (*CP* 373), and simultaneously seeks to tame this desire, attempting to convince it that it might find permanent satisfaction in the "now" of "midsummer come" and "arrested peace"— the very "grossness of peace" (*CP* 239), the peacefulness of "what there was," of "the silence before the armies" (*CP* 237) that Stevens rejected in "Man and Bottle" and "Martial Cadenza." Read in this context, the desire for "an eternal foliage," for "arrested peace," for "Joy of such permanence" (*CP* 373) could function as a self-correction of the wish to cast off "a grossness of peace," or perhaps as a way of settling the contradiction between this wish and another of Stevens's wartime desires, the desire to discover "the chants of final peace" (*CP* 259). Since there is no question of Stevens directing such desire toward a conventionally apocalyptic vision of fulfillment, its redirection toward an earthly pastoral of permanent peace functions as a kind of *askesis*, or self-disciplining, of that potentially destructive force.

   This reading of the relations between pastoral and apocalypse works from the assumption that the poem's primary impulse is apocalyptic and that the pastoral elements serve as a means of checking or re-channeling that impulse. Yet if one assumes instead that the poem is primarily pastoral, a different set of questions emerges, along with a different way of thinking about the relations between the two modes. In a largely pastoral poem, why should there be a question of terminations at all? Why must the value of a summer day in Oley appear only against this peculiar eschatological backdrop? One might begin to answer these concerns by suggesting that canto iv attests to Stevens's sense of his position in literary history and of the impossibility of simply stepping outside that history altogether: to turn against the past means to engage with the past. But more importantly, the very presence of this antiapocalyptic apocalyptic fiction indicates, as was the case in canto ii, the operation of a desire that cannot be satisfied within the realm of pastoral; in fact, it is only the speaker's eschatological position that allows him to assert the pastoral world's status as a final value, as a final locus of fulfillment: "Things stop in that direction and since they stop / The direction stops and we accept what is / As good" (*CP* 374). The pastoral world requires some kind of eschatological heightening in order to function as the mode in which "a *final* accord with reality" (*LWS* 719, my emphasis) can occur. Stevens makes a complex gamble by raising the stakes to an eschatological level; he escapes his pastoral mode and adopts an already problematic (for him) apocalyptic one in order to affirm the value of the former. If one considers this gesture in relation to the previous history of apocalyptic and pastoral modes, one would appear to encounter another version of that Stevensian tendency, noted by Cook in relation to Stevens's allusions, to avoid any straightforward reversal of conventions and instead to decreate his sources and then move "beyond, in order to retrieve what, after much testing, will hold" ("King James" 241). Canto i of "Credences" transposes this tendency from the level of allusion and trope to that of genre and mode. The possibility that this process marks a gap between apocalyptic desires and pastoral fulfillments may help clarify the strangely doubled stance toward the pastoral world in the first canto and elsewhere: the speaker's desire for absolutes, his need to eschatologically heighten the pastoral mode, places him outside that mode even as the text operates within it (or as it operates within the text). Something of this ambivalence may be involved in the *kind* of speaker who utters the first canto's words: he describes a conventional pastoral/erotic scene of "young broods," "roses . . . heavy with a weight / Of fragrance" (*CP* 372) and "lovers waiting in the soft dry grass," but does not himself occupy the expected position of masculine, pastoral lover internal to that world; instead, he emerges not just as a characteristically distant Stevensian observer but as an observer heavily invested in the ability to speak from a position of prophetic and apocalyptic certainty. The speaker wants to insist on the sufficiency of the pastoral world but finds that world insufficient to another set of poetic ambitions.

But the preceding claims seem to have forgotten the supposedly undecidable problem raised earlier—namely, the problem of deciding whether "Credences" is a predominantly pastoral poem with apocalyptic modulations, or an apocalyptic poem with pastoral modulations. Some refinement of this issue at least seems possible here: it may be more a matter of deciding whether the poem is predominantly a pastoral poem that undergoes apocalyptic heightening, or an apocalypse that is continually limited and confined within a pastoral world—a poem in which a sense of the world's sufficiency encounters a desire for "more," or one in which a desire for "more" is subjected to disciplining by the former sense. The poem may have its origins in a problematical and perhaps indecipherable relationship between desires for expansion and desires for self-limitation, or in a tension between two different relationships between these forces.

But if one cannot disentangle these motives, one can at least explore how the appeal of each is marked in the poem and indicate how the conflicts between them might function in the generation of meaning. Certainly, there are clear signs in the text of the poetic gains netted by placing pastoral fulfillments against the background of a problematical engagement with apocalyptic modes, by describing the world of "lovers waiting in the soft dry grass" from the position of seer rather than lover. A desire for absolutes involves both a desire to know the truth and a desire—especially important for a poet—to make truthful utterances, or utterances that have some of the forcefulness of truth; it involves a desire for a certain poetic or discursive power. And, as my first chapter argued, apocalyptic discourse claims for itself a unique relationship to truth: "The structure of truth here would be apocalyptic. And that is why there would not be any truth of the apocalypse that is not the truth of truth" (Derrida, "Apocalyptic" 84). One might think of the first canto's claim that "there is nothing left of time" as an apocalyptic thought experiment, a fiction self-consciously sustained in the name of the poetic project, in the name of establishing a certain position of poetic power through a relationship to an apocalyptic tradition of truth. Here, Kermode's concern throughout *The Sense of an Ending* with the capacity of eschatological thinking to retroactively grant order and meaning to what might otherwise be "vain temporality, mad, multiform antithetical influx" (115) indicates something of the discursive power to be gained by investing in such a fiction, as does the following observation by John Lynen: "An end is required, and the reader's problem arises from mistakenly thinking that the last day is just another day of the same sort—a caboose to the temporal train. Calling it the Day of Judgment is a way of describing the end as a point of view, a point from which the whole of history can be seen" (411–12).[3] In declaring that "there is nothing left of time" and "nothing more *inscribed*" (my emphasis), Stevens's speaker does not merely take his place in a tradition that defines this subject position by a privileged access to ultimate truth; he also marks himself as the terminus of that hitherto interminable tradition of the End, and marks his own text as the "this" after which "There is nothing more inscribed," adding one more voice to the eschatological going-one-better.

The relationship between an eschatological position and discursive power emerges with particular clarity in the tropes of power that reappear throughout "Credences," tropes that often displace figures of temporal extremity with figures of extreme height, or translate the former into the latter. In canto iii, for example, Stevens tropes "the refuge that the end creates" as a position of maximum height—"the natural tower of all the world, / The point of survey, green's green apogee" (*CP* 373)—and as a point of temporal extremity, or of temporal and vertical extremity combined: "It is the final mountain" (*CP* 373). The speaker flies to a similar refuge in canto vi, where we find "the rock of summer, the extreme, / A mountain luminous half way in bloom / And then half way in the extremest light" (*CP* 375). The shuffling back and forth between tropes of extreme lateness and extreme height suggests a doubled attitude toward the former: the speaker may betray some discomfort with the eschatological position and its theological baggage, and yet still desire the power associated with that position, the power that underwrites the declaration of final values. The desire for discursive power becomes particularly evident when the tropes of extreme lateness are displaced not just by tropes of extreme height but also by tropes of political supremacy. In canto ii, the "natural tower of all the world" becomes "The point of survey squatting like a throne" (*CP* 373), and in canto vi, the rock's highest heights become "the extremest light / Of sapphires flashing from the central sky, / As if twelve princes sat before a king" (*CP* 375). Still more problematical, however, is the fact that this shift does not abolish the end point's theological baggage—instead, these figures intensify the theological colorings of such language. The canto's final reference to princes and king seems more than merely "hieratic," as MacCaffrey suggests (428). If the "rock" of canto vi, with its allusion to the celebrated Peter/rock pun of Matt. 16:18 (noted by La Guardia [118], Riddel [*Clairvoyant* 220], and Fisher [*Intensest* 133]) calls to mind Christ's earthly relations with his apostles and the church Peter establishes, then the concluding lines must allude to the promise Jesus makes to his disciples concerning their exalted status in heaven and to the association between sapphire and the throne of God in the Old Testament:

> And Jesus said unto to them, Verily I say unto you, That ye which have followed me, in the regeneration when the Son of man shall sit in the throne of his glory, ye also shall sit upon twelve thrones, judging the twelve tribes of Israel. (Matt. 19:28)

> And above the firmament that was over their heads was the likeness of a throne, as the appearance of a sapphire stone: and upon the likeness of the throne was the likeness as the appearance of a man above upon it. (Ezek. 1:26)

Stevens's "sun, / Sleepless" (*CP* 373) also alludes to prophetic eschatology and apocalypse: after the last day, "Thy sun shall no more go down" (Isa. 60:20), "the light of the moon shall be as the light of the sun, and the light of the sun shall be sevenfold, as the light of seven days" (Isa. 30:26); and, in Revelation's new Jerusalem, "there shall be no night" (Rev. 21:25). If this reading is valid, canto iii's figures of power might well be understood to incorporate similar sources; the conjunction of a "point of survey squatting like a throne" with an "old man" whose "ruddy ancientness / Absorbs the ruddy summer" (*CP* 374) echoes the figure of the "Ancient of days" in the apocalyptic seventh chapter of the Book of Daniel: "I beheld till the thrones were cast down, and the Ancient of days did sit, whose garment was white as snow, and the hair of his head like the pure wool: his throne was like the fiery flame, and his wheels as burning fire" (Dan. 7:9). The poem shifts, then, from eschatological positions to positions of extreme height only to discover that apocalyptic echoes still resound on throne, tower, and mountaintop; and those echoes may indicate that these positions gain their peculiar status from their relationship to the end they seek to displace. They pose a question as to whether access to a certain level of discursive power always entails a relationship to eschatological and apocalyptic modes, whether the former can ever break free of the latter. And they suggest that there is still something apocalyptic about these attempts to displace apocalypse. Canto vii's "thrice concentred self" (*CP* 376) may also partake of this peculiar logic, at least if such a self has been through three concentred Dantean journeys. Stevens poses a more particular question, too, about the desires that generate "Credences," a question about the possibility of burning away or purging every potentially apocalyptic desire, every desire that still retains vestiges or traces of a desire for absolute, transcendent fulfillment.

Clearly, too, these figurations of power return the discussion to the problems raised by the "bristling soldier," since many of these figures offer alternatives to the soldier's version of masculinity and poetic power—a "sleepless" but distinctly masculinized sun, the "old man standing on the tower," the king and his princes, the "cock bright," the vanished gardener, the "inhuman author." As was suggested in my discussion of canto v, the relationships among these different figures, and particularly between the soldier and the rest, present a problem in interpretation, as does the relationship of the poem's speaker to all of these figures. In the first instance, it should be obvious enough that the theological echoes noted above place most of these figures within an ancient patriarchal tradition that conceives of truth in terms of a particular kind of relationship to a male deity; and it should be clear, too, that the soldier does not quite belong to this tradition. The contrast between the theologically haunted figures and the soldier might seem to articulate a difference between truth and "strength" or "heroic power," though a more Foucauldian reading would of course question the difference between the two categories—their puzzling copresence in the poem would mark a scarcely suppressed awareness of the mutual entanglements of power and truth. Yet there are other differences articulated here: a difference between age and youth, for example, and between the kinds of power available to old and young men, fathers and sons, "ruddy ancientness" and "filial form[s]," a man near the end of his life and one just beginning his prime. The man of "ruddy ancientness" can attain "an understanding that fulfils his age"—such understanding makes the last years of his own life fulfilling, or fulfills the entire historical era to which the man belongs—and can experience "a feeling capable of nothing more"; he has, more significantly, the capacity to be "appeased," to arrive at the "arrested peace" that can only be desired by the speaker of the poem's second canto and that might elude a "bristling soldier." At issue here, perhaps, is a need to make the strongest possible claims about the kind of poetry that can be written by an older, if not ruddily ancient, poet, the kind of poet Stevens would have been in 1946 (age sixty-seven). And while the poem's speaker does not identify himself with any one of the poem's masculine figures, but merely observes all of them and meditates on each, his repeated insistence on a rhetoric of terminations nevertheless aligns him most strongly with "ruddy ancientness" and fulfilled age, with seers and visionaries rather than "bristling soldiers." The poem opts for the achievements of age, for understanding, fulfillment, and appeasement. Generically, it opts for the heightening of pastoral by means of apocalyptic modulations (or a limitation of apocalypse by pastoral) rather than by setting pastoral love and leisure against a background of epic heroism.

And yet, as my reading of canto v suggests, "Credences" does not quite rid itself of a lingering desire for and anxiety about the "strength" and "heroic power" of the "youth, the vital son"—an anxiety reintroduced yet more faintly when canto x's characters speak "Their parts as in a youthful happiness" (*CP* 378). There may be some anxiety or ambivalence, too, behind the "feeling capable of nothing more" that forms part of the appeasement of the "old man"; the phrase is, after all, delicately balanced between plenitude and exhaustion. Writing late in a career and, perhaps, late in an "era in the history of the imagination," may offer a poet the power of being at the culmination of his own career or of an entire aesthetic dispensation, but might also raise anxieties that both the poet and his dispensation may now be "capable of nothing more" (*CP* 374). These last comments are not intended to suggest that anxieties about masculinity are what drive the poem; they are not meant to indicate that, for example, the apocalyptic heightening of the poem's pastoral mode merely masks a deeper need to conceive of the older self as possessing a greater degree of power than the younger, or to compensate for a loss of virility— the speaker is neither pastoral lover nor hero. The most one can say, perhaps, is that anxieties about different kinds of poetic speech and different versions of masculine identity are articulated together in the poem, and that considering the two together, but without reducing one to the other, may help to clarify some of the poem's more problematical elements. Finally, this treatment of the poem's figurations of masculinity has, I hope, suggested that a reading of gender in

Stevens that emphasizes the tensions between different versions of masculinity is at least as rewarding as one that emphasizes the tensions between masculinity and femininity. In "Credences," at least, it shows us a poem that remains ambivalently divided between two mutually exclusive figurations of masculinity even as its speaker aligns himself with "ruddy ancientness."

Other tensions emerge *within* some of canto iii's individual tropes of fulfillment, involving relationships between nature and artifice rather than between different versions of masculine power. In Stevens's visionary "natural tower," for example, one of the two terms must be understood to develop metaphorical predication—it is a natural pinnacle described as though it were a tower, or a tower described as though it were a natural pinnacle. According to the first reading, Stevens's phrase would record a shift from a desire that can be fulfilled within nature to one that must move beyond nature; the second reading would reverse this shift. The poem resists any attempt to privilege either of these two readings, but such irresolution itself remains significant as an indication that two equal and conflicting desires operate in the poem. A similar tension is marked in the speaker's redescription of the tower as "green's green apogee" (*CP* 373). The genitive doubling of Stevens's color of earthly reality leads further into the earthly pastoral, whereas the designation of the tower as "apogee" leads us, according to the word's etymology, away from the earth (*apo*, "off," is prefixed to *gaia*, "earth") and, according to its modern usage, as far as possible from the earth, at the point in any other planet's orbit at which it is most distant from ours—a movement away from centeredness and toward eccentricity.

It may be precisely this tension between a desire for the greatest possible discursive power and a discomfort with the theological burden of the apocalyptic position that transforms the poem's most intensely apocalyptic moment into its most intensely antiapocalyptic one and leads Stevens to invoke the beginning of a new age in language still redolent of the past:

> The trumpet of morning blows in the clouds and through
> The sky. It is the visible announced,
> It is the more than visible, the more
> Than sharp, illustrious scene. The trumpet cries
> This is the successor of the invisible.

This is its substitute in stratagems
Of the spirit. This, in sight and memory,
Must take its place, as what is possible
Replaces what is not. The resounding cry
Is like ten thousand tumblers tumbling down

To share the day. (*CP* 376–77)

Clearly, as Longenbach suggests, when Stevens "anticipates the unveiling of a new age," he surrenders to "an apocalyptic urge" (*Plain* 88)
and does so in biblical language, even though that urge is an urge to
do away with apocalypse. But Stevens's doubled discourse involves
something other than a purely intellectual paradox: it speaks, again,
of a level or mode of desire that cannot be fulfilled by the merely "visible." If Stevens has been defining "the visible" in largely pastoral and
topographical terms in this sequence, the adoption of the apocalyptic mode in canto viii would indicate that those modes remain inadequate to the desires that motivate the poem. Even the advent of
"the visible" must be heightened by a language "grown venerable in
the unreal" (*CP* 377), in "the invisible." Such irreducible desires are
marked, perhaps, in the curious play of modifiers and prefixes around
"the visible"; to move from "the invisible" to "the visible" is to move
through a morphological loss, to move semantically from the unbounded to the bounded, and this sense of loss apparently motivates
a further shift from "the visible" to "the *more* than visible, the *more* /
Than sharp, illustrious scene" (my emphasis). As has been suggested,
desire in this poem is related to questions of discursive or poetic
power, or is the desire for such power. It is worth remembering here
Kermode's and Derrida's awareness of how even an antiapocalyptic
discourse may reinscribe within itself (or inscribe itself within) the
very forms of discursive power it claims to reject. Kermode's suggestion in "Waiting for the End" that "if in addition we deny all
end-directed history we have apocalyptically eliminated apocalyptic
thinking" (261) implies that even an explicitly antiapocalyptic utterance still assumes the apocalyptic position that underwrites any declaration of final truth. And it is precisely this sense of the power
involved in both apocalyptic and antiapocalyptic positions that haunts
Derrida when he asks, "But then what is someone doing who tells
you: I tell you this, I have come to tell you this, there is not, there

never has been, there never will be an apocalypse, the apocalypse deceives, disappoints? There is the apocalypse *without* apocalypse" (94–95). One way of framing this problem, of course, would be to suggest that utterances like Derrida's, or, more pertinently, like Stevens's in canto viii of "Credences," retain a desire for the discursive power inscribed within apocalyptic discourse but not for apocalypse itself; they write of and out of a strangely hollowed apocalyptic desire. Yet it might also be argued that, in Stevens's case, an apocalyptic degree of discursive power is seen as necessary to the very rejection of apocalyptic discourse: in this tradition, one fights fire with fire, so to speak; one needs a position of unassailable strength and leverage in order to uproot the apocalyptic past. Later writers, of course, suggest that apocalypse can be dismantled only by avoiding or refusing all such positions of power, and Stevens's simultaneous use of and discomfort with a strategy that belongs to and prolongs the tradition it battles marks his peculiar position in the literary history of the twentieth century. It is a question of the relative force with which Stevens respectively adopts and questions the apocalyptic mode.

Canto viii's vacillation between tropes of visibility and tropes of audibility seems particularly instructive in relation to Stevens's divided stance. Stevens repeatedly insists on the vocalic quality of the trumpet's sound; "its diction's way" (*CP* 377) is etymologically a way of speaking or, in the canto's most frequent trope of voice, a way of crying. The question to be asked here is *why* "the *visible*" must be announced at all, and why that announcement must specifically be one that is *heard* rather than seen (announcements may be either oral or written). One might also ask why in this instance Stevens tropes the poem's own intertextuality, its interweavings of previous apocalyptic and prophetic texts, as a "re[-]sounding cry," as a vocal rather than textual phenomenon. The "more" announced by this trumpet's announcement of "the more than visible, the more / Than sharp, illustrious scene," may well be the "more" of poetic voice in its transcendence of the merely visible, the merely "there"; it may more specifically mark the transcendence of voice over writing, as the trumpet's "more" triumphs over and displaces the "nothing more" of canto i's terminal situation, a situation in which "There is nothing more inscribed nor thought nor felt" (*CP* 372). If one grants credence to Derrida's insistence that the earliest writings of what we have come to call poststructuralism announced the advent of an era of writing and textuality—

and even if this was not true before *Of Grammatology*, it has certainly become true since—and if one reads canto viii of "Credences" in relation to Derrida's analysis of the privileging of voice over text in the phonologocentric tradition, then Stevens's work in this instance would seem to align itself more clearly with that tradition in its association of truth with speech, its privileging of the vocal over the textual; he sings in that heavenly chorus that relates truth to vocality. And yet to the extent that Stevens also places himself *after* the end of the apocalyptic era as a prophet of "the visible," he also speaks *against* the apocalyptic tradition in which such vocalic privileging is inscribed and looks toward that "new modernism" which we now refer to as poststructuralism and postmodernism. Stevens's language leads us to read an agonistic element in this canto—a "cry as clarion" (*CP* 377) may be the cry of a military trumpet, and "stratagems / Of the spirit" are etymologically those of a military leader (from *stratos*, "army," and *ago*, "lead"); if such a battle is under way, Stevens would appear to place himself simultaneously on two different sides of the struggle.

Additionally, this doubleness marks the trope of the "inhuman author" (*CP* 377) in canto x. If throughout "Credences of Summer" Stevens has been continually displacing a problematical desire to speak from a position of eschatological and apocalyptic certainty onto non-eschatological figures of sublime or visionary power, then this figure would be the most transcendent or hyperbolic instance of such displacement. The canto's opening lines present one of the earliest versions of a figure that appears regularly throughout late Stevens, the "pensive nature, a mechanical / And slightly detestable *operandum*" (*CP* 517) of "Looking across the Fields and Watching the Birds Fly," the hypothetical enthroned imagination of canto vii of "The Auroras of Autumn," the title figure of "Presence of an External Master of Knowledge" (*OP* 131), or, in "The Region November," the north wind that blows "like a critic of God, the world // And human nature, pensively seated / On the waste throne of his own wilderness" (*OP* 140). These figures are among the strangest and most ambivalent in all Stevens, for they record opposing desires that are as strong as they are extravagant: a desire that there *be* a position of absolute authority like the one occupied by God in the Judeo-Christian tradition, and a desire that this authority be as foreign as possible to the Judeo-Christian tradition and the metaphysical philosophies descended from it—foreign, indeed, to any theological or metaphysical tradition. These

two forces emerge with particular clarity in "The Region November,"
which echoes scriptural accounts of God's throne room (*OP* 140)[4] in
its "revelation not yet intended" (*OP* 140) and places "a critic of God,
the world, // And human nature" (*OP* 140) on that throne. And since
"critic" is etymologically related to the words applied to God and
Christ as judge throughout the New Testament,[5] Stevens's "critic of
God" becomes the critic of The Critic, the judge of The Judge, in an
antitheological usurpation. As Roy Harvey Pearce observes, such
figurations are not instances of pathetic fallacy (131); they reinscribe
human thought within the generalized and strangely emptied non-
human thinking of a "pensive nature" engaged in "an inhuman meditation" (*CP* 521), so that we think "within the thought / Of the wind"
(*CP* 513) or "as wind skitters on a pond in a field" (*CP* 518).

In canto x of "Credences," Stevens's "inhuman author," though not
dressed in the heraldic "pales" of his characters, declares his own descent
from the ancient trope of God as author of the book of nature. And
Stevens again marks his ambivalence in the strange limitation imposed
on this figure—"He does not hear his characters talk" (*CP* 377). This
incapacity creates a locus of discursive power for "his characters" even
as the rhetoric of incompletion ("half pales," "Part of the mottled
mood," "speaking / Their parts" [*CP* 377–78]) limits those powers, too:
speech becomes the vehicle or mark of a freedom founded in desire,
freedom not just from the unhearing author but from the "malice" and
"sudden cry" that respectively create and result from human suffering—the malice and sudden cry, perhaps, that lead to and sound out
in war. The final canto's rhetoric of parts and wholes actually tropes
a *division* of discursive powers between "inhuman author" and "his
characters" (*CP* 377), figuring both an inhuman but absolute discursive power and a limited human capacity for freedom of utterance.

If there is a trope of discursive power in "Credences" that both displaces eschatology and remains untouched by any apocalyptic heightening, it is the trope of the "centre" that appears in cantos ii and iii.
Some other Stevens poems pit the rhetoric of the "centre" against
teleological and apocalyptic thinking; see, for example, the contrast
between "final belief" and "the central good" (*CP* 250, 251) in "Asides
on the Oboe" (1940), or in "Of Ideal Time and Place" (1947), in which
"the last man," maker of "the final choice" (*NA* 88) at an "exultant
terminal" (*NA* 89), will turn away from his terminal situation and
look back to the past—Stevens's own present—as "the *center* of ideal

time" (*NA* 89, my emphasis). Value and the fulfillment of desire are displaced from a terminus to a center. In a similar vein, canto ii of "Credences" replaces the terminal situation of canto i with a desire for "the centre that I seek" (*CP* 373), though this center itself appears to be in motion and exists in a "whitened sky" that can only be a metaphor for the absence of metaphor. And in canto iii, the speaker again figures the "refuge" created by the terminal situation of canto i as "the axis of everything." As has already been noted, the most significant and extended version of this rhetoric emerges in the latter portion of canto vii, and it is worth remembering that it functions there as part of a necessary disciplining of an irreducible desire, a final redirecting of desire away from the "woulds" of pastoral and toward the actuality of possession in and of the present. But what seems crucial here is that the speaker desires the sought-after center to be "Fix[ed] . . . in an eternal foliage" and that he proclaims this center to be "the barrenness / Of the fertile thing that can attain no more" (*CP* 373). It is, in other words, a center that functions simultaneously as an end, or a center that displaces an end. There are questions, though, as to whether any actual centering takes place in the poem. The last part of canto vii *describes* a "concentred" poetics, but does it *embody* such a poetics? The very abstract, theoretical diction would appear to (re)position the speaker outside the poetic mode he proposes, so that the poem remains divided from what it describes as its own "object" or objective through that very act of description.

"High poetry and low" (*CP* 490): "Credences" seems both a low poem that strains for the heights and a high poem that needs to be brought down to earth. Stevens faces a disjunction between, on the one hand, a recurring desire to occupy a particular masculine position of heightened imaginative power and, on the other, a long-standing mistrust of the theological and metaphysical foundation of this power. This disjunction also emerges in a later poem that could be considered a companion piece to "Credences" and "The Auroras of Autumn"—"Things of August" (1949), one of the more marginalized works in the Stevens canon. The title of the later sequence immediately marks its difference from "Credences": it offers not the whole of "Summer" but the smaller "region" of "August"; and it explores not the inner world of beliefs, with all its theological baggage and connotations of certainty and stability, but the mere miscellany of "things" as they exist in the world outside the self and its potentially exorbitant desires. As was suggested earlier, this poem, in examining the relative merits of "High poetry and low" (*CP* 490), unmistakably associates the latter with one of Stevens's characteristic pastoral topoi, "the penumbra of summer night," and its opening canto, quoted in full below, might well be read as a transposition at a lower pitch, a lower level of creative tension, of the opening of "Credences":

> These locusts by day, these crickets by night
> Are the instruments on which to play
> Of an old and disused ambit of the soul
> Or of a new aspect, bright in discovery—
>
> A disused ambit of the spirit's way,
> The sort of thing that August crooners sing,
> By a pure fountain, that was a ghost, and is,
> Under the sun-slides of a sloping mountain;
>
> Or else a new aspect, say the spirit's sex,
> Its attitudes, its answers to attitudes
> And the sex of its voices, as the voice of one
> Meets nakedly another's naked voice.
>
> Nothing is lost, loud locusts. No note fails.
> These sounds are long in the living of the ear.
> The honky-tonk out of the somnolent grasses
> Is a memorizing, a trying out, to keep. (*CP* 489)

Key elements of the opening of "Credences" return here—sexual desire, summer, "somnolent grasses," and so on; but Stevens's musical tropes place us more thoroughly in that pastoral world in which poetry is song, and, furthermore, do so in terms quite deliberately borrowed from popular or "low" culture—"August crooners" and "honky-tonk," for example. There is no eschatological or apocalyptic heightening of the moment, as in "Credences," and, some might argue, little even of "the dialectical, tensive structure characteristic of all worthwhile pastoral" (Toliver 5). If Stevens prefers here the "sun-slides of a sloping mountain" to its summit, he rejects figures of sublime height in still more certain terms in the poem's seventh canto, where an unnamed figure "turned from the tower to the house" (*CP* 493) because

He could understand the things at home.
And being up high had helped him when up high,
As if on a taller tower
He would be certain to see

That, in the shadowless atmosphere,
The knowledge of things lay round but unperceived:
The height was not quite proper;
The position was wrong. (*CP* 493)

Stevens does not deny the value of the position of height and power,
but gives it the paradoxical function of revealing its own limitations
and making, for those who turn from the tower, the "low" fully satisfying. There may be some sense, in the mere fact that Stevens thus
dramatizes the value of relinquishing the sublime, of a lingering nostalgia for the power provided by the tower, a desire for sublime heights
and revelations that must still be tamed, though in every way the
tone and diction of this passage seem to accommodate themselves to
the domestic realm to which the unnamed figure returns. The critical neglect of "Things of August" even in a period that has shown
increasing interest in Stevens's later work suggests, perhaps, that this
accommodation has been achieved too easily, that Stevens's pastoral-
ism here is too "soft," that the abandoned sublime has not been replaced, at least in most of "Things of August," by that uncanny poetic
strength that Stevens discovers in the domestic setting constructed in
so many of his great final lyrics.

"Credences," in its extravagant desire to achieve "a *final* accord
with reality" (my emphasis) appears, for the most part, to strain
against the dominant tendency of these other poems, a tendency toward recovery. Only in canto ix does Stevens produce a version of
pastoral untouched by any of the apocalyptic desires that have elsewhere marked the poem—Stevens investigates, in other words, the
versions of pastoral that emerge when pastoral has been purged of
any apocalyptic desires for complete and lasting fulfillment. Many
critics have noted the parodic aspects of this canto, and these are, as
Bloom rightly suggests, directed against all "the qualified raptures of
earlier cantos" (*Climate* 251), the apocalyptic trumpet of canto viii,
and the mountains and tower of vision of cantos iii and vi. Stevens's
parody is thus also *self*-parodic and as such has a self-purgative or

self-disciplinary force: the speaker commands the more aspiring aspect of himself represented by the bird to "Fly low" (*CP* 377) rather than seek "refuge" on the heights of cantos iii, vi, and viii, and, perhaps, to avoid the heavenly realms sought in sublime romantic versions of this trope, such as Shelley's in "Ode to a Skylark." If this apocalyptic desire is the target of Stevens's parody, then the "complex of emotions [that] falls apart, / In an abandoned spot" (*CP* 377) in canto ix is not the complex encoded in the pastoral mode, as Jarraway (235) suggests, but rather the one inscribed in the peculiar relations between the apocalyptic and pastoral modes that have developed throughout the course of this poem. This "abandoned spot," identified as "last year's garden" with its dead cat, "salacious weeds," "decay," and "the fund of life and death" (*CP* 377), calls to mind the elegiac version of the pastoral topos one finds in such works as Wordsworth's "The Ruined Cottage," Goldsmith's "The Deserted Village," or, in a more self-consciously artificial vein, in the topos of nature's mourning encountered in pastoral elegies from Virgil to Shelley and beyond. Canto ix thus offers the clearest instance of that "dark countersong" that Berger finds in "Credences"; it is the moment when the poem "discover[s] the significance of *et in Arcadia ego*" (Berger 83). In canto x, one could argue that the trope of the "inhuman author" has been pastoralized: his main activity is described by the Virgilian verb of pastoral contemplation ("meditates"), whose arrival this late in the poem indicates, perhaps, the extent to which the speaker's apocalyptic desires have denied the possibility of purely pastoral satisfactions. The world he and his characters inhabit includes some key pastoral topoi—"blue meadows, late at night" (*CP* 377), "sky and sun" (*CP* 378), and "youthful happiness" (*CP* 378), but does not relinquish the consciousness of time and the ephemerality of the pastoral topos.

Stevens also figures this disengagement of apocalyptic and pastoral modes as a more radical abandonment of poetic power. When "a complex of emotions" falls apart in canto ix, the disintegration opens its "listener" to "a sound, / Which is not part of the listener's own sense" (*CP* 377), a trope that recalls Stevens's self-emptying "listener, who listens in the snow" (*CP* 10) and foretells the still more detached listener in "The Course of a Particular," who "holds off and merely hears the cry" (*OP* 123). And the "cock bright" who may or may not make that sound is not the only figure of poetic activity in the canto; Stevens also introduces a departed "gardener" whose absence results in "The decay that you regard" (*CP* 377)—another version of the self-elegiac "planter"-as-poet and his "garbled green" in *Notes* II, v (*CP* 393) and, perhaps, of Stevens the avid horticulturist. But these tropes of the abandonment of creative power become, paradoxically, a means of maintaining that very power: as has already been suggested, such tropes are among Stevens's strongest and most individual figurations, and he exploits them in his late poetry with an uncannily unobtrusive strength that transcends even his best earlier work, like "The Snow Man." It might be preferable to suggest that canto ix explores the different means of gaining poetic power that emerge when pastoral and apocalypse are disengaged; it moves from self-parody to self-elegy in an exploration of what Marianne Moore calls "the power of relinquishing / what one would keep" (*Complete Poems* 144). Any effort at emptying the self is a curious means of imagining or gaining poetic power, since it assumes the existence of a still more powerful self capable of the most rigorous self-discipline, the discipline achieved by a self that can truly empty the self, much as the self-parody earlier in canto ix depends on the emergence of a new poetic self capable of discerning and reacting against the errors of the earlier, parodied self—a self that desires the power of sublime heights.

Stevens's self-parody suggests a certain caution toward the sublime figurations of "Credences," a caution born out of a sense that there is a certain risk of self-inflation for a poet who reaches after such heights. But sublime heights bring other kinds of risks, too, risks that emerge with particular force when the poet cannot figure the highest of the high as a locus for his or her own poetic power but only as a position already occupied by some other power. For Stevens, at least, the sense that the position of maximum height and maximum power may be occupied by something other than the human imagination transforms a Wordsworthian sublime of poetic power into a more Burkean sublime of terror, a version of the sublime in which the speaker turns his eyes upward to encounter a force that transcends and unsettles his own powers. Such a vision dominates "The Auroras of Autumn." It is a vision that is again paradoxically apocalyptic and antiapocalyptic, and, as my next chapter shall demonstrate, one that again shows Stevens seeking points of resistance to the possibility that he may be living and writing at "the end of one era in the history of the imagination" (*NA* 22).

chapter five

Mournful Making
Apocalypse and Elegy in "The Auroras of Autumn"

Critics have commonly, and understandably, treated "Credences of Summer" and "The Auroras of Autumn" as contrastive companion pieces, a reading best encapsulated in Vendler's sense of the "energy of repudiation" (Vendler, *Extended* 248) directed by the later poem against the earlier. But there may be a commonality beneath the contrast. The earlier poem articulates an ambivalent desire toward the position of patriarchal mastery and toward the discursive power encoded in apocalyptic rhetoric; the later work treats a peculiar post-apocalyptic position as a crisis and bids an ambivalently regretful farewell to the position of patriarchal mastery. Both poems thus make a similar sort of affective investment in the father's mastery and in the discursive power of apocalyptic language, despite the contradictory modes through which these investments are marked in the poems. Readings like those of Jarraway and Beehler suggest that "Auroras," of all Stevens's sequences, enters most confidently into a poststructuralist or postmodern textual space, but the poem's attitude toward what even Harold Bloom calls the "endless decentering of itself" (*Climate* 276), toward the "poison" of "disbelief" (*CP* 411) that leads Stevens to abandon his own master tropes, must, at the very least, problematize interpretations that seek to herd Stevens into the postmodern fold. Above all, the poem's elegiac elements—or, more properly, its peculiar configuration of elegiac and apocalyptic modes—and its figurations of gender prove to be the sites of the poem's strongest resistance to any movement outside of a modern or modernist aesthetic dispensation.

"Auroras" differs greatly in more than just mode (elegiac rather than pastoral) from "Credences of Summer"; above all, the earlier poem's desire for the discursive power associated with apocalyptic discourse is complicated by an intense eschatological fear. The precise source of this fear, and the reason why it should be inspired by a display of the aurora borealis, remains difficult to ascertain; Berger suggests in his chapter on the poem that the auroras symbolize the threat of nuclear annihilation, though in using them thus Stevens must also be relying on folkloric associations of the northern light with omens of disaster, war, and even the biblical End of Days.[1] B. J. Leggett's study of the influence of Henri Focillon's *The Life of Forms in Art* on "Auroras" seems helpful here, though I would like to revise Leggett's suggestion that Stevens sees the auroras as "a fearful phenomenon" because "he now sees the frailty of the individual imagination in the presence of an external intelligence that is of the same order as his one candle but that overwhelms it in its magnitude" (*Poetic Theory* 184). The auroras could elicit this sense of frailty without having any "intelligence" projected onto them, and could function as a symbol, rather than literal source, of the unpredictable disappearance and emergence of aesthetic and imaginative dispensations, a reminder that the imagination "is always at the end of an era" (*NA* 22). But one question would then remain: whether, as a symbol of "form gulping after formlessness" (*CP* 411), the auroral display represents the ordinary process of cultural change, or whether it inspires fears of a more radical break to come, another "collapse of our system" (*NA* 20) into "an ever-enlarging incoherence" (*NA* 17), a disappearance of Stevens's own aesthetic principles or of the aesthetic itself. Either possibility would make sense of the self-elegiac sequence of farewells to Stevens's own fictions in cantos ii–iv.

I would like to begin, then, with a detailed consideration of the conventional relations between elegy and apocalypse in order to clarify how Stevens's modifications of the traditional configurations help situate his position in literary history. David Shaw's excellent study of this poem in *Elegy and Paradox* demands detailed attention here, since it remains unique in its exploration of the poem's dual generic allegiances and thus opens a more general discussion of the affiliation between elegy and apocalypse. Shaw describes the Stevens of "Auroras" as "a poet who is trying to move from elegy toward apocalypse" (*Elegy* 158). Shaw's sense of the *direction* in which the poem moves— "from elegy toward apocalypse"—and his observation that "at its outer limits an elegy may turn into an apocalypse, which is a lament, not just for a dead person, but for the passing of a world" (*Elegy* 155) require further comment; they lead me to ask whether apocalypses, or at least biblical and intertestamental apocalypses and their more "conventional" descendants, do in fact lament the end of the world.

Revelation eagerly looks forward to the destruction of a sinful and corrupt world, its replacement by "a new heaven and a new earth" (Rev. 21:1), and the final (and just) punishment of the bad and rewarding of the good. But as I suggested in my first chapter's discussion of the comic and ironic aspects of apocalypse, only the *bad* lament the passing of this world—an understandable reaction, given the predicament that awaits them in the next one—whereas the faithful apocalyptic seer does not; if anything, from his perspective, the end of the world is as good a thing as it is inevitable. This antielegiac force is implied by Robinson, Patricia Parker, Derrida, Adela Collins, and any others who treat apocalypse as a means of encoding an excessive desire—a topic discussed already in my first and fourth chapters. This desire for the end of the present world and the beginning of a new, perfect order of things is at odds with the retrospective lament of elegy, and Tennyson's observation that "the song of woe / Is after all an earthly song" (*In Memoriam* 57, ll. 1–2) implicitly acknowledges just such a difference.

An elegy that crosses into apocalypse in the manner Shaw suggests would have to make significant departures from either of these genres, since the elegiac need to mourn is as antiapocalyptic as the apocalyptic desire for the end is antielegiac. Shaw's reading of "The Auroras of Autumn" and of the relations between elegy and apocalypse may assume or elide an elegizing of apocalypse that had already been under way by the time of their autumnal conjunction in Stevens's poem. The disengagement of the idea of the End from any concepts of judgment, reward, divine teleology, new creation, and so on—in short, the secularization of the End, the emergence of an eschatology that cuts short the apocalyptic plot and consigns the Christian promise to the abyss of vanished beliefs—this disengagement might well lead a writer concerned with last things to mourn, rather than celebrate. The tendency of this sort of "secularized doomsday" to undergo elegiac modulation appears in sections 3 and 123 of Tennyson's *In Memoriam*. In the first selection below, a purely scientific understanding of the cosmos produces an *anti*revelation, a revelation of the absence of any divine presence in nature, and of an eschatology of mere material entropy, rather than of divine fulfillment; in the second, Tennyson's geological studies lead him to raise a standard mutability topos to an apocalyptic pitch:

"The stars," [Sorrow] whispers, "blindly run;
   A web is wov'n across the sky;
   From out waste places comes a cry,
And murmurs from the dying sun:

"And all the phantom, Nature, stands—
   With all the music in her tone,
   A hollow echo of my own,—
A hollow form with empty hands." (3, ll. 5–12)

The hills are shadows, and they flow
   From form to form, and nothing stands:
   They melt like mist, the solid lands,
Like clouds they shape themselves and go. (123, ll. 5–8)

Shaw discusses the subtle ways in which Tennyson's elegies transgress the genre's norms (210–35), and the remaking of apocalyptic modulations in the preceding passages exemplifies such transgressions. Shaw's description of Tennyson's confrontation throughout *In Memoriam* with "the eclipse of any lodestar for faith in the burned-out universe predicted by the Second Law of Thermodynamics" (217) might well apply to the first of these passages; and in the second, Shaw finds a "pageant [that] seems about to end in terrifying absurdity" (213). The elegiac genre undergoes apocalyptic modulation in the passages just cited, but these apocalyptic modulations are already peculiarly elegized and doubly or paradoxically apocalyptic, since they also situate themselves *after* the end of any belief in the Christian apocalyptic promise and see that end as a cause for mourning. At one point in *In Memoriam*, Tennyson imagines God as "some wild Poet" who "works / Without a conscience or an aim" (34, ll. 7–8), and suggests that the only response to such a situation would be "To drop head-foremost in the jaws / Of vacant darkness and to cease" (34, ll. 15–16). Such concerns with teleology appear so often in the poem that the different senses of "end" sometimes constitute the thematic substance of *In Memoriam*; what is at stake is the possible closure of one of that word's senses—the one associated with goal, purpose, telos. These apocalyptic modulations, then, temporarily mark the end of a certain discourse of the end.

Tennyson moves beyond this impasse to find consolation in "The truths that never can be proved / Until we close with all we loved"

(131, ll. 10–11), in "one far-off divine event, / To which the whole creation moves" (epilogue, ll. 143–44), and it is precisely this kind of apocalyptic modulation within elegy which has been the dominant and conventional one in English poetry, and which "The Auroras of Autumn" rewrites. Some classic examples of the elegiac genre, such as "Lycidas," with its "unexpressive nuptial song" (l. 176) or the "November" eclogue from Spenser's *The Shepheardes Calender*, find consolation in the apocalyptic promise of a world-to-come. These modulations reinscribe the poem's losses within a discourse of profit, a discourse that turns all losses into a final gain (or does so, at least, for the good and faithful). Tennyson situates his own losses and his vision of a mutable universe within a master narrative of God's mastery over all losses, and submits his own intellectual doubt to the faith commanded by "One God, one law" (epilogue, l. 142) and represented by the "Strong Son of God, immortal Love, / Whom we, that have not seen thy face, / By faith, and faith alone, embrace, / Believing where we cannot prove" (prologue, ll. 1–4). The return to this Christian version of the End at the conclusion of Tennyson's elegy raises questions about that poem's earlier elegiac/apocalyptic modulation. *In Memoriam*'s third section momentarily blocks the elegist's progress toward that final consolatory apocalyptic modulation; the latter emerges only when the first has been overcome or rejected. Here again, Shaw's reading proves instructive; for him, the "elegist's habit of turning upon himself, questioning his own most cherished axioms" (67)—a habit that informs *In Memoriam*'s peculiar retrograde movement[2]—may finally serve to "strengthen resolve" (67) and lead the elegist back to a stronger, more fully consoling faith. The moments of doubt are thus subsumed by the poem's own teleology, which is a return to faith in God's plan. One might ask in this context, then, whether section 3's elegiac vision of a random and dying universe is *anti*apocalyptic, rather than apocalyptic, in its lament. Clearly, this question involves some assumptions about the importance of the stance or attitude adopted toward the end in apocalyptic and antiapocalyptic discourse. Is a poem that resists or mourns the end even as it contemplates that event still an apocalyptic poem, or does such a poem become post- or antiapocalyptic in thus rewriting the relationships between the two genres?

These considerations should, I hope, provide a basis for a more precise formulation of how "The Auroras of Autumn" rewrites the conventional relationships between elegy and apocalypse. I would argue, first of all, that Stevens's poem is not an elegy that turns into an apocalypse but rather a topographical poem (as Helen Vendler suggests)[3] featuring frequent apocalyptic modulations which are also already elegiac in mode; and, second, that this transformation of apocalypse leads to a self-elegiac sequence in cantos ii–iv that further rewrites the relationship between elegiac and apocalyptic modulations. The conjunction of the topographical and the apocalyptic is already unusual, since apocalypse imagines the end of all earthly topoi and their replacement by a utopia, or looks forward to the transformation of a hitherto imagined utopia into an actual place. In the context of the topographical poem, which seems founded on an *attachment* to this world, a foreshortened apocalypse could well become "a lament, not just for a dead person, but for the passing of a world," since such an end offers no hope of compensation in a "world to come." It announces our position in a very different "world to come" that has already come, a world in which such beliefs no longer operate. Such a poem would have to deal with a double bereavement, as the elegist/prophet confronts and mourns the death of the self, of humanity, of the world, as well as the death of the traditional consolation for those losses once provided by apocalypse. Stevens reads the aurora borealis as the harbinger of a postapocalyptic apocalypse, of an "apocalypse *without* apocalypse," of an end that transcends and exceeds the narrative of teleological fulfillment inscribed in the apocalyptic tradition, and his elegiac *mourning* of this end inscribes a certain *resistance* to that situation within the poem. The elegiac stance thus adopted does not merely serve as a mark of the poem's doubled position in relation to the apocalyptic tradition—participating in that tradition and turning against it simultaneously; it opens the speaker's need to further mourn the presence of difference. The final part of this chapter will consider how the search in "Auroras" for elegiac consolation revises the gendered aspects of elegiac conventions. But it is the realignment of elegy and apocalypse that I will explore now in greater detail, after first adding, as a corollary to Berger's comments on how Stevens deeschatologizes elegy,[4] the observation that Stevens also performs a concomitant elegizing of eschatology and of the *end* of eschatology.

A good example of Stevens's peculiar postapocalyptic apocalypse appears in canto vii, which constitutes the poem's most intense and textually specific site of both apocalyptic influx *and* antiapocalyptic resistance:

> Is there an imagination that sits enthroned
> As grim as it is benevolent, the just
> And the unjust, which in the midst of summer stops
>
> To imagine winter? When the leaves are dead,
> Does it take its place in the north and enfold itself,
> Goat-leaper, crystalled and luminous, sitting
>
> In highest night? And do these heavens adorn
> And proclaim it, the white creator of black, jetted
> By extinguishings, even of planets as may be,
>
> Even of earth, even of sight, in snow,
> Except as needed by way of majesty,
> In the sky, as crown and diamond cabala? (*CP* 417)

Eleanor Cook has given us our most detailed reading of Stevens's biblical allusions in this passage; here, she hears combative echoes of the visions of God's throne room in Ezek. 1–2, of the lamb of Rev. 5–6 ("King James" 246, 248), and the eschatological separation of the sheep and goats of Matt. 25:32–33 (247–50). But some questions remain unanswered. Stevens resists the scene of eschatological *judgment* associated with Christian apocalypse by replacing, as Cook suggests, Revelation's enthroned lamb with a goat, as well as by portraying this enthroned imagination as being itself simultaneously "the just / And the unjust"—there is no separation here of just souls from unjust souls. Here, one might remember Stevens's resistance to eschatological separations of good and evil in "Extracts from Addresses to the Academy of Fine Ideas" and "Esthétique du Mal." But in "Auroras" vii, Stevens does not resist the mere idea of the End. His "goat-leaper"/ imagination

> leaps through us, through all our heavens leaps,
> Extinguishing our planets, one by one,
> Leaving, of where we were and looked, of where
>
> We knew each other and of each other thought,
> A shivering residue, chilled and foregone,
> Except for that crown and mystical cabala. (*CP* 417)

Stevens makes his own eschatological separations here, isolating and rejecting some elements of the discourse of the End while retaining others—hearing what the apocalyptic genre has contained in the past and refusing those elements associated with notions of judgment and fulfillment. As such, canto vii can be read as a response to canto iv, in which Stevens presents a father who leaps "from heaven to heaven," but does not allow us to forget the "bad angels [who] leap from heaven to hell in flames" (CP 414). Those angels have already been judged, and the judgment passed upon them is the first such judgment and proves to be, in the Miltonic version of this narrative, the origin of the eschatological judgment that awaits the human race and is inextricably entwined with the serpent, the fall, and the poisons of knowledge and disbelief that dominate canto i of "Auroras." Canto iv, of course, judges against this judgment, and the father abandons any thought of "The heavens, the hells, the worlds, the longed-for lands" (CP 486) that might be encountered even on "An Ordinary Evening in New Haven" for the reality of "green-a-day," in which the "flights of eye and ear, the highest eye / And the lowest ear" (CP 414) displace the sublime heights and depths of heaven and hell. In canto vii, the comfortless vision of "A shivering residue, chilled and foregone" suggests the cost of Stevens's excision of judgment in the face of the End's persistence, or of the End's capacity to survive belief in a terminal judgment that confers meaning upon history. Such questions take on a very particular historical weight, as Eleanor Cook ("King James" 246, 250) and Charles Berger (67) point out, in a poem written some two years after the end of World War II and within a year of the Nuremberg Trials; these questions, too, put tremendous pressure upon the desire for "innocence" that dominates cantos viii and ix. Here, the speaker is left with an End that is itself a mere residue, chilled and foregone, except for the splendor of its auroral annunciation, suggesting that the mere thought of such an End reduces our world, in our imaginations, to mere ash, to a "universe of death," a universe in which certain possibilities of imaginative grandeur and significance are no longer tenable. These considerations raise questions about which is the site of the greater anxiety—the rejected scene of eschatological judgment, or the persistent idea of an eschatology *without* judgment, an "Extinguishing [of] our planets, one by one" which leaves only "A shivering residue, chilled and foregone"?

Canto vi, in contrast, works with the double sense of "end" and demonstrates the capacity of apparently apocalyptic fears to return despite the elimination of both eschatologies and teleologies:

It is a theatre floating through the clouds,
Itself a cloud, although of misted rock
And mountains running like water, wave on wave,

Through waves of light. It is of cloud transformed
To cloud transformed again, idly, the way
A season changes color to no end,

Except the lavishing of itself in change,
As light changes yellow into gold and gold
To its opal elements and fire's delight,

Splashed wide-wise because it likes magnificence
And the solemn pleasures of magnificent space.
The cloud drifts idly through half-thought-of forms.

The theatre is filled with flying birds,
Wild wedges, as of a volcano's smoke, palm-eyed
And vanishing, a web in a corridor

Or massive portico. A capitol,
It may be, is emerging or has just
Collapsed. The denouement has to be postponed . . .

This is nothing until in a single man contained,
Nothing until this named thing nameless is
And is destroyed. He opens the door of his house

On flames. The scholar of one candle sees
An Arctic effulgence flaring on the frame
Of everything he is. And he feels afraid. (*CP* 416–17)

Here, as various critics have remarked, Stevens rejects teleology and eschatology in such phrases as "the way / A season changes color to no end" (with the word "end" clearly serving multiple semantic ends) and "the denouement has to be postponed . . . ."[5] The auroras remain beyond all plots; they overflow our myths of beginnings and ends and resist any sort of "containment." They deny our desire for a sense of purpose as well, and there may be some question again as to which of these senses of "end" is the site of the greatest anxiety for Stevens. The figuration through which Stevens postpones denouement—"A capitol, / It may be, is emerging or has just / Collapsed"—resembles the omens of disaster so often associated with displays of the aurora borealis, and calls to mind the wars and massive political upheavals Stevens struggled to empty of apocalyptic associations during World War II, upheavals whose cultural and aesthetic implications he resisted. Here Stevens makes us wonder whether the postponement of denouements "to no end" is itself a disaster in the aesthetic realm, whether the most recent historical upheaval has done away with belief in denouements, in the ability to locate pattern and meaning in historical disasters. It is difficult to decide whether the "scholar of one candle" feels "afraid" at the end of the canto because fictions of "ends" have survived in the "flames" and "flaring" of the aurora's "arctic effulgence," or because those fictions are among the things destroyed in those flames. Here, the movement between "flames," "effulgence," and "fear" may be instructive, since—at least in the *OED*—the middle term has no association with any destructive force but with splendor and glory; in Milton it is associated with the creative powers of God and the relation between man and God (in *Paradise Lost* III, 388 we learn that "on thee / Impresst the effulgence of his glorie abides"). Stevens's "effulgence," of course, is "arctic," not divine, and this difference may inspire the anxious questions associating the auroras with an enthroned imagination at the beginning of canto vii. If this is a purely natural effulgence, Stevens's scholar may experience the sublime terror of neither the End nor of divine glory but of a universe of endless and uncontainable flux, a universe in which beginnings and ends, the emergence and collapse of capitols, can no longer be distinguished, in which the linearity of "corridor[s]" and the clear demarcations provided by "portico[s]" are occluded by the intricacy of webs. It is worth remembering here that during World War II, Stevens associated "our sense of evil" with a feeling that time was nothing more than "water running in a gutter, / Through an alley to nowhere, / Without beginning or the concept of an end" (*OP* 112). "Auroras" vi would appear to present a peacetime version of such a terrifying encounter with the unbounded, and to present that encounter with greatly increased poetic and emotional power and complexity. It also offers a heightened or expanded version of "the pit of torment that placid end / Should be illusion" (*CP* 292) that opens in "Dutch Graves in Bucks County": in "Auroras" vi, torment now arises not just from the disconfirmation of a "*placid* end" (my emphasis) or of "An end of evil . . . / In a peace that is more than a refuge" (*CP* 291), but from the disconfirmation of any end at all. The end of the canto goes still further: the scholar views a force irreducible to any human meaning, a terrifying and meaningless "nothing" whose containment will come only at the cost of his destruction and reduction to namelessness.

This reading of canto vi does not resolve the problems raised by canto vii, but it does help clarify the key interpretive issue in this part of "Auroras": namely, how to read the tension between the two very different crises presented in cantos vi and vii. A possible solution may emerge by situating these crises in relation to the apocalyptic rhetoric that recurs throughout the poem. These two cantos, in fact, are the focal point of a conflict among several different stances toward the apocalyptic past. Michael Hobbs has described two of these strains—the discourses of the end and of the absence of any end—and associated them with two separate voices, termed, respectively, "a voice of doom" (126) and an "antiapocalyptic voice, the prophet who resists endings" (126). But there is just one voice "in" this poem, a voice that speaks a splintered, contradictory discourse, a discourse full of gaps, slippages, irresolvable tensions and uncertainties, sudden shifts in tone, all of which occur in relation to the idea of the end. Read against canto vi, the first part of canto vii appears to resolve the tensions that surround the loss of belief in "ends," retaining the idea of terminations while troping against biblical figures of a purpose-giving final judgment. Yet a rhetoric of necessity and telos continues to haunt the canto; when Stevens proclaims that the enthroned imagination "dare not leap by chance in its own dark," or insists that "It *must* change from destiny to slight caprice" (*CP* 417, my emphasis) and "move[s] to find / What *must* unmake it and, at last, what can" (*CP* 418, my emphasis), the rejection of destiny is strangely compromised by the rejection of chance and the reiterated modal auxiliary. And these concerns return in canto ix's "sense of the activity of fate" and "disaster" (*CP* 419) and in canto x's "The full of fortune and the full of fate" (*CP* 420), each of which I shall later discuss in more detail. They emerge elsewhere, too. The antiterminal rhetoric of canto ii's beach is trumped by the eschatological "ice and fire" (*CP* 412); and the crumbling house and burning books of canto iii, as well as canto ix's "disaster" (*CP* 419), make the aurora a harbinger of the End—though in the latter case, the advent of the End is figured not as an unveiling but as a reveiling: "The stars are putting on their glittering belts. / They throw around their shoulders cloaks that flash / Like a great shadow's last embellishment" (*CP* 419). The poem's first canto remains delicately balanced between figurations of natural flux and some more absolute, final change. It dismantles some aspects of apocalyptic thinking while leaving others, at the very least, in a state of suspension: when the speaker beholds the serpent "Skin flashing to wished-for disappearances" (*CP* 411), it proves difficult to decide whether the speaker or the serpent desires those disappearances, or whether the speaker projects his own desires onto the metaphoric serpent.

An extraordinary and conflicting range of stances toward the apocalyptic past thus emerges in the poem—a stance that rejects finality, one that fears finality, one that rejects finality but not destiny, one that rejects eschatological judgment but not a secularized eschatology, and one that fears the *absence* of finality; in addition, I would suggest that this conflict—a conflict generated by the auroras' illegibility—is the locus of the poem's crisis. The "fear" felt by the "scholar of one candle" at the conclusion of canto vi has something to do with the auroras' illegibility and with Stevens's sense of his peculiar position in literary history. When Stevens's scholar "opens the door of his house // On flames" and sees "An arctic effulgence flaring on the frame / Of everything he is" (*CP* 416–17), part of that "frame" is an intellectual and aesthetic framework that helps make the world interpretable. And, as Bloom suggests (*Climate* 271–72), the scholar is everything that is most Emersonian in Stevens, everything that links his creative project to a sublime tradition of discursive mastery. The auroras in canto vi emblematize the possibility of an absolute randomness, and by so doing they usher in the end of the age of the scholar and his entire intellectual and cultural inheritance, the structure of knowledge and the imaginative dispensation within which he has his authority. Read against this context, canto vii appears to snatch a vestigial belief in ends out of canto vi's "Arctic effulgence" and to reduce the poem's complex of conflicting stances to a single but still problematical position. It makes the first of these gestures in particular in the name of a minimal capacity to maintain clear boundaries and limits, to find something in the world other than "mad, multiform antithetical influx" (Kermode, *Sense* 115)—a condition that James

Longenbach describes as "intolerable" in his work on Jorie Graham: "If we really could step outside of narrative, if we could live without any sense of an ending, attaining some sense of the given, of pure being, we would be in hell" ("Jorie Graham's" 110). Stevens either needs or cannot avoid the End, but imagines a version of the End that itself ends earlier versions of the End and becomes thereby a disturbingly doubled discourse of the End.

Between canto i's initial encounter with an auroral desire for formlessness and canto vi's recognition of its implications for the scholar/poet, Stevens composes a series of self-elegies that work out the implications for his own "master fictions" of the auroral situation. This gesture could be read as a celebratory escape from the poet's own past and from a restrictive tradition, but the rhetoric and tone of most of this sequence-within-the-sequence calls such an interpretation into question. The elegiac characteristics of these cantos, the mere decision to mourn the postapocalyptic situation announced by the auroras—these most basic modal gestures suggest Stevens's nostalgic rather than celebratory stance toward the "end of an era in the history of the imagination." Each "farewell" to a master fiction is a double gesture, since it keeps that fiction alive in its own death. The element of nostalgia, along with the sense of crisis aroused by Stevens's postapocalyptic situation, is deeply at odds with the postmodern attitude toward the past. Hutcheon, for example, insists that postmodernism's stance toward the past "is as far from 'nostalgia' as anyone could wish" (*Poetics* 39), and her formulation of postmodernism's tendency to "install and then destabilize" (23) past discourses clearly indicates its counternostalgic force. Jameson, in discussing the retrospective orientation of much postmodern art, makes a distinction between its attempts at a merely "stylistic recuperation" (19) of the past and a "properly modernist nostalgia" (19).[6] Stevens's nostalgia in this part of "Auroras" must, at the very least, complicate any attempt to read him as a postmodern writer even at this late stage of his career.

Stevens's farewell to the cabin in canto ii is an elegy for a personal fiction and oeuvre as well as for a whole tradition, a particular imaginative dispensation in which the individual oeuvre participates. Jarraway writes of the house of canto iii as a "Jamesean house of fiction" (239), but this is a specifically Stevensian version of that trope, ironically and self-deprecatingly diminished to a mere "cabin," and a "deserted" one at that (*CP* 412). Stevens is, more specifically, elegizing a particular aspect of his house of fiction, the "whiteness" that Bloom (*Climate* 262) convincingly reads as "that ever-early candor" (*CP* 382) of "the first idea" (*CP* 382), an imaginative capacity for *askesis*, for reduction and abstraction, "a pure power" that "gives a candid kind to everything" (*CP* 382)—described in "Auroras" ii as "the accomplishment / Of an extremist in an exercise" (*CP* 412) and identified as the sole aspect of the cabin that grants it visibility in a darkening world. But in noting that the cabin comes by its whiteness "As by a custom or according to // An ancestral theme or as a consequence / Of an infinite course" (*CP* 412)—the course, perhaps, of a fictive "particular"—Stevens signals his oeuvre's participation in a poetic tradition of "whiteness," of the "pure power" of abstraction. An elegy for the white cabin—now deserted, open to the elements, surrounded by flowers (of rhetoric?) "trying to remind, of a white / That was different" (*CP* 412)—thus becomes an elegy not just for Stevens's own poetic powers or his own belatedness but for a whole imaginative dispensation already fallen into desuetude. Yet for all the tone of nostalgia and regret that dominates the first part of the canto, the decision to turn away from the cabin and toward the aurora's "blue-red sweeps / And gusts of great enkindlings" (*CP* 413) brings an extraordinary access of poetic power, one of the greatest of Stevens's sublime moments. Stevens's "man who is walking" is also a man who "turns" (*CP* 412), who tropes, and does so between the nostalgia for the white cabin of fictions and the illegible auroras, between two imaginative dispensations. He emblematizes the peculiar power located in the position of betweenness, the position that involves or facilitates a doubled stance of desire and resistance toward both the old and the new cultural dispensations.

The elegy of canto iv encompasses a similar literary historical scope, bidding adieu, as it does, not only to the kinds of masculine figures of discursive power that were so crucial in "Credences," but to a whole patriarchal tradition of visionary poetic mastery. As in "Credences," then, the possibility of mastery or of belief in a particular fiction of mastery is at stake, and, while one cannot take Stevens's references to "masters" and "mastery" as a conscious entry into this debate, his attitude toward these terms in "Auroras" helps place him in relation to the postmodern problematizing of "mastery." But first, the location of an elegy for both a private fiction and a history of poetic mastery in canto iv helps make sense of a more particular problem, an apparent contradiction in this section that has yet to be satisfactorily explained. Critics have identified the father with some of Stevens's sublime seekers, such as Canon Aspirin of *Notes* III, v–vi, Whitman (Stevens's "more severe, // More harassing master" [*CP* 486]), the crowned humanity of "Crude Foyer," or the angel of *Notes* III, vii;[7] but they have also noted that the father first appears as one of Stevens's Jehovah-like figures, echoing *Notes* III, i and iii, for example;[8] furthermore, at the end of "Auroras" iv, he again resembles the "voluminous master folded in his fire" (*CP* 381) who was rejected in *Notes* I, i. This strange conflation of positive and negative figures makes sense if we imagine Stevens as creating a palimpsest in this canto, inscribing different versions of the father on top of each other, or, perhaps, allowing that earlier and oft-rejected version to show through the more properly Stevensian sublime seeker. Stevens compresses, in a single figure, a history of fathers leading right back to the Father even as he bids that history farewell, thus establishing a visionary lineage for himself, the "ancestral theme" of a lineage in which "One father proclaims another, the patriarchs / Of truth" (*OP* 120). If this concealed genealogy of the visionary imagination seems unusual for Stevens in its inclusion of the usually *rejected* Jahweh figure, the apocalyptic context may provide a framework for interpreting the latter's presence in the canto. If what is problematic here is the survival of a univocal discourse of "single, certain truth" (*CP* 380), the survival of the greatest possible degree of discursive mastery, of the power to affirm affirmation by saying "yes to yes" and to deny negation by saying "no to no" (*CP* 414); if what is at stake here is the expression of that mastery in the voice of the male creator/poet, then surely it is appropriate that the loss of that masterful discourse's foundation, or at least of the figure for that foundation, should thus appear in the presentation of this crisis. Such an interpretation helps explain, too, the fact that so little in this canto sounds elegiac; the poem's visionary rhetoric and dominant concern with the father's sublime imaginative achievements suggest the extent to which Stevens still identifies with the father—he does not just write *about* the father, but writes *as* another visionary father. If the canto is marked by a desire for the position of visionary mastery to which it bids adieu, it seems unlikely to support a reading of Stevens as a postmodern skeptic who radically questions all fictions of mastery.

It may be objected that the preceding readings unduly privilege the elements in cantos ii and iv that lend themselves to the location of an essentially modernist aesthetics and poetics in the text—that they privilege the elegiac mode and visionary rhetoric while ignoring the ways these elements are ironized. It might be claimed that my reading does not fully acknowledge the way each farewell marks the ephemerality of these tropes, indeed of all tropes. But my purpose is not to deny readings like Beehler's and Jarraway's, for example, which see in cantos ii–iv the bottomless ironizing characteristic of postmodern and poststructuralist thinking. Stevens's farewells are necessitated by an ironic sensibility; the diminished stature and decayed condition of the house/cabin of fiction indicates an ironic stance toward his own fictions and his fictions of those fictions, as does the more thorough emptying of the father's powers at the end of canto iv—clearly, his "company, / In masks" (players, perhaps, in his "Theatre / Of Trope" [CP 397], whether Crispinesque comedians or "insatiable actor[s]" [CP 240]) cannot "choir it with the naked wind" (CP 415), and the absence of any response to the canto's terminal question silently inscribes the silence to which Stevens's usual poetic troupe is so tellingly reduced. But these readings still need to be placed alongside those (Vendler's, for example) that find the notes of elegy and nostalgia in this sequence, and serious consideration needs to be given to the possibility that both these interpretations are generated by equal and opposing forces at work in the poem, the possibility that the poem is "double-voiced," to use Linda Hutcheon's term, in a way that is more characteristic of modernist than postmodern texts.

In *A Poetics of Postmodernism*, Hutcheon refines her earlier sense of the "double-voicing" (*Parody* 97) characteristic of *both* modernist and postmodernist literature and distinguishes the different parodic *ethoi* of modernist and postmodern texts: in contrast to the "wishful call to continuity beneath the fragmented echoing" of Eliot's "The Waste Land," postmodern parody often reveals "ironic discontinuity . . . at the heart of continuity, difference at the heart of similarity" (*Poetics* 11). Clearly, what is at stake in these distinctions is not a straightforward opposition between univocality and polyvocality but between or among different kinds of polyvocality, between continuity at the heart of discontinuity and discontinuity at the heart of continuity. A similar construction emerges within the different context of Charles Altieri's reflections, in *Postmodernisms Now* and "Why

Stevens Must Be Abstract; or, What a Poet Can Learn from Painting," on the impact that modern and postmodern thought have had on lyric subjectivity. For Altieri, Stevens's essentially modernist "imperative to abstraction" ("Why" 87) functions as a safeguard against an excessive or unmasterable irony. Altieri thinks of the process of abstraction as an imaginative *activity* that remains free from the incessant ironizing otherwise attendant upon the decreation of individual fictions, fictions created by abstraction itself—in his own words, the "final negation" of "Examination of the Hero in a Time of War" "at once affirms the compositional force of decreation and indicates how that force leads well beyond the unmakings of infinite irony" ("Why" 94). In "Auroras" ii and iv, it is not a question of arguing for the presence of a nostalgia that undermines or undoes the ironizing force that sweeps through the text, rather than for an "infinite irony" that undermines the elegiac mode; rather, it is a question of the copresence of two equal and contradictory forces, a copresence that could not exist in a text categorizable as postmodern. According to Hutcheon's reading of postmodernism, even a text in which irony finally triumphed over an elegiac mode might still be best read as modern rather than postmodern.

Here, it may be instructive to attempt to locate the position of the Stevensian speaker in these two cantos more precisely. In canto ii, as was noted above, the "man who is walking turns blankly" between two aesthetic or imaginative dispensations. The speaker might appear to identify with this position of "betweenness," but his actual position seems still more distant, further abstracted from that of the character; the speaker is "present" as the person who *sees* and speaks not just of the two dispensations but of the position between them as well. His position is not one of "betweenness" but one of "bothness," and if he makes a choice here, it is "not a choice // Between, but of" (*CP* 403). It may involve a perilously fine distinction to claim that this position is not that of the infinite ironist but rather one who wields a "compositional force" that "leads well beyond the unmakings of infinite irony." But I would like to hold to this distinction and claim that the speaker of canto ii attempts to establish himself in a position beyond the endless self-unmakings of the auroras, a position that can, at least momentarily, contain them or sustain a fiction of their containment—nearer, perhaps, to the quintessentially modernist, "new critical" understanding of irony as the totality of often contradictory meanings contained by a given text. If the conclusion of canto iv seems less poised than that of canto ii, it may be because in canto iv the speaker, even though he adopts the stance that permits him to present both the father *and* the auroras, has invested too intensely in the paternal position for the same degree of distance to be maintained—the lack of distance being marked not just in the cry of "Master O Master" (*CP* 414) but in the fact that the voice of "bothness" here maintains the biblically sponsored trope of apocalyptic "throne" (*CP* 415) as a means of figuring the aurora's supreme power. This speaker, then, acknowledges a more thorough participation and investment in one of the two imaginative dispensations he beholds, even as he witnesses omens of its collapse into silence.

The possible presence of a "wishful call" or of something "beyond the unmakings of infinite irony" seems especially significant in relation to canto v, since Stevens's tone here differs greatly from the heightened and biblical rhetoric used to empty the figure of the father in canto iv; in fact, I would suggest that here, to borrow the terms used by David Shaw in his discussion of elegy and apocalypse, the final question of canto iv has led not to a breakthrough, but to a breakdown—not into apocalypse, but into self-parody.[9] While the stylistic disjunction between self-elegy and self-parody may seem enormous, Berger's sense of the close relationship between self-disparagement and self-elegy in his chapter on Stevens's last lyrics suggests how the two modes overlap (cf. Berger 146). Reading the poem as self-parody means, of course, identifying aspects of the father with Stevens himself, and if my reading of canto iv has not provided sufficient reasons to do so, it might be useful to remember that Stevens himself was a father, and in particular a father who, as his letters reveal, was fond of "fetching" exotic and entertaining gifts, both for himself and his family, at all times of the year, though most particularly as part of the Stevens household's Christmas festivities.[10] There is poetic self-parody, too, as Stevens turns bitterly against his own more festive or celebratory moments, denigrating these efforts with such epithets as a "tinny time" and "loud, disordered mooch" (*CP* 415)—the latter suggesting Stevens's own "mooching" of Prospero's pageant and the prophetic "trumpet's touch" (*CP* 415) of Shelley's West Wind (itself mooched from the Bible). But even in the most bitterly ironized moments of canto v, Stevens preserves an aspect of the imagination from "the unmakings of infinite irony":

What festival? This loud, disordered mooch?
These hospitaliers? These brute-like guests?
These musicians dubbing at a tragedy,
A-dub, a-dub, which is made up of this:
That there are no lines to speak? There is no play.
Or, the persons act one merely by being here. (*CP* 415–16).

Stevens's tone is difficult to read here; "A-dub, a-dub" sounds like a
nursery rhyme, but could also be merely echoic of the funeral drum-
ming appropriate to a tragedy. But to continue to consider the *absence*
of tragedy tragic is to take it seriously—to see in it a weight and dignity or, to use a key word from "The Noble Rider," a "nobility" that
goes beyond the incessant ironizing that would be more characteristic of a postmodern writer and even, perhaps, of some modernist
writers, such as the Eliot of "Prufrock," who allows his speaker only
the knowledge that he is *not* Hamlet. The way the canto's conclusion
turns on the question of tragedy's continued viability suggests that
even in its loss, tragedy retains a value that is not ironized. In Altieri's
terms, the tragedy of tragedy's absence demonstrates the imaginative
force, the determination to invest the world with meaning, that survives even the "unmakings of infinite irony." The persistence of tragedy
and, perhaps to an even greater extent, the cry of "Master O Master"
at the conclusion of canto iv have an affective force that speaks of the
"powers of intensification" ("Why" 100) that we come to understand,
according to Altieri, in reading a poet like Stevens—powers that invest
reality with meaning, that reveal the "heroism and nobility" (103) the
human mind can achieve. Such forces may be operative in canto x of
Stevens's "Esthétique du Mal," where they facilitate the capacity to
say, after the speaker acknowledges that "The death of Satan was a
tragedy / For the imagination" (*CP* 319), that "The tragedy, however,
may have begun, / Again, in the imagination's new beginning" (*CP*
320). The capacity to begin again despite the full knowledge that the
"new beginning" will prove as ephemeral as the old fiction, and, furthermore, to continue to name this ephemerality a "tragedy," bespeaks
an investment in these fictions and in this capacity that is something
other than ironic, something Stevens identifies as "a passion for yes
that had never been broken" (*CP* 320). Such a "passion for yes" may
be part of the "what will hold," as Eleanor Cook puts it, that Stevens
"retrieves" after decreating his sources ("King James" 241).[11]

Something of this desire for a position beyond irony dominates canto viii's search for innocence, which critics have commonly treated as the poem's climax—for Bloom, in fact, it is almost the climax of Stevens's entire career, "the most radical instance in Stevens of the undoing of an earlier trope by a later play upon it" (*Climate* 277). Critical debate over both the significance and quality of this passage has been especially intense. Those critics who express dissatisfaction with this passage for its too-easy undoing of the auroras' apocalyptic threat tend to simplify Stevens's concept of "innocence," and might be best answered by observing that Stevens does not so much change the auroras' meaning as redefine "innocence" along the lines of Yeats's "murderous innocence," as Berger has suggested (67).[12] But most relevant for my purposes is the mere fact that the poem is marked by a *desire* for innocence, a desire that there be some "thing" or nonthing that remains unharmed, uninjured, untouched, pure. The logic of canto viii's search for "innocence" is homologous to the search in "The Noble Rider" for a "nobility" that can survive the disconfirmation of each historical embodiment of that quality. As a "thing of ether that exists / Almost as predicate" (*CP* 418), "innocence" remains, despite (or because of) Stevens's ambiguously positioned "Almost," separable from and subsistent in each individual and ephemeral instance, a strangely impure and unsettled "pure power" (*CP* 382) The great peculiarity of this canto is not, as Berger and Leggett claim, the speaker's insistence that "innocence" has a visible existence, but that a "pure principle" should take such a concrete and visible form; the move disrupts what Altieri has described as the essentially modernist logic of abstraction that leads Stevens to the nonrepresentable "force" and "pure power" of "Noble Rider" and *Notes*, a logic that has been operating in the poem since the encounter with the "poison" of disbelief first began to work in the first canto of "Auroras." If the "pure principle" of "innocence" is visible, it runs the risk of disconfirmation. It may be that the intensity of the crisis Stevens faces in "Auroras" leads him to seek something more tangible than an unrepresentable force or power in his search for a nonironizable activity, and that the auroras' own restless self-undoing provides a sufficiently fluid image for such activity—it cannot be disconfirmed because it is never the same as it was. In fact, as I shall explore later, the initial designation of innocence as "pure principle" may itself suggest a dissatisfaction with the reliance on the unrepresentable.

Much of my discussion of "mastery" in "Auroras" has proceeded at the thematic level, the level that for Altieri is less significant than the performative one he investigates, though it may be that the full complexity of Stevens's poetry emerges through the relationship between "what" the poem says and "how" it says it. In cantos iv and v, Stevens's poetry demonstrates the same powers it bids farewell; it is an abstract and visionary farewell to the abstract and visionary father. If it bears witness to the death of a kind of nobility, it nevertheless invests that death with a tragic dignity. The mere act of bidding farewell remains paradoxical, since the farewell actually brings back, momentarily, the very thing it leaves behind. And the poem continues by reimagining forms of mastery and nobility that "will hold" after this initial farewell. Mastery reappears not only in the unmasterable "enthroned imagination" of canto vii, in the "rabbi"—literally "my master" in Hebrew—who opens canto x, and in "The vital, the never-failing genius, / Fulfilling his meditations, great and small" (*CP* 420) who brings it to a close, but also in the act by which Stevens names the auroras "innocence" in canto viii. Here, both the act of naming and the quality named move the poem beyond the ironies of canto v. For Bloom, this moment signifies Stevens's transumptive victory over his poetic anxieties, an instance of trope-making as the sheer assertion of poetic will (*Climate* 276–78). It is unclear whether one should be more surprised at the appearance of another master at the poem's conclusion or at the questioning of the father's mastery in cantos iv and v. As I have already suggested, the absence of "a central control" is at times problematical in Stevens, providing both an exhilarating freedom and a disturbing uncertainty.

If Stevens's doubled stance toward the father involves a simultaneous recognition of the value and limits of a patriarchal tradition of mastery, the more obviously nostalgic tone of the farewell to the mother in canto iii situates that stance in relation to an "other" tradition. The rest of the poem, in fact, remains deeply divided in its attitudes toward its male and female figures and in the values assigned to each. Stevens says farewell to the masterful father in cantos iv and v only to allow other male figures of mastery to return, albeit with a difference, at the end of the poem; and similarly, the mother is "dissolved" and "destroyed" (*CP* 413) only to reappear—again with a difference—at the end of canto viii.

What is at stake in this construction of gender in the poem's rejection and restoration of its male and female figures? Apocalyptic literature, of course, articulates its vision of a perfect world and of the author of that world in terms of gender, and here one might wonder about the extent to which the role played by the "innocent mother" (*CP* 419) in canto viii of "Auroras" marks a break with apocalyptic discourse—a break that might still be interpretable as a new kind of apocalypse. Alice Jardine claims that "the space 'outside of' the conscious subject has always connoted the feminine in the history of Western thought," and that "any movement into alterity is a movement into that female space" (114–15); Kristeva finds just such a version of femininity constructed within Plato's discourse of space, which is "designated by the aporia of the *chora*, matrix space, nourishing, unnameable, anterior to the One, to God and, consequently, defying metaphysics" ("Women's Time" 16). According to Derrida, the dominant "philosophical, onto-eschato-teleological interpretation" ("Apocalyptic" 83) of apocalypse constructs that discourse as a resistance to such alterity, a desire for closure in the final "truth" represented by a single, male deity. Mary Carpenter and Martin Jay have observed that Revelation portrays such closure only after expelling everything that is perceived as negative in female sexuality (or, for Carpenter, everything that the apocalyptic believer unconsciously fears about his own sexuality); such qualities are projected onto the figure of the whore of Babylon, thereby being separated out, named, and eschatologically eliminated.[13] And in "Of an Apocalyptic Tone," Derrida suggests that Kant's apocalyptically antiapocalyptic discourse assumes "an excluded middle" in the form of the veiled goddess Isis, the feminine "other" which must be excluded by a "non-emasculated *logos*" (79), the logos of the Western phallogocentric tradition. Such an understanding of "the feminine" is double-edged: it can be a means of marginalizing the female and the feminine, or a means of challenging the patriarchal tradition with a set of values that radically disrupt all the assumptions of that tradition. What seems more important for the present context, though, is the way the theorists considered immediately above share, despite their differences, an assumption that a movement beyond the kind of metaphysics in which "the modern" and modernism invest so heavily must involve an undoing of or radical departure from an essentially masculine and patriarchal discursive tradition, a tradition that figures itself, its power, and the social and discursive operations that both support it and are supported by it in terms of a relationship to a masculine Absolute. Such a claim may appear to subsume feminist theory to postmodern and poststructuralist theory, but it could just as easily seem to do the opposite—to make, for example, Derrida's questioning of a (phal)-logocentric philosophical tradition a mere subset of the feminist critique of this tradition. It needs to be remembered, at the very least, that feminist thinking has its own distinct history and that there are earlier and even contemporary versions of feminism that partake of the metaphysical assumptions that theorists like Cixous and Butler insist on leaving behind, and that the relationships between specific versions of feminist theory and between these theories and postmodern and poststructural theory are extremely complex. Nevertheless, even in the face of an acknowledgment of such historical complexity, these considerations suggest how Stevens's figurations of gender may tell us something about his position in relation to postmodern and poststructuralist discourse, about the extent to which he is able to leave behind a masculine, patriarchal discursive tradition. To what extent does Stevens's farewell to and resurrection of the mother register such a "movement into alterity," a movement necessitated by the auroras? To what extent do Stevens's figurations of gender align him with the position of the father, or participate in a more general metaphysical construction of difference?

A movement "outside" a patriarchal tradition may begin in canto iii. Here, Stevens says farewell not so much to the mother/muse[14] as to the idea that her children can possess her or at least possess a proper image of her, an image that has, therefore, been entirely contained within a patriarchal tradition:

> Farewell to an idea . . . The mother's face,
> The purpose of the poem, fills the room.
> They are together, here, and it is warm,
>
> With none of the prescience of oncoming dreams,
> It is evening. The house is evening, half dissolved.
> Only the half they can never possess remains,
>
> Still-starred. It is the mother they possess,
> Who gives transparence to their present peace.
> She makes that gentler that can gentle be. (*CP* 413)

Again, the speaker takes a position of "bothness," a position that embraces both the children's possession of the mother and the incompleteness and brevity of that possession, qualities that necessitate the canto's elegiac farewell. But to whom does Stevens ascribe belief in this myth of possession? Is this myth of possession one of Stevens's own? The interior location of this epiphany of the mother's face is familiar enough, since, after *Harmonium*, Stevens's muse is almost invariably an "Interior Paramour" (*CP* 524); but for all the ubiquity of such muses in Stevens's work, I know of no similar appearance of the mother's or of any muse's face in Stevens's poetry and particularly not one that declares that face to be "The purpose of the poem" and shows her thus possessed by her children.[15] In fact, Stevens's female figures and muses tend to be far more evasive and elusive, characterized by their capacity to remain beyond the poet's attempts at possession, linguistic or otherwise. Even in the moments of most complete rapprochement with these figures, Stevens's rhetoric does not denote possession but rather a meeting of equals in which "we forget each other and ourselves," "In which being there together is enough" (*CP* 524); the other usually appears "in difference" (*CP* 406). And in the passage which this part of "Auroras" iii most strongly resembles—the epigraph to *Notes toward a Supreme Fiction*—Stevens does not attempt to name the bringer of "transparence" and "peace":

> In the uncertain light of single, certain truth,
> Equal in living changingness to the light
> In which I meet you, in which we sit at rest,
> For a moment in the central of our being,
> The vivid transparence that you bring is peace. (*CP* 380)

It is puzzling, in other words, that Stevens should bid farewell to a myth of the possessed muse/mother in which he has never apparently invested. Even if the mother's possessors represent a tradition that thus lays claim to its muse, Stevens would seem to misread the dominant figuration of the poet's relationship to the muse—the male poet is more likely to be possessed by, not of, a muse always beyond him. Such is certainly the case for Whitman, who consistently tropes his muse as a potentially annihilating oceanic mother. But perhaps canto iii offers not a misreading but a critique; a suggestion that even such figurations as Whitman's and Stevens's own take all too certain a grasp of poetry's finally unknowable source. Canto iii would thus make explicit a tendency toward containment of the feminine that has always been covertly under way, and may do so in order to move away from that tendency, suggesting, as Jarraway notes, that something has always remained outside these tropes: "The house is evening, half dissolved. / Only the half they can never possess remains, // Still-starred."[16]

When the mother returns at the end of canto viii, Stevens thoroughly reconfigures her relationship to speaker/child, so there is no longer any question of possessing the mother within a patriarchal house of fiction:

> That we partake [of innocence],
> Lie down like children in this holiness,
> As if, awake, we lay in the quiet of sleep,
>
> As if the innocent mother sang in the dark
> Of the room and on an accordion, half-heard,
> Created the time and place in which we breathed . . . (*CP* 418–19)

As creator of "the time and place in which we breathed," the mother could never become an object of possession; she creates the conditions of possibility for any fiction of possession. In fact, the last line of this passage should be weighed against a similar description of the father: in canto iv, he is "in space and motionless and yet / Of motion the ever-brightening origin" (*CP* 414). Has the mother usurped the father's place? Has a patriarchal dispensation given way to the rule of an "other," to a feminine and matriarchal dispensation? The association of the auroras with "holiness" and of the latter with the mother transfers the poem's religious rhetoric—the rhetoric of masters and mastery—from father to mother. The auroras are not "A saying out of a cloud" (*CP* 418) such as Ezekiel hears, not a prophetic or proverbial truth uttered by a male deity dwelling in the sky or heard and recorded by a prophetic father, but the music of an innocent female earthiness. Gender also marks Stevens's subtle contrast between two versions of innocence in canto viii: one exists "in the idea of it, alone," "As pure principle" for "the oldest and coldest philosopher"—another version of the emasculated thinkers of "Figure of the Youth"—and is "not a thing of time, nor of place" (*CP* 418); the other proves to be "visible" in the "time and place" created by the mother as an "innocence of the earth." The "innocence of the earth" displaces the earlier and inadequate "pure principle" of innocence, an innocence associated with an abstract philosophical tradition that Stevens consistently understands as a masculine or patriarchal discourse cut off from any relation to the feminine. As I indicated in my second chapter, it is unwise to identify Stevens with "the oldest and coldest philosopher." Stevens later demonstrates a wariness of "pure principles" (*OP* 137) in "Solitaire under the Oaks" (1955),[17] and also writes of what one assumes to be his own heart as the "oldest and the warmest heart" (*CP* 523) in "A Quiet Normal Life" (1952). "I am not a philosopher" (*OP* 275), Stevens wrote in his 1951 essay "A Collect of Philosophy," a work which, for all its interest in the poetic nature of some philosophical concepts, nevertheless suggests why "the oldest and coldest philosopher" might not be a positive figure for Stevens:[18] this thinker sounds a little like a Snow Man with a Ph.D. It may be for these reasons that Stevens later associates the "rendezvous" with an unnamed "she"—variously identified by critics as either "the beloved" (Berger 71) or as the mother (LaGuardia 137, Jarraway 240–41)—with the experience of freedom:

> The rendezvous, when she came alone,
> By her coming became a freedom of the two,
> An isolation which only the two could share. (*CP* 419)

This freedom, perhaps, is the freedom of what Jardine calls a "movement into alterity," of the movement outside the patriarchal, visionary discourse of apocalypse and toward a vision of an earth that need not be subject to eschatological judgment or apocalyptically redeemed, since it is already innocent. This movement constitutes the poem's most complete undoing of canto vii's scene of eschatological judgment, and marks its greatest distance from the discourse represented by canto iv's father, its greatest remove from a modernist dispensation.

But there are elements in canto viii that also strain against this movement into alterity and that strain against the suggestion that in "Auroras" Stevens is moving into a postmodern textual space when he thus aligns himself with the maternal "other." Stevens's figuration of the mother in canto viii remains profoundly ambivalent, particularly in the liminality that either enacts or resists—or does both simultaneously—the "movement toward alterity" (and away from the father) that Jardine associates with a feminine space. Many critics have observed that the mother's presence in this passage is greatly attenuated through the "as if" of simile. In fact, one can hardly speak of the "presence" of the mother here, since the innocent mother does *not* "[sing] in the dark / Of the room"; instead, Stevens *compares* some other event to the mother's singing—or rather, Stevens, writing in the imperative mode, suggests that we perform an action ("Lie down like children in this holiness") which might provide an experience similar to that of hearing the "innocent mother." Is this extraordinary evasiveness (an evasiveness heightened by the mother's position "in the dark" and her only "half-heard" song) a way of registering a "movement into alterity" without taking possession of that alterity and thereby altering it? Or does it reflect a profound discomfort with this movement, with the space "outside" the patriarchal order, outside the house of fiction, and a discomfort with the consequences of rejecting fictions of patriarchal mastery and the concomitant reduction of the self to a childlike state? The poem may maintain a deliberate distance from something that both consoles and threatens. At the very least, an irresolvable tension emerges here between a desire to bring back the mother and a desire to keep her at a distance, a desire of the masculine self for a relationship to an engulfing feminine presence and a desire to maintain an essential separation from that presence. In the extremely disjunctive ninth canto, the speaker shifts abruptly between constructions of the masculine self as a relation to a feminine other—the mother, the unidentified "she" of the fifth tercet's "rendezvous"—and, in the middle of these two figurations, an essentially homosocial construction of identity, a world of "hale-hearted landsmen," men who "thought alike" as "brothers . . . in a home / In which we fed on being brothers" (*CP* 419). The disjunctive syntax proves especially difficult to read: the dismissive "We lay sticky with sleep" (*CP* 419) may reject the "drama" of "Danes in Denmark" (apparently not a tragic drama) or the "quiet of sleep" created by the "innocent mother." The "rendezvous" of the fifth tercet might illustrate *or* break free of the "activity of fate." As "an isolation only the two could share," the rendezvous separates the speaker from the fraternal society of the canto's opening tercets, thereby maintaining an irreducible tension between competing versions of masculine identity. And the liberating rendezvous also opens the poem again to the possibility of disaster. Apocalyptic omens reappear in the anxious question about imminent "disaster" and the eschatological preparations seen in the auroras:

> The stars are putting on their glittering belts.
> They throw around their shoulders cloaks that flash
> Like a great shadow's last embellishment. (*CP* 419)

By the end of the canto, the speaker's ability to invest in a fiction of maternal, earthly innocence has been greatly reduced, and he can only hint that the unnamed disaster may come "*Almost* as part of innocence, almost, / Almost as the tenderest and the truest part" (*CP* 420, my emphasis).

If these marks of anxiety or resistance raise questions about the extent to which Stevens is willing to move outside a modern aesthetic or imaginative dispensation, the male figures of mastery—a "rabbi" (translatable as "my master," as was mentioned earlier) and a "spectre of the spheres / . . . / The vital, the never-failing genius" (*CP* 420)—who preside in canto x might transform these questions into a confirmed doubt:

> An unhappy people in a happy world—
> Read, rabbi, the phases of this difference.
> An unhappy people in an unhappy world—
>
> Here are too many mirrors for misery.
> A happy people in an unhappy world—
> It cannot be. There's nothing there to roll
>
> On the expressive tongue, the finding fang.
> A happy people in a happy world—
> Buffo! A ball, an opera, a bar.
>
> Turn back to where we were when we began:
> An unhappy people in a happy world. (*CP* 420)

If one of the central problems of the poem has been the difficulty of leaving behind the discourse of the father, and of allowing the "m/other" to be heard singing in the poem, then canto x would seem, by returning to male figures of poetic speech and creativity, to signal its author's awareness of his distance from the mother and, thus, his decision to align himself again with the visionary company he left behind in canto v. This change also involves a movement away from the poem's most radical reconfiguration of the relations between elegy and apocalypse. As was already discussed, elegies such as *In Memoriam* and "Lycidas" close the mourning process only when the elegist aligns himself with the discourse of God the Father and Christ the Son, that is, with the prophetic and apocalyptic discourse, the patriarchal discourse of truth that promises compensation in a perfect, unchanging world, a world without loss that restores all losses. Stevens's initial return to the consoling fictions of the mother and of an innocent earth—an unfallen earth, an earth that need not be judged, destroyed, redeemed or replaced—departs from this tradition. But by displacing a feminine, earthly innocence with the "rabbi" and "spectre of the spheres," Stevens moves back toward a more conventional elegiac/apocalyptic configuration of gender, even while maintaining his difference from any theological content; he aligns himself with a sort of vestigial remnant of a near-exhausted tradition, a tradition that survives only in the form of a masculine position of discursive power and that can do nothing to eliminate the gap between an "unhappy people" and a "happy world." Furthermore, that gap displaces sexual difference with an ontological difference, or rewrites the former as the latter—the difference between "a happy world" and "An unhappy people," in other words, is a nongendered version of the gap between an innocent mother and a male speaker who cannot quite believe in her or must maintain an uneasy distance from her, speaking of her within a paradoxical "as if." This change is not exactly a forgetting of sexual difference, but it may nevertheless constitute a movement away from a site of greater anxiety. In this regard, the rabbi of canto x bespeaks a different mastery from that associated with a father who "leaps from heaven to heaven." Like the speaker of canto iv, this final master may have looked on the "present throne" of the auroras and incorporated a knowledge of difference into his discourse, or recognized, perhaps, the difference that lies outside his discourse.

The treatment of closure in the preceding paragraph is far too straightforward, however, to be useful in relation to a discussion of Stevens's position in literary history; if, as Barbara Herrnstein Smith says, twentieth-century poetry, in general, has a tendency to resist or refuse closure, it seems necessary to invoke something other than a clear-cut opposition between closure and its absence, and, instead, to ask whether modernist and postmodern texts demonstrate different kinds of resistance or refusal, whether they encode different affective stances toward the absence of closure. To rephrase Hutcheon's discussion of parody, it may be a matter of the presence or absence of a "wishful call" to closure even in acknowledgment of the impossibility of closure. In the final tercets of "Auroras," Stevens inscribes an insistence on irreducible differences alongside a rhetoric of wholeness and completion that makes one wonder whether the rejection of closure or the *nostalgia* for closure is the stronger force in the poem:

> Read to the congregation, for today
> And for tomorrow, this extremity,
> This contrivance of the spectre of the spheres,
>
> Contriving balance to contrive a whole,
> The vital, the never-failing genius,
> Fulfilling his meditations, great and small.
>
> In these unhappy he meditates a whole,
> The full of fortune and the full of fate,
> As if he lived all lives, that he might know,
>
> In hall harridan, not hushful paradise,
> To a haggling of wind and weather, by these lights
> Like a blaze of summer straw, in winter's nick. (*CP* 420–21)

Stevens's rhetoric of completion—extremity, spheres, balance, whole, fulfilling, full, all—accumulates as the poem approaches its conclusion; we have arrived at "this extremity," an end point. And the poem shows other signs of having come full circle; the echoes of its first cantos recall the serpent's hypothetical and relentless "possession of happiness" and "His meditations in the ferns" (*CP* 411) as well as canto ii's "accomplishment / Of an extremist in an exercise." When the poem suggests that we "Turn back to where we were when we began," it speaks not just of returning to the first aphorism proposed at the canto's beginning, nor of returning to the entire poem's opening, in which we encountered a "master of the maze . . . / Relentlessly in possession of happiness" (*CP* 411); it tells also of a return to human origins and the beginning of human history. But the poem does not achieve the closure suggested by these figures. For Stevens, this circle of return differs from the closure of the apocalyptic plot; it does not return us to the lost innocence of a "hushful paradise" (*CP* 421), of "a happy people in a happy world," but leaves us in an already fallen world of "unhappy people," or, in the absence of belief in a fall, a world in which "It is the human that is the alien" (*CP* 328). Does Stevens fulfill his own meditations, great and small? Or is there something a bit contrived about the language of completion in this "contrivance of the spectre of the spheres"? We might remain wary, too, of the spectre who "Contrive[s] balance to contrive a whole," or of the economic motif in the "haggling of wind and weather" of the penultimate line. If we are still haggling, the deal is not complete, the bargain not struck, the balance still lacking. And when Stevens describes this world as a "hall harridan" rather than a "hushful paradise," the introduction of a more negative version of femininity than the one embodied in the figure of the "innocent mother" reopens the poem's anxious division across gender lines. Thus, different tensions emerge in the poem's closural movement: a tension between a rhetoric of wholeness and one of incompleteness, and a tension between the poem's figures of closure and the degree of closure (or nonclosure) it actually attains. The distinction involved in reading this tension as a modern rather than a postmodern one is, no doubt, perilously fine; a reader might, with reasonable conviction, decide that the text's closural or anticlosural complexities and contradictions are characteristics of the postmodern condition, that the gaps, tensions, slippages are all introduced into the text as a means of ironizing and problematizing the rhetoric of completion and closure. But such a reading would be making an equally perilous distinction and closing off the possibility of an affective orientation toward closure in the poem's language, a "wishful call" rather than an ironic critique. In fact, the difficulty of making such a distinction is, perhaps, an indication of the ways in which the poem resists categorization as postmodern; an equal division between contradictory desires—a desire for closure and a desire for nonclosure— would still, at least according to Hutcheon's and Altieri's versions of postmodernism, belong to a modernist aesthetics.

The presence or absence of closure in an elegiac text also needs to be situated in relation to the difference between mourning and melancholia and particularly in relation to the different stances taken toward these terms by, on the one hand, Freud and Julia Kristeva, who place melancholia within a therapeutic teleology whose end is the closure of mourning and the return to psychic health, and, on the other hand, Hélène Cixous, who insists on an affirmation and celebration of the melancholic position.[19] Cixous proposes a liberation of melancholia from any Freudian teleology. Cixous begins with a rather Kristevan description of the feminine text, which "takes the metaphorical form of wandering, excess, risk of the unreckonable: no reckoning, a feminine text can't be predicted, isn't predictable, isn't knowable and is therefore very disturbing. It can't be anticipated, and I believe femininity is written outside anticipation it really is the text of the unforeseeable" (355).

Cixous also moves from text to consciousness and life (if these can be distinguished from each other), making a distinction between Man, who "has to mourn" (355), and Woman, who "does not mourn": "She basically *takes up the challenge of loss* in order to go on living: she lives it, gives it life, is capable of unsparing loss" (355). My purpose here is not to reduce Stevens's text to a set of symptoms of the poet's psychological state, or to suggest that Stevens was a melancholic person. I am interested in the *stance* taken by the text toward what has now been identified as the difference between melancholia and mourning—toward, on the one hand, an interpretation of the inability to name and of an absence of closure as a lack, as a *negative* moment within a dialectic of recovery, and, on the other hand, a reinterpretation of this "lack" not as a lack at all but as a means of liberation. To understand the elegy of cantos ii–iv in such terms is to situate it in relation to postmodern suspicions of teleologies, master narratives, and mastery in general. "Auroras" *does* name a series of losses, but the poem neither moves beyond this naming to full closure and consolation nor interpret its situation as being unambiguously liberating. "Auroras" occupies a peculiar intermediary space *between* melancholia and mourning, or between celebratory and mournful stances toward the melancholic position. If closure eludes the "Auroras," the poem nevertheless remains marked by a desire for the very sort of closure it cannot attain, thereby constructing an absence within itself. Martin Jay's claim that postmodern apocalypses are characterized by melancholia proves suggestive here, though his analysis of *all* apocalyptic discourse as either melancholic or manic—the two contrasting manifestations of the same underlying cause—too readily collapses

the profound differences between postmodern and Christian apocalypse; for Derrida, after all, the latter is the instance par excellence of
the logocentricism that postmodernism sets itself against.[20] Could
postmodern texts be understood as being melancholic in Cixous's
sense, joyously refusing the closure of mourning?

I have explored three different aspects of "The Auroras of
Autumn"—its rewriting of apocalypse and elegy, its concern with mastery, and its construction of gender—and suggested that in each case
the poem arrives at a paradoxical space between the traditions it engages. It is a poem that gestures toward something "outside" of the
tradition of a masculine, visionary discourse that plays such a crucial
role in "Credences of Summer" and that functions as a problematical
stay against the threat of aesthetic collapse during the war years. And
yet the stance it takes toward that "outside" position is deeply divided
and troubled. The struggle with the apocalyptic past opens the self
to the greater fears of an "apocalypse *without* apocalypse" and thus
becomes such an apocalypse; the farewell to Stevens's "Master O master" is informed by the desire for what it rejects; the final opening of
the poem to "difference" is nevertheless closed by its reinscription of
a metaphysical concept of gender and sexual difference and a tradition of mastery. If the reconfiguration of elegy and apocalypse means
that the elegy cannot find any traditional form of closure, Stevens
can nevertheless reinscribe this radical brokenness within a consoling and familiar myth of gender. Unlike the postmodernist, who, in
Hutcheon's formula, "uses and abuses" the past, Stevens would seem
to reverse the order and importance of the two terms—to return to
Cook's phrase, he "decreates" in order to "find what will hold." I trust
that it is clear that I am not condemning Stevens for being conservative, for failing to fully realize the more radical implications of his
poetic practice; to do so would be to assume a teleology of literary
forms and styles that would be questionable not only from a postmodern perspective but also from that provided by the "facts" that
make up our fictive past.

Part III: Going after Apocalypse

chapter six

Past Apocalypse, Past Stevens

Jorie Graham's *The Errancy*

My readings of modern and postmodern stances toward apocalypse would be incomplete without some effort to test them in the work of at least one more recent poet. Jorie Graham's oeuvre provides a particularly appropriate laboratory for such an experiment, even though her differences from Stevens, as this chapter shall demonstrate, cannot be constructed within a straightforward distinction between modernism and postmodernism. Graham belongs to a postmodern generation; her work is unmistakably marked by the logic of post-modernism and poststructuralism; she has an explicit and overriding concern with the role of eschatological and apocalyptic thinking in the construction of aesthetic objects and historical narratives, as well as in everyday life and contemporary politics. Like Stevens, Graham takes an antiapocalyptic stance, but her work betrays a different kind of self-consciousness about its possible complicity with apocalyptic discourse, as well as a different understanding of the aesthetic and political implications of any lingering investment in the End. And conveniently enough—at least for my purposes—Graham does not just openly acknowledge her admiration for Stevens's oeuvre, but quotes from or alludes to "Martial Cadenza," "Dutch Graves in Bucks County," "Credences of Summer," "Things of August," and "The Auroras of Autumn." Graham appropriates material from poems in which Stevens engages with apocalyptic discourse. I will suggest in par-ticular that Stevens's resistance to apocalyptic rhetoric is, for Graham, still deeply entangled in the discourse of the End, as well as in an aesthetics of "closure" that Graham considers complicit with that discourse. Most of this chapter will be devoted to Graham's 1997 collection, *The Errancy*. However, Graham's quotations from Stevens need to be understood in relation to that volume's concern with a particular kind of cultural exhaustion or collapse, with Graham's own sense that she is writing at and about the end of one era of the imagination; the discussion of Stevens's presence in that volume will, therefore, be preceded by an account of that collapse and its relationship to Graham's own historical situation. Both of these aims, however, necessitate a still more general starting point, namely, a more general account of Graham's engagement with the discourse of the End.

Graham's engagement with that discourse is anything but straightforward. Critics have been quick to point out not just the anticlosural element in Graham's work, but the tension between closural and anticlosural desires.[1] And a concern with endings is often enough marked in Graham's titles: "The Sense of an Ending," *The End of Beauty*, "What the End Is For," "Eschatological Prayer," "Manifest Destiny," "The Phase after History." These titles indicate a concern not just with aesthetic closure but with a broader notion of ends, telos, as well as with eschatology and apocalypse (Graham, "Interview" 89) and, in particular, with the relationship between eschatology and an aesthetics of closure. According to Graham, such an aesthetics has not just dominated Western art but is synonymous with it. Graham herself acknowledges the presence of all these forces in her work, and, in an interview with Thomas Gardner, articulates her understanding of the link between apocalypse and aesthetic closure:

> Well, the way the sentence operates became connected, for me, with notions like ending-dependence and eschatological thinking. With ideas like manifest destiny, westward expansion. Imperialisms of all kinds. I began to notice how the forms our Western sensibility creates are, for the most part, ending-dependent, and that such notions of form—however unconsciously—give birth to historical strategies like the Christian one: the *need* for the conflagration at the end that takes what appear like random events along the way and turns them into *stages* . . . when we start realizing that by our *historical* thinking we have created a situation whereby we are only able to know ourselves by a conclusion which would render *meaningful* the storyline along the way—it becomes frightening. . . . It forced me to recognize the little wind in myself which I think blows through many people living today—that secret sense of "well, let's get it over with so that we might know what the story was, what it was *for*"—apocalypse as the ultimate commodification. (Graham, "Interview" 84)

A resistance to "narrative" and "closure" is of more than merely aesthetic significance to Graham, and she hopes that poetry like hers may prove capable "of affecting the consciousness of the race so that we might not destroy ourselves" (89)—a hope that she simultaneously acknowledges as "absurd," and, in a more ethically self-critical moment, as "a delusion I create for myself in order to get myself off the hook" (89). Graham's anticlosural stance, then, is an antiapocalyptic stance, and one that has for her an inescapable social and political dimension.

But there is another and more important paradox at work here. The paradox is not simply that there are alternating, opposing tendencies toward closural and anticlosural (or apocalyptic and antiapocalyptic) strategies at work in Graham's poetry, but that the antiapocalyptic stance is simultaneously apocalyptic and could not be otherwise. The comments from the interview, for example, hint at an implicit teleological narrative of Graham's own. This teleology emerges with particular clarity in her antiapocalyptic reading of the relationship between ordinary end-directed narratives and the specific version of such narratives known as apocalypses: narrative "gives birth" to eschatological prophecy and apocalypse as though the latter forms were in narrative's genes, or as though the emergence of apocalypse were narrative's own predetermined eschaton, a necessary culmination and a ne plus ultra. Apocalypse tells us "what the story . . . was *for,*" and, for Graham at least, the advantage of her own postapocalyptic historical position lies in the way it permits her to state what apocalypse, too, "was *for,*" and to use her late position in the history of story to undo or neutralize apocalypse. Such considerations suggest, then, that Graham does not tell the full story of her *own* desire for the safety and pleasure of closure; she does not acknowledge, that is, that "the little wind" of apocalyptic desire is blowing "in [her]self" not just when she speaks of the apocalyptic desire to "get it over with" but also when she makes her most antiapocalyptic pronouncements. That wind also blows when Graham claims that "this moment in our culture" is one "in which the female is ascendent" and, as a result, is a moment characterized by a widespread "desire for loss of hierarchies" (87); it is "a period of history when the hero, the ascendent rational mind, has gotten so far along in its quest that the female has to ask for him back—or risk total psychic disintegration" (88). Graham does not exactly figure an absolute break with the past here, a wholesale movement into an "alterity" that the Western tradition, according to Alice Jardine, constructs as a "female space" entirely "'outside of' the conscious subject" (Jardine 114–15); Graham is, in her own self-confessedly "exaggerat[ed]" words, attempting to "reincorporate the *hero* part of [her] psyche back into the unconscious, uroboric female. Not in some foolish way in order to dissolve 'him'—*the mind*—but to keep everything alive, to keep the tension alive" (88). In other words, Graham does not imagine an overthrow of the realm of the hero, or an absolute break with the era of the hero, the master, of narrative and master narratives; instead, she undertakes a reconfiguration of the relationships *within* the existing cultural and philosophical opposition between male and female. But as is clear from Graham's language, she reads this moment as a crux of unique importance in human history, one that promises a kind of salvation not heretofore available. In fact, she invests her present with a double eschatological significance: all preceding history has led to the brink of "conflagration" and absolute destruction, but it has also led to the turning point that may prevent that conflagration. In both of these interpretations, the present becomes charged with a special significance that imposes a new meaning and pattern on all that precedes it; as in 2 Corinthians, "now *is* the accepted time" (2 Cor. 6:2), and, as in Mark 1:15, "The time is fulfilled" and the kingdom "is at hand"—not the kingdom of God, but of what Graham calls "materialism."

Clearly, I am suggesting that Graham's antiapocalyptic stance becomes another version of the apocalyptic "going-one-better" discussed in my introduction, that in resisting ends she still adds her voice to the apocalyptic chorus, proclaiming the end of the end, the dawning of a new era or the opening of a new cultural space, a space that she maps with particular clarity in *The Errancy.* There is, in fact, something unsatisfying in Graham's comments on apocalypse. Here, she tends to adopt a totalizing perspective and to ignore the subtleties, complexities, and nuances of this discourse and of its history— Graham's thinking here is itself apocalyptic in its search for a single, fundamental cause of our contemporary crisis. Graham's apocalyptic atavism may also arise at least in part from a lingering nostalgia of the kind I have been tracing in Stevens's texts, a nostalgia for something noble, for what Graham calls the "incredibly noble and beautiful idea, the idea of Progress, the love story we call History" (Graham, "Interview" 86). But I do not mean to suggest, as I may seem to be doing, that Graham's and Stevens's apocalyptically antiapocalyptic stances are identical. The figurations of gender in some of Graham's preceding comments indicate the locus of at least one significant difference between the two poets. In fact, Graham's strategies of resistance to apocalypse are almost diametrically opposed to Stevens's characteristic strategies; as I have already suggested, the elements of the apocalyptic and eschatological tradition that remain as vestigial presences in Stevens's texts are the very elements Graham attempts to eliminate from her own. And the most apocalyptic elements in Graham's poetry—above all, her far from unequivocal desire to step "outside" the aesthetics of closure and experience the radical "openness" possible in an age without apocalypse—depend upon the kind of aesthetic collapse against which Stevens tends to defend himself. But these differences, I hope to demonstrate, prove resistant to any easy categorization in familiar literary historical terms; it is difficult, at least, to read the differences between Stevens and Graham in terms of the presumed differences between modernism and postmodernism. This difficulty is already hinted at in the present critical uncertainty concerning Graham's work—an uncertainty, to be specific, concerning just where to situate her oeuvre in relation to modernism and postmodernism.[2] Graham's poetry often operates within the characteristic conceptual structures and logic of poststructuralist thought, though it may be preferable to say that Graham puts that logic to work within her texts. But the ends to which Graham employs it do not belong within the logic of poststructuralism or postmodernism. Graham's poetic territory includes an unmistakably metaphysical province—"the ground of being," "a more genuine reality" (Graham, "Interview" 85)—that has no place in the geography of poststructuralism or postmodernism, no matter how Graham might define that metaphysical territory.

Graham claims that territory again toward the end of her introduction to the 1990 edition of *The Best American Poetry*: "Each poem is, in the end, an act of the mind that tries—via precision of seeing, feeling, and thinking—to clean the language of its current lies, to make it capable of connecting us to the world, to the *there*, to insure that there be a *there* there. For it is when we convince ourselves that it is not really wholly there—the world, the text, the author's text, the intention—that we are free, by the mere blinking of a deconstructing eye, to permit its destruction" (xxviii–xxix). This passage is haunted by the ghosts of modernism: Graham's rhetoric of "cleansing" and "connection" is the rhetoric of Pound's and Williams's early essays, and perhaps, too, of the first canto of Stevens's *Notes toward a Supreme Fiction*; and the presence of this rhetoric should remind us that "the poem of the act of the mind" (*CP* 240) must, according to Stevens, be a "finding" (*CP* 239) rather than an "imposing." One could thus observe that Graham's apparently poststructural and anti-teleological unsettling of the relationship between "hurry" (narrative) and "delay" (a non-narrative stasis), between closure and an absolute openness or gap, finally involves a classically philosophical privileging of the "real." In contrast, what Derrida's "White Mythology" discovers in the ruins left by the "*other* self-destruction of metaphor" (270) is not "a more genuine reality" but a reign of metaphor "without limit" (270). There is nothing outside of the text, nothing outside of metaphor's wanderings. Graham's desire in "Annunciation" to find a position "outside of *outside*" (*EB* 77) can seem to hover between, on the one hand, a desire to collapse the classical philosophical distinction between inside and outside, *and*, on the other, a desire to experience an actual unmediated contact with "reality," to move entirely outside discourse's position "outside" of "reality." The hovering is not permanent, and when Graham touches ground she does so on the side of "the ground."

But the passage from the introduction also highlights the peculiar difficulties involved in Graham's desire to place her work outside both the apocalyptic enclosure and the deconstructive (poststructuralist, postmodern) one. For Graham, the Western philosophical and aesthetic traditions need to be questioned and resisted because of their inherently apocalyptic program; and yet deconstruction, perhaps the dominant mode of such resistance in contemporary academic circles, carries its own apocalyptic risk, the risk that we might, "by the mere blinking of a deconstructing eye"—a less "comforting" version of 1 Corinthian's apocalyptic "twinkling of an eye" (15:52)?—"permit [the world's] destruction." Graham, then, is caught between eschatologies. In *The Errancy* in particular, she observes the collapse of the old apocalyptic threat at the hands of the new one; yet she attempts to write that new eschatological force *out* of her work even as it operates *in* that very text. Here, Vendler, despite her understanding of Graham as a postmodern writer, may best capture Graham's position; Vendler describes "Self-Portrait as Both Parties" (*EB* 14–16) as a poem "mark[ed] . . . with the signature of a postmodernist generation" ("Married" 241), a comment that leaves open the possibility that

Graham's works are not themselves postmodern, that Graham's texts attempt to recontextualize the postmodern signature (if there can be such a thing within a discourse that so problematizes the signature) within a project that is not itself postmodern. Graham has gone through the postmodern era, or at least thinks, to paraphrase Pound, that she can get through postmodernism in a hurry; she has absorbed poststructuralist and postmodern thought as thoroughly as anyone could, but is seeking, *through* postmodernism, a position *outside* postmodernism. But that position cannot be considered an unequivocally "modernist" one either, since a modernist ambition that has already absorbed postmodernism can be neither continuous with nor identical to the modernism of the first half of the twentieth century; it can only call to that modernism across a sizable gap of historical and cultural difference, never forgetting that its call originates from a radically different political and cultural realm.

A few last comments should be made on the broader implications of the preceding discussion. The first such implication is that the real locus of tension in Graham's poetry may not lie simply between the opposing pairs of philosophemes that play such a crucial role in her poetry,[3] but between different ways of configuring these oppositional pairs, between modern and postmodern constructions. A sense of whether this observation is accurate will, I hope, emerge from my readings of relevant poems. The discussion thus far may also seem to make rather extravagant claims for Graham, as though she truly were the avatar of a new aesthetic dispensation or, perhaps, were participating in the completion of Fredric Jameson's projected dialectical movement from modernism, through the negative moment of postmodernism, to an era of renewed modernist ambition and political agency. No such claims are intended here. Nor are my questions about the postmodernity of Graham's work intended to carry any sort of evaluative import, either positive or negative. My purpose is simply to make some sense of a cultural and literary historical context in which Graham's double engagement with the apocalyptic past and with Stevens's texts can be read with reasonable accuracy. That task shall take up the remainder of this chapter.

Thomas Gardner offers the best description of the cultural situation Graham confronts in *The Errancy*, though, as I shall demonstrate shortly, the book has a specifically American element that Gardner overlooks. Gardner notes that *The Errancy* "seems to be written from within the exhaustion or wreckage of what it calls the dream of reason" (*Regions* 202), from within a recognition of "the failures of the drive to name and colonize and map" (205). To put it in Lyotardian terms, Graham situates *The Errancy* at the moment after the delegitimation of the "grand narratives of legitimation—the life of the spirit and/or the emancipation of humanity" (Lyotard 51); she situates it, in other words, within the postmodern "moment," or at least within a particular understanding of that moment. But Gardner's reference to the "drive . . . to colonize" touches on the ways in which *The Errancy* is a peculiarly American book, perhaps the most American book Graham has written. This status derives not merely from the book's exclusively American setting and the relative scarcity of allusion to European myth and art, but from the fact that the collapse of the "dream of reason . . ." is also, in one of the book's recurring tropes, the collapse of a uniquely American dream, the dream of the New World as the site of "the *city on the hill*" (*TE* 65). *The Errancy* is concerned, in other words, with the nonrealization of the Puritan topos of America as the place of millennial and eschatological fulfillment, the place where a saintly community of the elect living by God's law would serve as a sign of the coming completion of God's plan (or would actually be that completion)—a hope famously embodied in John Winthrop's allusion, in a 1630 lay sermon ("A Modell of Christian Charity") delivered on board the *Arbella*, to Christ's words in Matt. 5:14 ("Ye are the light of the world. A city that is set on an hill cannot be hid").[4] *The Errancy* is concerned, too, with the dissolution of any vestigial belief in that unrealized ideal, with a culture that has lost faith in a guiding principle. This trope, then, as well as an eschatological rhetoric of "first fruit[s]" (cf. *TE* 5, 8), "harvest" (*TE* 8), and missionary zeal (*TE* 5), continually reminds us that in *The Errancy*, as in *The End of Beauty*'s "Eschatological Prayer," we are situated "late in the second millennium / of a motion measured / by its distance from the death / of a single young man" (*EB* 35). There is in *The Errancy*, though, the crucial difference that comes with living in "the American moment," the moment of a culture "both in history and somehow beyond it" (Graham, "Introduction" xxix)—the moment after the wavelike motion has shattered against the American continent and dispersed its now attenuated energies across that landmass. And Graham characteristically marks the text with reminders of the appropriative, colonizing urge that has driven "the whole adventure" (*TE* 9)—"galleys, slaves, log-books" (*TE* 9), the presence of "a tyrant or a tyranny that won't reveal itself" (*TE* 79), the "stirring rhetoric" that celebrates in song the history of owner-ship in the "new world" ("This is your land, this is my *my*" [*TE* 65]), and so on. In these terms, then, *The Errancy* is a postapocalyptic book; it situates itself after the collapse of this particular embodiment of the apocalyptic urge and, by implication, of the myth itself; it is con-cerned, therefore, with what comes after apocalypse and eschatology, as well as with the ways in which the dream of the "city on a hill" might, despite its collapse, continue to function unconsciously in everyday thought and action. And as I have already suggested, it takes a complex stance toward that collapse, remaining suspicious both of the dream's fragmentary survival and of the forces that have shattered the dream. The dream of the "*city on the hill*" is complicit with an urge to order, to dominate and appropriate, an urge that carries, in Graham's view, an apocalyptic threat; yet Graham cannot rest in the state of collapse that is the postmodern situation, which is itself a new kind of apocalypse, the end of the End.

Among the loci in which that dream continues to function are the everyday construction of selfhood and a particular set of aesthetic concepts, concepts of imagination and poetry as isolated, protected, interior realms set apart from the externality of the material world. These concerns are perennial features of Graham's writing, and, since they have been analyzed in the critical literature on *The End of Beauty* and *Materialism* in particular, I wish only to outline here, as briefly as possible, some of the particular forms they take in *The Errancy*. It is no accident, obviously, that "The Guardian Angel of the Little Uto-pia" serves as *The Errancy*'s first speaker, that she is one of Graham's own "figure[s] of capable imagination" (*CP* 249), and that "the upper floors" (*TE* 2) where she dwells somewhat conventionally trope the imagination and the products of the imagination as autonomous, in-terior, elevated spaces, restlessly redescribed in Graham's poem as "the created place, / in which to make a life—*a liberty*—the hollow, fetish-ized, and starry place" (*TE* 2). This ruling demon's obsession with "arrang[ing] the / thing" (*TE* 1), with eliminating the natural decay and disorder of dead flowers (cf. *TE* 2), with "fix[ing] it" (*TE* 3), further associates this already enclosed realm with an aesthetics of closure, of finished form, or at least a realm of the desire for such values. Graham also conflates this angelic construction of imagination with the Puritans' millennial hopes and with the longer "motion" to which those hopes belong—an identification made when the angel tropes her interior realm as "a bit gossamer with dream, a vortex of evaporations, / oh little dream, invisible city, invisible hill" (*TE* 2), and made again when the speaker of a later poem tropes selfhood as "a sort of city" (*TE* 84). Graham thus suggests that this concept of imagination is complicit with destructive and appropriative aspects of the colonial imperative, as, for example, when she later figures thought as "an oar, this ship the last of some / original fleet, the captains gone but some of us / who saw the plan drawn out / still here" (21).

What most concerns Graham here, however, is the sense that this aesthetic dispensation is coming to an end; the angel—a common figure in apocalyptic texts—is, somewhat comically, "A bit dizzy from the altitude of everlastingness . . . here on the upper floors," and the poem ends with the following desperate plea:

Oh knit me that am crumpled dust,
the heap is all dispersed. Knit me that *am*. Say *therefore*. Say
philosophy and mean by that the pane.
Let us look out again. The yellow sky.
With black leaves rearranging it. . . . (*TE* 3, ellipses in original)

If the Eliot of "The Waste Land" knew "only a heap of broken images" (63), Graham's guardian angel is even more thoroughly impoverished, facing an absence of images and dwelling at the verge of dispersal as a mere handful (or more) of dust. The distorted quotations from Henry Vaughan's "Distraction"—Graham substitutes "crumpled" for "crumbled" and, in the second line, quotes rather than uses "*am*"—might be taken as a demonstration of dispersal and its effects, an emblem of time's and history's effects on an original text and meaning. And Graham's angel speaks from within an aesthetic dispensation that has lost or is losing its own capacity to construct the textile/textual forms that narrow the generality of being into the specificity of the individual "*am*"; lacking, too, is the power to create links between the world's disordered or disconnected particulars through the logic of "*therefore*," as well as the poetic energy that can trope a window's barrier as "*Philosophy*," and therefore remain on the "inside" of philosophy's inside/outside boundary. The fact that the "Guardian

Angel of the Little Utopia" pleads for the restoration of these powers tells us, of course, that they are already gone, that it is too late, that the angel herself cannot provide herself with the tools of her own trade; in this regard, the angel's concluding turn to the "outside," where she encounters a different *kind* of arrangement or rearrangement in the darkening sky, prefigures the turn toward openness that will be the dominant project of the first part of *The Errancy*—a turn that differs from Stevens's response to the eschatological fears of the 1930s and World War II.

It is here that the question of Graham's relationship to postmodernism and poststructuralism becomes significant, since this "collapse" and the turn to "openness" appear to participate in a logical structure that strongly resembles some of the characteristic textual strategies of poststructuralism. Crucial in this regard is an early poem in *The Errancy*, "So Sure of Nowhere Buying Times to Come" (*TE* 11–13), in which a traffic jam looks "As if a stairway had collapsed / . . . / (by the shell of measurement, by the dream of passage) as if we / were the rungs, the individual upwardgoing steps, / now crumbled in a heap / down here" (*TE* 11–12). If the cars caught in the traffic jam function as a sort of late, debased, and specifically technological emblem of the human capacity for "forwarding"—Graham's trope of human beings as "steps" and "rungs" conflates Victorian Christianity's appropriation of Darwinian evolution with Jacob's vision of the heavenly ladder—and if the cars serve, too, as symbols of our self-enclosure in ideals of individual identity, power, wealth, and ownership, then one of the implications of this traffic jam is that the collapse of the "dream of reason" may be inherent in the dream itself; the collapse is a necessary part of its program rather than an accident imposed on it through "error" or some sort of outside interference. Similarly, in *The Errancy*'s title poem, Graham tropes the roads as "cadaverous swallowings of the dream of reason . . . / hot fingerprints where thoughts laid out these streets" (*TE* 4), thereby suggesting that reason's self-realization in the material realm leads to its own collapse in the traffic jam that clogs these roads. What Graham is proposing, then, is an alternate teleology—or, perhaps, an a-teleology—that lies concealed within the positive teleology of "the dream of reason," a fault or weakness that is woven into the fabric from the outset, a fault that will eventually open onto the radical "openness" that the teleological projects of religion and reason have attempted to cover over.

In the midst of reason's collapse, Graham tropes a classical topos of poststructuralist thinking—the logic of the "outside" that is already "inside." She writes of

> our single destination at the core,
> there inside the car—
> (the point-awaiting-us now beating at the core),
> (beating above the hum, mid-air, mid-car, yet wrapped by the
>   ticking, honking shell)—
> (by the shell of measurement, by the dream of passage) . . .
>   (*TE* 11)

The "destination at the core" reappears throughout *The Errancy*, and for Graham it is a strangely a-teleological telos, a "zero / at the heart of the christened bonfire" (*TE* 5), a "zero at the core" of "these desperate, aimless ones" (*TE* 14) who subject themselves to the linear rule of "their paper calendars" (*TE* 14). As the "point-awaiting-us," this destination seems less a goal that her "forwarding" characters actively seek than one that will erupt unexpectedly into their lives. It functions as another version of what Graham refers to in the interview with Gardner as a "*real* gap" (85), the kind of gap Graham associates with the "more genuine reality" (a concept definitely *not* tenable within poststructuralist thought) mentioned earlier in this chapter. In the same interview, Graham identifies "the zero" as "the value which negotiates between being and non-being" (79); in "Pollock and Canvas," she explains, it is "the space between the end of the brush and the canvas on the floor beneath him" (79), the space that Graham identifies as "Maya," the authentic gap, the genuine "rip in the fabric" between "the desire to create and the created thing," "a flash, a woman, an opening" (Graham, "Interview" 80)—a gap, Graham speculates, where something "could come alive . . . that Western thinking has refused to let in for so long" (80). In the passage from "So Sure of Nowhere," Graham gives this "zero" a multiple location, both *inside* the "ticking, honking shell / of measurement" and *outside* that shell; furthermore, the external position is subdivided to a multiple "midness" in "mid-air" and "mid-car." This "zero," then, is a force or a movement that defies and questions the construction of such boundaries, an outside that is already inside, and vice versa, an outside whose eruption from within the "dream of reason" leads to an unsettling reinscription of that dream within the absolutely outside, an outside that is "outside of *outside*" (*EB* 77). Graham playfully inscribes this multiple locus in the poem's grammar and form as well. The car and the tropes for the car ("shell of measurement," "ticking, honking shell") are placed both inside and outside the parentheses, and both the interior and exterior locations of the "hum" are identified within another parenthetical comment. It seems safe to suggest, then, that Graham's poem participates in the collapse it describes, or that Graham allows the logic of that collapse to operate within her text. In closing off one version of apocalypse, it opens another.

A similar logic is inscribed in the figurations and formal procedures Graham employs at the outset of the same poem, though what is particularly significant here is the claim that these lines articulate what the speaker "understood" in the traffic jam described in the poem's succeeding three sections:

I understood that there must have been.

And then the two folds of this world.

Towards us, thus marking time in time.

A gaping hole:

the *yes* suspended in the amniotic sac:

the end.

That there must have been.

That there might have been. (*TE* 11)

Here, Graham brings into play the poetic devices she characteristically employs when attempting to move her language as close as possible to the openness that exists outside of time, narrative, and reason: wide spacing between lines, fragmented syntax, abstract diction, and so on. But it is the ordering of the lines that proves particularly instructive: the "two folds of this world," "time in time," are framed by references to a "must have been" and "might have been," the unknowable and unnameable openness that precedes and exceeds—or can only be assumed to have preceded and to exceed—all closure, all form, all philosophy, and whose strange force bends language away from its normal grammatical trajectory. And yet further within these folds Graham suspends "a gaping hole," the "*yes* suspended in the amniotic sac: / the end," a moment of suspension *between* the mere idea of conception and conception itself *before* the teleology begins; gaps exist, again, both inside and outside "the two folds of this world." The metaphor of the "fold," of course, is cut from the same poststructuralist fabric, serving as a locus classicus among figurations of the inside that is an outside, the outside that is an inside, of the mutual permeability of all apparent oppositions.[5] This trope figures significantly throughout *The Errancy*, above all in "The Guardian Angel of the Swarm," where it forms part, as Graham's own notes indicate, of a "conversation" with Gilles Deleuze's *The Fold*, and in particular with his treatment of self or subjectivity as a fold, as an outside made inside—a conversation whose aim is both "to review, and in spots to argue with" Deleuze's "brilliant intuitions" (*TE* 112). I shall return later to the specifics of Graham's argument with Deleuze, but wish only to note here that what the speaker understands in the first two lines of "So Sure of Nowhere" is the relationship between inside and outside embodied in the metaphor of the "fold." She understands the fold as the paradoxical structure that makes it possible for the "zero" to exist both inside and outside the interior realm of car and self; she understands the role that this mutually constituting permeability of the two has as the foundation of "this world." What the speaker "understood," then, in the traffic jam's "unmaking" and "stalling" (*TE* 13) is not just the existence of "the spot outside consequence" (*TE* 12)—a spot also "inside," at the very center of the traffic jam; she understands the structure in which this spot participates. She understands that it is not just a limited "delay" that can be safely absorbed within the dream of reason's teleology, but is the opening, within the dream of reason, of the inside/outside relationship that exceeds and absolutely unsettles the dream, a rupture whose force causes "the parts of the picture the glance sews up / . . . to break into separate puddles" (*TE* 12–13) until they are lost in "featurelessness" (*TE* 13). This moment provides the context through which all of *The Errancy*'s moments of opening need to be interpreted—the moments when "*what breaks down breaks down*" (*TE* 13), when the ink-stained mouth sends "its crisp inaudible black zeros out" (*TE* 47).

This logic has not always been present in Graham's work, and it may be worthwhile to trace the differences between *The Errancy*'s inside/outside figurations and Graham's earlier rhetoric of "gaps," "rips," "tears," and "delays." I hope it is possible to read these differences simply *as* differences, as a series of shifts or reconfigurations, rather than as a necessary development toward a "true" or "proper" understanding of the issues involved, or toward an "authentically" Grahamesque position; if, for Graham, "each book is a critique of the previous" (Graham, "Interview" 82), one would not expect her to arrive at a definitive position, and certainly the much more fragmented poetics of *Swarm* questions some aspects of *The Errancy*. Graham's idea of a "*real* gap" suggests that her poetry initially works with a binary logic, a logic of polar oppositions. In the interview with Gardner, Graham hopes that her poetry can "keep [the gap] alive, hopefully—or ideally—as a *real* gap, not one invented for the purposes of extending the delicious moment between the beginning and the ending. The deliciousness of that moment was the thing I was trying to mess with. The imperialist pleasure" (85).

Here, Graham distinguishes between two kinds of "delay" that can open within a narrative structure (85); one is the kind of "delay" or "digression" that does not disrupt or explode the narrative structure but merely keeps it alive and, perhaps, strengthens it, heightening the desire for closure by means of a temporary deferral of the promised end. It is the kind of "digression" or "delay" that the classical philosophical tradition treats as an accident or negative moment within a teleology whose completion is always possible or taken as a given condition of discourse. The "*real* gap," for Graham, is characterized by its uncontainable disruptiveness; it is a delay, digression, or gap "without reserve," a generalized gap, an interminable detour and originary wandering, a "genuine risk" (93), something like Derrida's "apocalypse without apocalypse." It is a gap in which we are "*not* safe" (85): the poet who takes this risk "might not, in fact, *get a poem*" (93). Implicit in this contrast is a larger opposition between narrative (which for Graham includes all kinds of aesthetic forms and closure) and the "openness," the "*real* gap" that lies outside of all closed forms. This oppositional logic is at work throughout much of *The End of Beauty*, as, for example, when Daphne thinks of Apollo's "hurry" (which includes the kind of "delay" that keeps "hurry" alive) as "a quick iridescence / on the back of some other thing, unimaginable" (*EB* 32) and consigns him to "the freedom // [with] his autograph all over it, slipping, trying to notch it" (*EB* 33); it reappears in *Materialism* when the speaker of "The Break of Day" figures herself as "the sill of nothing to nothing" (*M* 125); when, in "Annunciation with a Bullet in It," Graham figures "A brief history of mankind" as "a doorway in the air, a graduation / from nothing to nothing" (*M* 66); or when the form of Helen's "living face" (in "Event Horizon")—a mere "stain on the flames" (*M* 54) in which Troy burns—gives way to "the smoky upslanting void" (*M* 54). In all these instances, Graham consistently tropes her "*real* gap" only as an outside, as an unknowable, unmasterable, absolute exteriority that surrounds all human attempts to create closed aesthetic structures, or within or over which those structures are perilously suspended.

In fact, something more complex than a straightforward oppositional logic operates in *Materialism*. This is not to suggest that there are no moments in *Materialism* when Graham locates "freedom *within* narrative," as James Longenbach suggests ("Jorie Graham's" 110, my emphasis); exemplary instances include the speaker's attempt, in "Concerning the Right to Life" to feel the paradoxical and punning "immaculate spot within—the freedom of / choice, illustrious / sleep, bloody spot" (*M* 16), and, in "Annunciation with a Bullet in It," the moment when the speaker's ten-year-old self, reading *Anna Karenina*, discovers that in Anna's first meeting with Vronski, Anna's

black waist

    blocked the whole view,

    black hourglass the stillness would use to enter,
swirling, breathless
      yet in itself nothing,
not fear, not desire (I knew that even then),
      not hope, not even an awakening—just

 a rip where evidence exists,

    but not *of* anything. (*M* 74–75)

Presumably, when the speaker "tried to see past" Anna, she was trying to "see" the narrative structure in which Anna participates and which gives her appearance here a determinable meaning within that closed structure; the "stillness" thus represents an opening "*within narrative*" ("a flash, a woman, an opening") in a quite literal way, a momentary suspension of the ability to treat the written marks of language as something other than merely material, to treat them as marks of a nonmaterial "meaning." Yet it seems necessary to ask about the relationship between the "nothing" of this "stillness" and the "nothing" that lies outside the "doorway" of human history at the beginning of the same poem, to inquire where the "stillness" enters *from*, particularly since the speaker later describes the printed words as part of "one universal, stubborn black / out of which—*in* which?—the dark words *seem* / . . . as feathers on a wing / are packed" (*M* 75). Here, the moment of suspension becomes part of a larger, "universal, stubborn black," so that the narrative is itself located within a greater darkness: there is stillness both within and without the narrative. The same logic operates in "The Break of Day," when an external darkness becomes "a tautology for / what is trapped in this sealed skin of mine (INSIDE)," something the speaker remains unable to name: "What is it / is corporeal but still concealed? // Does not involve error? / Perfectly hollow?" (*M* 124). This "freedom *within* narrative" thus opens onto a freedom *outside* of narrative; it is the opening of the outside within the inside, and it offers a glimpse of an outside that, presumably, can be identified with what Graham calls "a more genuine reality" or "the ground of being" (Graham, "Interview" 85). If there is a shift in Graham's poetry, it is a shift away from the more straightforward logic that opposes narrative to "openness," and toward the tripartite construction in which the "outside" also erupts from inside the "inside."

Such then, is the ruined textual space of *The Errancy*, the space from within which Graham engages with Stevens's texts. It is a space in which the "dream of reason," the millennial hopes of the Puritans, and a whole range of related (according to Graham) concepts have collapsed as the strange logic of poststucturalism opens within them. And to the extent that this space begins "the phase after history" (Graham, *Region* 111) or inaugurates a new "era in the history of the imagination," to the extent that it marks or is marked by the disruptive force of the "nothing," the "black," the "stillness" that lies outside the doorway of "history"—to this extent it remains, as I have suggested already, a strange sort of *other* apocalypse, an "apocalypse *without* apocalypse." Perhaps Graham might be best understood, then, not as a straightforwardly antiapocalyptic poet, but as a poet inhabiting or negotiating a strange space *between* apocalypses, between an old End and an end of that End in which there is no "forwarding" and hence no End. In the next section, I hope to show that these negotiations are also a series of negotiations with Stevens, with the modernist past, and with the versions of apocalypse they both contain and are contained within.

The preceding paragraphs might seem to have lost sight of this chapter's initial claims—in particular, of the claim that the differences between Stevens's and Graham's responses to eschatology's collapse cannot be construed as a straightforward difference between the modern and the postmodern. That claim would appear to have been repudiated by my insistence that Graham deliberately and self-consciously participates in the poststructuralist logic that *is* the collapse of the "grand narratives of legitimation"—the "dream of reason" being one of these narratives. But it is still my intention to demonstrate how Graham recontextualizes that poststructural logic within a distinctly non-postmodern and non-poststructural project; I will show, in other words, that Graham's poetry makes a "wishful call" to particular aspects of modernism, as well as to particular elements of Stevens's poetry. But that "wishful call" makes sense only in the context of Graham's questioning and critical reinscription of some of Stevens's wartime tropes. As the latter comment suggests, Graham's most intense disagreements with Stevens—at least in *The Errancy*—center around his wartime poems, and particularly around their construction of heroic, masculine figures of creativity that can withstand the threat of cultural collapse. Yet even here, Graham's relationship to Stevens is anything but straightforward; it involves a complex, ambivalent, doubled desire for both continuity and discontinuity with the aspects of the poetic past that Stevens seems to represent for Graham. I want to begin, then, by examining those Stevensian passages in which *The Errancy* wanders furthest from the modernist way, but will eventually begin to map the ways in which Graham's apparent erring is simultaneously a mission of errancy, an attempt to rescue some valuable treasure from the long-dispersed modernist heap.

In "Spelled from the Shadows Aubade"—the first of a sequence of aubades in *The Errancy*—Graham's disagreement with Stevens's wartime tropes seems immediately evident and is worked out first on the level of genre. Graham recontextualizes Stevens's tropes within an aubade, a genre which, on the evidence of such loci classici as *Romeo and Juliet* III, v, Donne's "The Sun Rising" and "The Break of Day," or even Auden's more nocturnal "Lay your sleeping head, my love," seems to constitute a poetry of "delay" (to borrow Graham's term), a genre whose speakers often begin by refusing to relinquish the erotic and ecstatic world of "Beauty, midnight, vision" (Auden 157) for the daylight world of reality, reason, narrative, politics, commerce, and so on. Graham's speaker in "Spelled from the Shadows Aubade" lies in a darkened bedroom at daybreak, resisting the call to join the outside, daylit world, a world in which she hears a Stevensian "furious machine" (*TE* 34), "banners where the strong go by" (*TE* 35), and "shrivelings of place" (*TE* 35). By peppering the realm of daylight with quotations from Stevens's "Dutch Graves in Bucks County"—passages that contrast the violent, heroic struggles of the present to the deadness of Stevens's buried ancestors—Graham's speaker does not merely reverse the values inscribed in that poem but levels the very opposition between past and present that dominates Stevens's text. Both the "doubly killed" (*CP* 291) ancestors' "shrivelings of place" and the "banners where the strong go by"—presumably a collective allusion to all of Stevens's tropes of the present's "violence," "glory," "hullaballoo," "force," "powerful heart," and "flags" (*CP* 293, 292, 291)—are relegated to the world outside the darkened room, which in turn symbolizes the speaker's resistance to or rejection of daylight and all the values (rationality, narrative, empire, eschatology, closure, masculinity) associated with it. For Graham's speaker, then, Stevens's opposition between past and present is not a genuine opposition, since both the past and the present participate in the "ancient story-line" (*TE* 35), in the erring of history's unfolding narrative; both involve, to borrow a phrase from Graham's "Le Manteau de Pascal," an undesirable "narrowing of infinity" (*TE* 66). One of Stevens's most apocalyptic visions of the aurora borealis is absorbed into the daylight world, too; the "Arctic effulgence flaring on the frame / Of everything he is" (*CP* 417) becomes "a glittery arctic yawn, effulgent, blazing" (*TE* 35). If all teleology belongs to the masculine, daylit world, then so, too, does Stevens's eschatological fear, though Graham's sense that this "yawn" is "slack" (*TE* 35) comments, perhaps, on the enervated state of teleological thinking in her culture, its loss of its original force or significance.

The only elements from Stevens's world that Graham's speaker associates with the positive values of the aubade's resistance to daylight are the figures of "defeat" that Stevens offers in the seventh of the poem's longer stanzas:

> other soldiers, other people,
> Men [who] came as the sun comes, early children
> And late wanderers creeping under the barb of night,
> Year, year and year, defeated at last and lost
> In an ignorance of sleep with nothing won. (*CP* 291)

Yet even here, Graham differs from Stevens's version of defeat. When the speaker of "Aubade" describes her enclosed world as one of "ignorant sleep," a "sleep where nothing's won, / or lost" (*TE* 35), her last two words—whether they represent a rearrangement of Stevens's own or an addition ex nihilo—construct out of the ruins of Stevens's text a sort of middle way, a space in which neither victory *nor* loss have any place because the speaker's position is, like the one discovered in "So Sure of Nowhere Buying Times to Come," "outside consequence" (*TE* 12). The aubade's speaker steps outside of all narrative, all agon, all struggle, all goals or telos, outside of loss and gain. Such a position is located outside of knowledge, too, or at least outside knowledge as it is constructed within the Western philosophical tradition: Graham conflates Stevens's "ignorance of sleep" with his "merciless triumph" (*CP* 291)—"In the end must come merciless ignorance" (*TE* 35)—to posit a paradoxical telos of self-emptying and unknowing, a telos which is at the same time not a fulfillment of time but an emptying into "time wasted utterly" (*TE* 35). The daylight world, in contrast, is the realm of loss and gain, the realm where time is saved or turned to profit and, at least for Stevens, "not wasted in your subtle temples" (*CP* 293).

Yet the poem makes a still more specific and pointed critique of Stevens's tropes of imaginative power, a critique that hinges on Graham's choice of war poems as the locus for her resistance to the daylight world. Here, the phrases that echo Stevens's "Martial Cadenza"—"*life came back*," "not as if evening had found me," "You are to walk and talk again, and breathe, and move" (*TE* 34, and cf. *CP* 237 and 238)—associate Stevens's tropes of erotic and poetic power with the daylight world that the aubade's speaker seeks to escape or resist. If, in Stevens's poem, the return of "sudden time" (*CP* 237) brings a welcome access of youthful vitality and imaginative capacity, in Graham's poem that return becomes, through a simple modal shift, a hectoring command, the mark of a less desirable kind of power, as though poetic speech, or a particular kind of poetic speech, were something forced upon consciousness by an imperium—the kind of power encoded in Stevens's allusive title and the poem's "martial" situation. Graham's association of this trope not with evening and the erotic evening star but with dawn and sun suggests, perhaps, that Stevens—at least in Graham's view—has not quite realized the true source of the poetic power he experiences here, not quite realized that such speech implicates him in larger and more destructive systems of political power, in the linkages between day, closure, reason, telos, war. Such may be the implication of Graham's later incorporation of a phrase from the opening of "Dutch Graves":

It held you, once, the other side,
in its gossipy arms,
it seemed to gaze with its taut wide-awakeness
straight into your furious machine,
it wasn't a shabby love—it held—
sentences poured from it in alleyways, sometimes in avenues,
the carpenters moved through them always needed,
joinings held,
cashiers added up the sum and it rose up from calculation
onto limpid sleek receipts—we paid—the eucalyptus shone—
the walkie-talkies heard each other clearly and the road got fixed
     (*TE* 34)

Graham's collation of tropes for narrative, logic, linearity, for all the artificial means by which the daytime world is held together and holds us in it are, despite their uniquely Grahamesque presentation here, hardly startling within the conventions of the aubade genre. And yet the speaker's figuration of her own daytime consciousness in terms of the "furious machines" of "Dutch Graves" (*CP* 290)—machines of war—goes further insofar as it associates this consciousness with an irreducible and specifically military violence. This gesture, however, conforms with Graham's sense of the relationship between the colonizing, imperial impulse behind the ideal of the "*city on the hill*"

(*TE* 65) and the establishment of selfhood (troped as "a sort of city" [*TE* 84] in "The Guardian Angel of the Swarm"); it proves consistent, too, with the analogical association between selfhood and Columbus's colonizing imperative in parts 6 and 7 of "The Dream of the Unified Field" (cf. *M* 85–87), to offer just one other example. Graham's speaker, then, appears to hear an unsettling relationship between Stevens's response to military violence and the maintenance of that violence in more subtle, less directly threatening, yet more pervasive and inescapable forms, such as the construction and maintenance of selfhood. Facing a situation of cultural anomie, facing the "ever-enlarging incoherence" that results from the collapse of both "the dream of reason" and the Puritans' millennial dreams, Graham responds by questioning and refusing Stevensian figurations of identity and poetic power.

However, it seems essential to acknowledge that the crises confronted by Graham and Stevens differ greatly in historicopolitical terms—to acknowledge, in other words, that the differences in their responses to a possible cultural collapse are informed by the differences between their respective cultural and social situations. When Stevens announces "the collapse of our system" (*NA* 20) and its replacement by an "intricacy of new and local mythologies, political, economic, poetic" (*NA* 17), an "ever-enlarging incoherence" (*NA* 17), "a new world so uncertain that one did not know anything whatever of its nature, and does not know now" (*NA* 20), he does so in the context of the solidification of a totalitarian version of communism in the Soviet Union, the social and economic collapse of the 1930s, the rise of fascism in Europe, and the outbreak of World War II. It seems safe to say, I hope, that in Stevens's situation the stakes were higher than in Graham's, the human danger more immediately physical; in this perspective, the collapse of a cultural and aesthetic dispensation was merely a minor result of political forces that were leading to or had already led to an immense and far more wide-ranging human suffering. Furthermore, for Stevens the forces of destruction were elsewhere: the imperial dreams of Soviet communism, Japanese imperialism, and Italian and especially German fascism could be contrasted (as long as one forgot America's colonial and imperial origins) with a comparatively "innocent" American liberal democracy that felt itself able to maintain a peaceful isolation from the European and Asian disasters. For Graham, in contrast, the dominant example of an imperium in her own lifetime is an American one. The realities of late twentieth-century American military, political, economic, and cultural power contribute to Graham's greatly heightened and more immediately self-critical sense that her own culture and the aesthetic practices of that culture are implicated in the maintenance of an imperium. Thus, if Graham's response to the dissolution of an aesthetic dispensation founded on "closure," on "the solace of good forms" (Lyotard 81), seems closer to that of the Lyotard who would "wage a war on totality" (82), this difference has much to do with the specific political and social context within which postmodern aesthetics operate—not just with the different ideologies but with the different historical "accidents" that both produced and were produced by those ideologies. Graham's tendency to implicate her own culture and, more generally, art itself, in the eschatological, colonizing, imperial urge, her tendency to move more decisively toward an investment in "openness" and an opposition to "closure," need to be understood within this cultural framework.

Yet Lyotard, since he is to a large extent responding to the atrocities of World War II and the Holocaust, reminds us that those atrocities function as a common reference point for Stevens and Graham, even though the two poets' temporal relationship to that point differs; and he thus reminds us that the responses formulated by Graham differ on fundamental political and philosophical points, and that the differences between her work and Stevens's cannot be ascribed exclusively to the accidents of history. Stevens's response to the immense human suffering and cultural upheaval of the war involved an effort to find the elements within an aesthetic tradition of closure and mastery that could withstand such disruptive forces, and to give these elements poetic embodiment in masculine figurations of poetic power and in a poetry that exercised some version of that power; Graham's response, in contrast, is to identify those elements in the literary tradition and in herself that seem complicit with the totalitarian urge— the very elements that Stevens invests in so heavily—and then unsettle them through an ironic recontextualization and self-questioning.

Yet Graham's speaker in "Spelled from the Shadows Aubade" is also implicated in such figurations of poetic power, and implicated in a way that suggests the presence of a lingering desire for that kind of power. In the long quotation above, the speaker herself—or at least some aspect of herself that she now addresses as "you"—has not only lived on "the other side" but even now continues to recognize a certain value in that world: for all the irony directed toward such items as "the walkie-talkies" who "heard each other clearly" (not just cell phones, presumably, but poets who heed the call to "walk and talk again"), the speaker still feels that the cohesive force offered by this world "wasn't a shabby love." Furthermore, if it is possible to read everything in the poem as a figuration of a state of consciousness, somewhat along the lines of the "Self-Portrait" poems of *The End of Beauty*, then the "Aubade" would figure a resistance not merely to an external call but to a call from within the speaker herself, from the conscious, rational, "daylight" self. This sense that the poem presents a consciousness already divided within itself would be implicit even in a reading that refuses to internalize the "outside" world as an aspect of Graham's self, since the speaker would have no need to struggle against a call that she feels no interest in heeding. Finally, and most significantly, this inner agon comments on the divided or shifting allegiances of Graham's own poetry or poetic career; it acknowledges a previous alignment with the "sun" aspect of Stevens's oeuvre and suggests that such an alignment, or at least a desire for such an alignment, remains an operative force in her poetry.

One need not look far through Graham's poetry for marks of this earlier alignment with Stevens's tropes of poetic power and for an association of that kind of power with narrative and eschatology, though again Graham's alignment with Stevens emerges only in the context of an equally forceful critique. The most notable example of such a critique appears in the first poem of *The End of Beauty*, "Self-Portrait as the Gesture between Them." Graham's characteristic linking of eschatology, teleology, and the category of "the aesthetic" is evident in the volume's title, though in this first "self-portrait" Graham is more concerned with the beginning of beauty than with its end, or, more properly, with how the end is already inscribed in the beginning: troping her divided selfhood and her divided stance toward eschatology, narrative, and beauty in terms of Eve's offering of the apple to Adam, Graham reads in the initial "rip in the fabric where the action begins" (*EB* 3) a simultaneous and punning positing of the action's "denouement" (*EB* 3)—an end, but also, at least etymologically, an untying, unknotting, unweaving of textile/textual strands, and revelation, to again evoke the etymology of "apocalypse." To a similar end, the later "Noli Me Tangere" echoes the description of that denouement in

"Self-Portrait" as a "sweet appointment": when Mary Magdalene's obedience to the title's divine command allows the risen Christ to again "posit the sweet appointment" (*EB* 44), Graham's self-echo reminds us that the Second Coming, the end of the narrative and of all narratives, is alike implied not only in Christ's resurrection but in the Fall itself. To begin is to close. To place Stevens in this mythical/theological context, then, to describe the story of history—the "digression," the "new direction," the "error" (*EB* 7), the story "outside the true story" (*EB* 3)—as a Stevensian "filial form" (*CP* 375) is to situate Stevens's form and his version of poetic power *within* the apocalyptic trajectory that begins with Eve's gesture; this gesture identifies Stevens's "Credences," or at least this part of it, as the continuation of the apocalyptic and eschatological tradition of aesthetic closure that Graham hopes to resist or at least question. Graham may be remembering, too, that Stevens's "filial form" is also a "bristling soldier" who "looms / In the sunshine" (*CP* 375), "The youth, the vital son, the heroic power" (*CP* 375)—the versions of masculinity that, for her, are most complicit with apocalyptic thinking. Graham's echo of the "rigid inscription" of "Things of August" (*CP* 495, *EB* 6) has a similar force in this context. Stevens's "inscription," in "Things of August" ix, is "A new text of the world" (*CP* 494), a break from Christian tradition; but Graham, by figuring a "rigid inscription" as the founding gesture of a closural aesthetic and theological dispensation, suggests that Stevens's inscription is older and more eschatological than his poem allows, that the masculine poetic power of "intelligent men / At the centre of the unintelligible" (*CP* 495) is too much a part of the apocalyptic fold. Stevens's conception of masculine poetic power, then, becomes part of that long playing out of an eschatologically oriented process of westward expansion, manifest destiny, and so on. Stevens's "filial form" becomes both a product of that process and a means of its continuation.

But even as Graham questions Stevens's text, she reminds us that her Eve is an aspect of herself, an aspect that has read and been influenced by Stevens, and that her text thereby maintains a relationship to the eschatological tradition opened by "the gesture between them." In making "the gesture between them" the locus of self-definition, Graham makes her own complexly doubled and redoubled gesture. She aligns the self with the moment prior to "beginning," with the moment before the first step in the narrative, with the still unformed and unexpressed; yet she simultaneously aligns herself with Eve's desire for a beginning, a story, and an end, for a closed or at least closable form. And by portraying Eve as "loving that error, loving that filial form" (*EB* 7), Graham further underlines her own sense of the value and appeal of a Stevensian "formal understanding" (Graham, "Interview" 94). This value emerges again in *The End of Beauty* when, in "Self-Portrait as Hurry and Delay [Penelope at Her Loom]," "the long body of the beach grows emptier awaiting [Ulysses] / gathering the holocaust in close to its heart growing more beautiful / under the meaning" (51). Here, Graham identifies a key trope from Stevens's most apocalyptic poem with the limited narrative delay that only extends narrative or keeps masculine desire and the desire for the End alive. And yet she nonetheless acknowledges the power and attraction of that delay: it is, in a trope from canto i of "Auroras," "a possession of happiness" that Graham equates with "shapeliness," "a body of choices," "a strictness," "an edge," "something that is not something else" (*EB* 50). In "Self-Portrait as the Gesture between Them," then, Eve's love for "that error" indicates Graham's own sense of her investment in this version of poetic power and the apocalyptic narrative in which it is caught up; even as she situates herself at or after "the end of beauty," she marks her engagement with a tradition of ends, her own desire to join that tradition. The last part of Graham's title—"the gesture between them"—may adumbrate a second gesture that shadows Eve's, a gesture in which Graham reaches out to accept something from Stevens even as she marks the gap between her text and his. Graham, or at least her text, becomes a "filial form."

If there is some sort of progression or development over the course of *The Errancy*, it does not involve any easy resolution of the complexities and ambivalences discussed above, or any decisive choice in favor of either light or darkness, form or formlessness, closure or openness, apocalypse or "apocalypse *without* apocalypse"; it is a matter instead of a slight shifting of the balance among the various affective stances taken toward any of these realms of figuration, or perhaps a mere shift in the perspective from which that balance is observed. In "Spelled from the Shadows Aubade," it is the desire for darkness that speaks and regulates the poem's affective current even as the countercurrent of an opposing desire flows through the poem. A further shifting is evident in a later "aubade," titled "The End of Progress Aubade (Eurydice to Orpheus)": in this poem, Orpheus, the hero /

poet aspect of Graham, the representative of "forwarding" and of the dream of reason, is held within hell's darkness by Eurydice, who herself will not "ever touch [Orpheus] / and risk awakening the song again" (*TE* 57). Here, the desire for darkness speaks still more forcefully; we are at the farthest remove from any eschatological teleology, and most deeply embedded in the space of the ascendent female, the figure who presides over the paradoxical end of the End. And yet the poem seems to embody Graham's desire, expressed in the interview with Gardner, to "reincorporate the *hero* part of [her] psyche back into the unconscious, uroboric female. Not in some foolish way in order to dissolve 'him'—*the mind*—but to keep everything alive, to keep the tension alive" (88). This poem functions as a pivotal moment in the slow shifting of balances that takes place over the course of *The Errancy*, the point when the desire for darkness most outweighs the countervailing desire for daylight. Yet the "tension" remains "alive" here, and the succeeding poems continually redistribute the relative strengths of the forces operative within that tension—as, for example, when the elegiac speaker of "In the Pasture" recognizes the voice that commands, "*You have to live*" (*TE* 89), and admits to herself, "I love the uniforms my thoughts are wearing. / . . . I love / the stitching-in" (*TE* 90–91). The stance taken toward the military "uniforms" and the "stitching-in" tip the affective balance in favor of the speaker's—and Graham's— attachment to "forwarding," to heroism, to an aesthetics of closure, an aesthetics that covers over the seam, the rip, the gap, but without permitting us to forget the negative products of the military and colonizing impulse. To return to "The Guardian Angel of the Little Utopia" with these observations in mind is to realize that the entire poem occupies a peculiarly doubled position, since even as the angelic speaker asks to be "knit" through the metaphoric or predicative "*am,*" she and every element in the poem operate *as* metaphor, as an appropriation of materiality (or at least the "reference" to materiality) in the name of "meaning" and of the poem's internal symbolic coherence—its closure. To reread "Spelled from the Shadows Aubade" is to sense more strongly Graham's attraction to the daylight world and the daylight Stevens, despite the privilege given to the desire for darkness. One might even read the earlier aubade's refusal to enter the daylight as a failure that is overcome only in the later parts of the collection. The most satisfying reading, however, might be one that finds both these stances precariously balanced in the text.

Some sense of that balance emerges again in *The Errancy*'s final figurations of the world of daylight, figurations that turn to Stevens but not to the Stevens of "filial forms" and "furious machines." This balance appears in the opening lines of the final poem of *The Errancy*, "Of the Ever-Changing Agitation in the Air":

The man held his hands to his heart as he danced.
He slacked and swirled.
The doorways of the little city
blurred. Something
leaked out,
kindling the doorframes up,
making each entranceway
less true.
And darkness gathered
although it does not fall. . . . (*TE* 109, ellipses in original)

Dance becomes a means of "blurring" but not destroying forms: "darkness gathers though it does not fall" (*CP* 412). Here, Stevens's presence corrects the preference for darkness and formlessness expressed by some of *The Errancy*'s earlier speakers, particularly the one who, in "The End of Progress Aubade," wishes to keep the hero/poet Orpheus enveloped in permanent and total darkness. It offers this correction without aligning the self with the world and tropes of daylight and unadulterated masculine poetic power. The Stevens of "Auroras" ii—or at least of its first six tercets—thus offers Graham a midpoint between her own tropes of complete formlessness and Stevens's tropes of sun and strength, a midpoint where both light and darkness, form and formlessness, are held in balance, both alive in their mutual opposition. The moment may be emblematic, at least for Graham, not so much of the "marriage" Stevens enacts in his poetry—the "marriage . . . between being at genuine risk *and* having all his formal understanding operative" (Graham, "Interview" 94)— as of the moment of risk itself, the moment of suspension between the creation of a form and the dissolution of form, the moment of "genuine risk" (93) when the poet "might not, in fact, *get a poem*" (93). And it should not be forgotten that Graham has selected this phrase from Stevens's most intensely eschatological poem, that his "darkness [that] gathers though it does not fall" hovers ambiguously at the brink of dissolution and terrifying visions of destruction. Graham, in other words, might be understood as rescuing this phrase from the apocalyptic context in which it originally appeared, as correcting not just herself but Stevens, too.

The whole of Graham's "Ever-Changing Agitation," in fact, is a sequence of tropes for these moments of balance, though with another significant shift in perspective from the beginning to the end of the poem. If the poem's opening lines present the moment when form hovers at the brink of its own dissolution or even desires that dissolution, the final lines offer instead a moment when the urge to create a form awaits the unformed material it must seize. Graham tropes this new balance in the predatory "cat in the doorway who does not mistake the world, / eyeing the spots where the birds must eventually land" (*TE* 109). Here, Graham revises her earlier tropes of the birds' "manyness" (*TE* 10), their "red currency" (*TE* 60), their song of "*no forwardness*" (*TE* 80), but this time presents the tense balance between her two forces—the desire to create form and the desire for the dissolution of form, the desire for the End and the desire to exist outside the End—largely from the perspective of the former. The two forces exist here in their mutually constituted independence. Such moments of balance are, perhaps, the most antiapocalyptic or nonapocalyptic in Graham; they speak of a desire for neither the End nor the end of the End, but for continuity, for—as Graham puts it in the interview with Gardner—the ability "to keep everything alive, to keep the tension alive" (88). They speak of a desire to continually negotiate between two apocalypses, between two extremes, or to find a path between the two extremes. The final action in "Recovered from the Storm" seems emblematic in this regard: in choosing to "pick up and drag one large limb from the path" (*TE* 108), the speaker makes a gesture that will help keep a possible route of "forwarding" open. It is a gesture toward order, toward the recovery of form out of the formless upheaval of the storm; yet it is far removed from the dangerous extreme of conventional apocalypticism. A minimal, practical, social gesture, it facilitates the continuation of ordinary life without erasing or denying the marks of the storm or preventing another such disruption.

These moments of balance can still seem, of course, to participate in a characteristically postmodern or poststructuralist logic: they refuse, after all, to grant an absolute privilege to either the formless or the formed, "the one" or "the many." Another such balance emerges in the figure, in "Studies in Secrecy," of a point both

> dwindling yet increasingly aswarm,
> the chittering of manyness in it as it is made to clot
> into a thrumming singleness—the secret—the place where the
>   words twist—. (*TE* 54)

In this erotic/philosophical poem, Graham is concerned with the space between individuals and, more significantly, with the space of sexual difference in general; what the passage demonstrates is not so much the ascendancy of the female as the ascendancy of difference. Graham's eschatological association of this space with Nietzsche's trope of "the last men" (*TE* 55) suggests its disruptive force, its capacity to unsettle the humanist project and its "dream of reason"; as a nonrational knowledge attained by means of the body, it remains "outside" any conventional philosophical construction of knowledge.[6]

The latter observations appear to gravitate again toward a postmodern reading of Graham's poetry, but the fact that "Of the Ever-Changing Agitation in the Air" reaches back into the modernist past in order to figure its own in-between textual space suggests that some qualification is necessary. The quotation from Stevens's "Auroras" rehabilitates Stevens as a poet of betweenness; it establishes a tradition of betweenness and places Graham's own tropes in that tradition. It suggests a need to rescue something of unquestionable value from the modernist past, something that, unlike the Stevens of "Dutch Graves" and "Martial Cadenza," Graham need not trope *against* so rigorously. It suggests, perhaps, a need to create a textual space in which an unequivocal nostalgia for the past can remain operative, to find a certain locus of uncertainty that can become the object of a nostalgic longing. Graham tropes this locus as a space of difference, but also tropes it as "the point devoid of ancestry" (*TE* 54), and elsewhere in *The Errancy* it appears as the moment "without chronology" (65), as the moment when the idea is "starting just to fold and pleat and knot itself / out of the manyness—the plan—before it's thought, / before it's a *done deal*" (22), "before the credo, before the plan" (22). Graham is concerned, in other words, with a moment "before" as well as a moment or space "between," and, for all its doubleness, for all its status as a moment of pure difference, this moment tends to become caught up in a particular kind of nostalgia, a nostalgia for the "impossible place of origin" (37). In fact, it may be more accurate to suggest that there is a tension in Graham's poetry between two nostalgias, between a nostalgia for pure difference and a nostalgia for something prior to difference—to borrow the language of "So Sure of Nowhere," for a "must have been" or a "might have been" (11) prior to the "two folds of this world" (11). The shifts in Graham's rhetoric at the end of the passage prove significant: "must have been" suggests a realm of necessity, or a realm that necessarily exists, whereas "might have been" figures a realm of possibility, or a realm whose existence is only possible—as though the initial formulation were too assertive, or made too certain and strong a claim to knowledge, attempted to take too strong a hold of this space "before" the folds that construct our cognitive capacity. The nature of this tension may be best grasped by comparing this "might have been" to another trope of the doubled origin—an origin more like the "two folds" of *The Errancy*—from *The End of Beauty*:

You see, there *is* a veil, or no, there is no veil but
there is
a rip in the veil,
which is the storyline,
what the lips just inconceivably apart can make
that cannot then, ever again, be uncreated. (46)

This passage appears in "The Veil," approximately at the midpoint of *The End of Beauty*, and seems to gloss or clarify the logic of "rips" and "tears" that dominates that volume: it tells us that the "rip" and the "veil" are both mutually constituting, that neither exists without the other, that there is only this doubled relationship "in the beginning." But at the beginning of *The End of Beauty*, there is also a "before," a "time" when Adam and Eve are always "beginning, / revolving in place like a thing seen, / dumb, blind, rooted in the eye that's watching" (3). These contradictory figurations of origins share a common feature: as tropes not of ontological truth but of desire, they bespeak an unwavering desire for an origin, a desire that there *be* an origin of some kind, whether it be the doubleness of the fold and the torn veil, or some unknowable "before." There is a strange consistency to Graham's apparent inconsistency here. Taken alone, the tropes of the torn veil and the fold indicate not just a desire for an origin but a desire that the origin *be* double, that it be something that keeps all the contradictory desires that mark Graham's poetry alive— the desire for closure and the desire for openness, and so on. The shift to the desire that there also be a "before" repeats the doubleness of this doubled desire but does so "outside" of that initial doubleness; it opens, in other words, another double desire, a desire that there be a double origin and that the double origin should itself have an origin.

It may seem strange to go on claiming that these complexities help identify the moment at which Graham's poetry leaves postmodernism behind. If the persistence of a desire for origins does not clinch the point, further support may emerge from the interview with Gardner. There, Graham identifies the "*real* gap" (85)—the sort of gap troped with Stevens's help at the end of *The Errancy* and opened elsewhere in the moment "before"—as the place where "the ground of being" might uncover itself, where "a more genuine reality" might make itself known. As I noted at the beginning of this chapter, such concepts do not have a place within poststructuralist and postmodern discourse (except as objects of deconstruction), and perhaps the greatest peculiarity and the greatest site of tension in Graham's poetry lie in the way this nostalgia for the real, for something like a conventional apocalypse, a revelation or unveiling, is articulated through the strategies of poststructuralism. Finally, these nostalgias have some bearing on Graham's final quotation from Stevens. If Graham is reading Stevens's suspended darkness as an earlier trope for the double origin, for the space of suspension where being might appear, then the reinscription of Stevens's trope may mark a nostalgia for "being" or for a poetry of being, for a capacity to speak or write unself-consciously of "being" rather than ask, as Graham does in the interview with Gardner, "Can we use the word *being*? The ground of being. The river of rivers" (85). Graham's "river of rivers" may or may not be the one Stevens located in Connecticut, but her words here are nevertheless marked by a nostalgia for poetry as the place where being might appear, and therefore involve a construction of the "*real* gap" that would be impossible, as I suggested at the outset of this chapter, within the logic of postmodernism and poststructuralism. And by locating this space in *The Errancy* by means of Stevens's trope of suspended darkness, Graham, in a sense, displaces a nostalgia for being with a textual nostalgia; she gives that first nostalgia a specific location in literary history and thus marks that nostalgia more emphatically *as* a nostalgia.

Graham's movement outside of postmodernism and poststructuralism may also be framed in terms of irony, in terms of her search for a position *outside* of the bottomless ironizing of postmodernity. This is not to suggest that irony does not operate within Graham's texts; in fact, Graham sounds like a postmodern skeptic when, in the interview with Gardner, she criticizes "the old (fake?) objectivity of simple representation—representation as a coded statement of beliefs (agendas really) (usually the dominant culture's) trying to pass for an objective picture of reality" (90). Yet Graham does not sound postmodern when she contrasts "the old (fake?) objectivity" to "a *whole view*, a view which arrives at objectivity via all the failures, all the archeology of multiple subjectivities" (90), a multiplicity that Graham tropes somewhat more disparagingly in "Oblivion Aubade": there, "every glance [is] a skin, a rag thrown on the pile, / which raises in place of the world its gigantic debris" (*TE* 37). Later in the same interview, Graham suggests that "what leaks in between the attempts at seizure *is* the thing, and you have to be willing to suffer the limits of description in order to get it" (97). Graham's frequent self-reflexive addresses to her reader, too, though they may appear to involve a postmodern ironization of the text, function as part of an attempt "to recover the faith of the reader, his or her good will" (99), an attempt to transform the skeptical postmodern reader "who doesn't necessarily even believe in literature" or "doesn't believe that words are telling the truth" (99). Graham wants to tell the truth, rather than to ironize all possible constructions of truth, and her desire to do so bespeaks a sensibility that, despite a redefinition of "truth" that does not belong within the classical philosophical understanding of "truth," is straining against the logic of postmodernism and poststructuralism.

There may be other calls to Stevens, other differences, and other qualifications of both. The argument of "The Guardian Angel of the Swarm" with Deleuze's *The Fold*, for example, involves an angelic insistence on a more autonomous version of subjectivity than Deleuze can permit:

> when inclusion is accomplished, is it not done
> so continuously

it includes the sense of a finished act that is not the site,
not the place, not the point-of-view,

but what remains in point-of-view—

what *occupies* point-of-view—

necessarily a soul, a subject—

a power of envelopment *and* development. (*TE* 83)

Graham seems to posit against the more purely poststructuralist logic
of Deleuze's text some sort of vestigial autonomy, some uniquely
individual force that can be abstracted or isolated from or within the
outside that folds itself to make an inside, something similar, perhaps, to Stevens's "pure power" (*CP* 382) of abstraction. And the gestures toward the creation of form and order made by Graham near
the end of *The Errancy*—the decision, for example, in "Recovered
from the Storm" to "pick up and drag one large limb from the path"
(108)—resemble in their modesty some of Stevens's final claims for
the imagination's autonomy, for its "unobserved, slight dithering" or
"puissant flick" (*CP* 517), its "actual candle" (*CP* 523). I have said little, too, about Graham's poetics—discussed extensively in Vendler's
The Breaking of Style—but it may be worthwhile to point out the
extent to which *The Errancy* is marked by a mark—the dash—whose
function in Stevens's poetry received some comment in my third chapter. Stevens's dashes are all, finally, contained or containable within
the functioning of a grammatically "normal" sentence, however
supple and self-undermining those sentences may be; their force
depends on their capacity to mark a disruption *within* a structure
that nevertheless remains intact. Graham's dashes seem to explode
normative syntax altogether; her "sentences" are all interruption, a
kind of poststructuralist ruination of the English sentence. And yet
if this strategy is part of an attempt to open the "*real* gap" through
which "a more genuine reality" might be glimpsed, this stylistic peculiarity cannot be construed as poststructuralist.

It may be worthwhile to remember that Stevens's texts are not
without their own complexities and ambivalences, and also that the
differences between the two poets are most pronounced when the
stakes for both authors are raised to an apocalyptic level. Under less

extreme pressures, Stevens—as I hope my readings thus far have acknowledged—is more than just a poet of imaginative mastery, a poet who invests unequivocally in his own identification with masculine figures of poetic power. Stevens is also the master of an unmasterable verbal play; he is a deeply skeptical and ironic poet, a poet of endlessly restless intelligence, feeling, and imagination. He is also, like Graham, a poet strongly drawn toward the world outside the imagination, to the "unnamed flowing" (*CP* 533) of the river of being, the "harsh reality" "outside of the legend" (*CP* 506), "A nature still without a shape" (*CP* 514), "an element . . . not planned for imagery or belief" (*CP* 518), the "escent—issant pre-personae" (*CP* 522) of February, or "a scrawny cry from outside" (*CP* 534)—the latter being the last sound heard, or the last trope of voice, in the *Collected Poems*. One of the great challenges in reading Stevens lies in balancing the opposing forces at work in his oeuvre—centripetal and centrifugal forces, perhaps. Thus if, in late Stevens, we sense an increasing opening of the imagination to what lies outside it, an increasing sense that the mind is no more than "A glass aswarm with things going as far as they can" (*CP* 519), this capacity for openness is nevertheless inscribed alongside a continuing lineage of male figures of poetic power and mastery, evidence that "the masculine myths we used to make" (*CP* 518) are still in currency—as in "The Irish Cliffs of Moher" that Stevens tropes as "one of the race of fathers" (*CP* 502), in the metaphor-making imagination's "puissant flick" that Stevens accords "A name and privilege over the ordinary of his commonplace" (*CP* 517), in a world "Too much like thinking to be less than thought, / Obscurest parent, obscurest patriarch" (*CP* 518), and so on. There is a strong sense, too, despite his tropes of openness and his celebration of "the dizzle-dazzle of being new" (*CP* 530) that closure retains a positive value and power for Stevens, providing "a kind of total grandeur at the end" (*CP* 510), the "Total grandeur of a total edifice" (*CP* 510), a positive value that lingers even in the more equivocal "stale grandeur of annihilation" (*CP* 505) of "Lebensweisheitspielerei"; there is a sense, too, of the value of closed forms, of poems that can "take the place of a mountain," where "inexactnesses" become "the exact rock" (*CP* 512) desired by the imagination.

The fact that both Graham and Stevens are responding to eschatological and apocalyptic discourse is not merely fortuitous. If modern and postmodern engagements with the End differ as I have suggested throughout this study, and if Graham nevertheless makes a "wishful call" back to other aspects of Stevens's modernism, then the fact that the two poets diverge most strongly at this eschatological point only confirms the power and longevity of the End, as well as the importance of the idea of ends in the self-definitions of modernity and postmodernity. The Graham of *The Errancy* is a poet who has been through and participated in the collapse of the "dream of reason," the collapse of the great millennial and eschatological narrative that has been such a powerful force in Western culture; she has absorbed and appropriated the theoretical writings that have proclaimed that collapse, that have produced and been produced by it, writings that have provided the most intellectually sophisticated analyses and embodiments of that situation. But she also sees a continuing eschatological risk in the postmodern situation. Graham takes that situation as seriously as Stevens takes the "ever-enlarging incoherence" of his own time, and yet her different historical situation, her different sense of the ways in which her own culture is implicated in the worst or most dangerous aspects of the delegitimated dream make it impossible for her to invest in the same strategies of resistance that one finds in Stevens's most antiapocalyptic poems. My readings of Graham's poems have clarified, I hope, the way their "wishful call" to Stevens's version of modernism can only occur after the more heroic, masculine, imperialist aspects of Stevens's poetry have been rigorously questioned and recontextualized, if not utterly rejected. And yet my readings have not forgotten that the great peculiarity of Graham's poetry lies in the way it locates poetry's new possibilities—the possibilities that grow out of the collapse of the dream of reason—in an idealized past, a less immediate past than the one in which poetry was permeated by a "strictly secular sense of reality," by an "almost untenably narrow notion of what that in between space is capable of" (Graham, "Interview" 81). Graham looks back to a time when poetry offered a "mystery and power" with which contemporary writers must "reconnect" (81) themselves. Graham's immediate targets here are confessional poetry and some versions of the "new formalism," but that desire for "mystery and power" must also have a peculiar force when uttered by a poet who has so thoroughly absorbed the critical and theoretical writings that have set out to demystify all mysteries, to short-circuit all existing sources of or claims to cultural power. Graham's "wishful call" to Stevens's modernism has something to do with the "re" of her "reconnect," with the desire to invest in a source of mystery that will remain a mystery or not prove subject to demystification. Such a call is a call to something outside of the dominant tendencies in the postmodern cultural situation.

Afterword
Ending with Strand and Ashbery

I want to begin my conclusion by quoting from a response to an earlier article of my own—"Wallace Stevens' 'Puella Parvula' and the 'Haunt of Prophecy'"—that appeared in the *Wallace Stevens Journal* special issue entitled *Approaching the Millennium: Stevens and Apocalyptic Language* (23, no. 2, fall 1999). In his "Afterword: Last Words on Stevens and Apocalypse," Langdon Hammer wrote that the difficulty of distinguishing between apocalyptic and antiapocalyptic strains in Stevens's work (such was the main concern of my article) "looks ahead to the postmodern condition, defined as a certain impasse: the break with apocalyptic thinking in postmodernism remains a mode of apocalypse, Woodland argues, 'in its very desire to transcend history.'" (194). Hammer's response is in every way fair and judicious, but I want to question two words—"looks ahead"—just as in my introduction I questioned Tyrus Miller's observation that late modernism "anticipates" postmodernism. In my article, I had not been thinking of Stevens as a poet who looks ahead to postmodernism; and I hope that one issue that becomes clear in this book is how the apparent resemblances between modernism and postmodernism have more—in fact, everything—to do with postmodernism's status as a development of and reaction against modernism. As Hutcheon puts it, "modernism literally and physically haunts postmodernism" (*Poetics* 49) or "is ineluctably embedded in the postmodern" (38); postmodernism "marks neither a simple and radical break from [modernism] nor a straightforward continuity with it: it is both and neither" (18).

It seems important to remember, too, not only that "our sense of what modernism was remains . . . fluid," as Longenbach rightly notes ("Jorie Graham's" 101), but that some of this fluidity is generated by the tensions and contradictions within modernism. This is hardly a new point; Linda Hutcheon gives a useful summary of canonical readings of this aspect of modernist aesthetics on page 43 of *A Poetics of Postmodernism*, and Charles Bernstein's brief "Pounding Fascism:

(Appropriating Ideologies—Mystification, Aestheticization, and Authority in Pound's Poetic Practice)" offers, in its understanding of how "Pound has systematically misinterpreted the nature of his own literary production," a penetrating account of one of modernism's main sites of tension:

> Pound, or part of him, wished to control the valuation of the materials he appropriated by arranging them in such a way that an immanent or "natural" order would be brought into being. As Pound seems to acknowledge in the final movements of the (for the moment) standard version of the poem, *The Cantos* never jells in this way. For Pound this was a measure, no matter how ambivalent he may have been about the evaluation, of the failure of *The Cantos*. In contrast, the success of *The Cantos* is that its coherence is of a kind totally different than Pound desired or could—in his more rigid moments—accept. For the coherence of the "hyperspace" of Pound's modernist collage is not a predetermined Truth of a pancultural elitism but a product of a compositionally decentered multiculturalism. (*Poetics* 122–23)

Bernstein's ironizing of Pound's "failure" has its charm, though there are reasons to question its assumption of a certain teleology of cultural history, a teleology that seems to culminate in the work of Charles Bernstein, among others. The tensions and contradictions in Pound's *Cantos* may be best conceived not in terms of a failure to be postmodern but in terms of a successful realization or embodiment of the contradictions inherent in modernism: the modern is that discourse that breaks with the aesthetics of the past in order to preserve them more effectively. My readings of Stevens attempt to show how this tension operates in his work. Admittedly, Pound and Stevens would appear to operate at almost opposite extremes of the range of poetic practices employed in the first half of the last century—Pound an apparently radical disrupter of formal conventions, Stevens one who stays closer to certain syntactic, metrical, and stanzaic norms—and are nearly as far apart in their overt political ideologies. Yet in its own way, Stevens's poetics enact an endless questioning of the poetic and intellectual past and of its own formulations while—again in its own way—seeking to preserve something from that past, trying to find "what, after much testing, will hold" (Cook, "King James" 241).

In Stevens's poetry, then, this modernist tension tends to be greatest when not only the individual products of Stevens's creative process but the very foundation of his aesthetics are called into question by a radically unsettling force, by a situation in which consciousness bears the burden of an apocalyptic and eschatological dread concerning both a historical and an aesthetic dispensation. The works studied in this book show a Stevens whose poetry is, on the one hand, as open as possible to the forces that threaten to undo its foundations and, on the other, most thoroughly entrenched in a defensive posture against those forces. If this doubleness is to be understood as a genuine contradiction, it must be acknowledged that the unsettling force cannot come exclusively from "outside" but must also originate from within Stevens's own "never-resting mind" (*CP* 194), just as much as the counterforce that resists the initial force must originate internally. My readings of Stevens's apocalyptic modulations have, I hope, had at least reasonable success in reading this contradiction *as* a contradiction, in acknowledging the contradictory forces at work in Stevens's resistances to apocalypse, and in suggesting that this contradiction is a contradiction inherent in modernist aesthetics—if it is not, in fact, the very substance of that aesthetics.

The kind of contradiction I have argued for in Graham's poetry can, on a superficial consideration, appear homologous to the one I have associated with modernist aesthetics—a contradiction between a desire to break with the past or to let the past destroy itself and a desire, to revise one of Graham's titles, to recover something from the storm. But Graham's sense of the eschatological risks inherent in the dominant discourses of both past and present—in the eschatologically inclined aesthetics of closure and in the eschatologically inclined aesthetics of poststructuralism and postmodernism—necessitates a wary stance toward Stevens's own gestures of recovery, his investment in heroic, masculine forms of subjectivity; it leads Graham to seek modes of antiapocalyptic resistance quite different from Stevens's own. And, as I have already suggested, the mere fact that Graham has been through and absorbed postmodern and poststructuralist discourse, the fact that she lives in a postmodern culture, means that she can call to Stevens's modernism only across a historical and cultural gap that can never be truly closed; her gestures toward the past's "poetic ambition" (Graham, "Introduction" xxx) must always be shaped by the later historical situation to which they belong. I do not mean to suggest that Graham's way of dealing with apocalyptic and eschatological discourse is somehow representative of the generation to which she belongs, and still less that it is representative of the poetry written since World War II and written, therefore, in the shadow of the atomic bomb. This is not to say, however, that her work is not marked by her time, or that it could have been written at any other time or in any other place; Graham's engagement with apocalypse is the product of the late twentieth-century Euro-American situation, but what she makes of that situation, or how it articulates itself through her discourse, differs from what others have made of it.

The preceding summary might create the expectation that a different stance toward apocalypse would emerge in the generation between Stevens and Graham, a stance unlike Stevens's and Graham's ways of resisting apocalypse—a stance, perhaps that does not resist at all. A good way to test this expectation might be to look briefly at a few apocalyptic moments in the work of Mark Strand and, still more briefly, John Ashbery, poets who both acknowledge the influence of Stevens on their work. Strand's "When the Vacation Is Over for Good" (from his 1964 collection, *Sleeping with One Eye Open*), and "The Way It Is" (from the 1970 *Darker*) both present the aftermath of nuclear war; in the earlier poem, the speaker imagines a post-apocalyptic future, whereas the later speaker situates himself *in* such a world, speaking of and from the ashes and ruins. Here, Strand's response to apocalypse should be weighed against not just Stevens's wartime investment in figures of heroic masculine subjectivity but also against one of Stevens's few comments on the reality of living in the "atomic age": "I cannot say that there is any way to adapt myself to the idea that I am living in the Atomic Age and I think it a lot of nonsense to try to adapt oneself to such a thing" (*LWS* 839). If Stevens's war poems attempt to adapt to living in a time of war, to make the fact of war somehow manageable or containable—a point made by Longenbach, Ramazani ("War Elegy"), and Filreis—then the absence of any poems in Stevens's oeuvre that directly name the possibility of nuclear war might suggest that Stevens, at least in his poetry, lived up to his refusal to adapt to the "Atomic Age." Of course, in saying nothing on the subject in his poetry, Stevens still says or implies something; taken in conjunction with the comment in the letter, Stevens's poetic silence on this issue constructs the possibility of nuclear war as a sort of sublime unsayable, a source of terror that absolutely transcends the mind's capacity for containment: it precludes all possible forms of consolation, whether through figurations of heroic engagement or of "final peace." Strand's response to the possibility of such a disaster falls somewhere between Stevens's comments in the letter and his silence in the poetry, and in doing so differs considerably from the stance of Stevens's war poems. The speaker of "When the Vacation Is Over for Good," for example, imagines the lives of those who survive the initial disaster thus:

> we will not have changed much, wondering what
> Will become of things, and who will be left to do it
> All over again,
>
> And somehow trying,
> But still unable, to know just what it was
> That went so completely wrong, or why it is
> We are dying. (*SP* 5)

Strand's speaker inhabits a world in which heroic resistance or even fictions of resistance have become impossible, a world completely emptied of any possibility of mastery, either through action against or understanding of the situation and its historical causes. The speaker's belief that "we will not have changed much" argues against even the most minimal, secularized version of the apocalyptic hope of 1 Cor. 15:51 ("we shall all be changed"), any notion that the End will confer added insight or understanding or will provide a perspective that reveals the meaning of history.

A similar sense of passive subjection dominates "The Way It Is," but even more noteworthy is this poem's critique of masculine figures of power and authority—a critique that has more in common with Graham's than with Stevens's treatment of such figures. A large part of "The Way It Is" focuses on the contrast between the speaker and his "neighbor," a parodic embodiment of American patriotism and military might, who

> marches in his room,
> wearing the sleek
> mask of a hawk with a large beak.
> He stands by the window. A violet plume

rises from his helmet's dome.

. . . .

His helmet in a shopping bag,
he sits in the park, waving a small American flag.
He cannot be heard as he moves
behind trees and hedges,
always at the frayed edges
of town, pulling a gun on someone like me. (*SP* 79)

Stevens, of course, would never have invested in and never did invest
in any figure that even vaguely resembles the one Strand presents here.
In fact, Strand's phallically beaked (and conventionally married) figure
of militaristic patriotism resembles the "pagan in a varnished car"
(*CP* 170) and the "profane parade" (*CP* 278) that Stevens himself parodies in (respectively) poem x of "The Man with the Blue Guitar"
and poem xi of "Examination of the Hero in a Time of War." But
unlike Stevens, Strand does not offer as an alternative to such mind-
less authoritarianism a more palatable, less jingoistic version of the
hero, the soldier, the patriot; nor does Strand seek to identify or access
the "force" of "nobility" that makes any individual version of heroism possible—the force Stevens calls "a feeling" (*CP* 278) of "brave
quickenings, the human / Accelerations that seem inhuman" (*CP*
279), "The life that would never end, no matter / Who died, the
being that was an abstraction" (*CP* 289). Instead, Strand investigates
the following two positions of resistance:

> I crouch
> under the kitchen table, telling myself
> I am a dog, who would kill a dog? (*SP* 79)

> . . . .

> I see myself in the park
> on horseback, surrounded by dark,
> leading the armies of peace.
> The iron legs of the horse do not bend.

> I drop the reins. (*SP* 81)

The first passage tropes a purely animal instinct for self-preservation, though the speaker's delusional gesture of bleakly comic cowardice also literalizes Strand's earlier trope of poet-as-dog in "Eating Poetry" (a trope that returns in the "Five Dogs" of *Blizzard of One*). In the second passage's dream vision, the speaker's counterheroism or anti-military heroism finally comes to nothing: the "iron legs of the horse" figure the futility of such resistance, the impossibility of mastery over an unmovable object or an unchangeable situation; more significantly, the "iron legs" and the decision to "drop the reins" may also signal the speaker's recognition that leading "the armies of peace" traps him in the same rigid authoritarianism represented by his "neighbor" and by the quasi-apocalyptic "horsemen" who tell the populace "why / They should die" (*SP* 80). If Strand's stance here seems characteristic of the antinomian politics of the 1960s and 1970s—a time when the "public name" of Strand's anxieties was "Lyndon Johnson, or the government of the United States" (Brooks 25)—then Strand's sense of his own culture's culpability may have some role in the speaker's inability to invest in any sort of position of power at all, his inability to see any sort of positive value in efforts toward mastery of or resistance to the situation. His speaker "drop[s] the reins" and disappears from the poem as an "I," doing nothing other than observe that "Nothing is done" (*SP* 81)—a nonaction reported, appropriately enough, in the passive voice.

Passivity, or the decision to trope a situation in which passivity becomes the only possible stance; an inability or refusal to resist forces beyond one's control, or a decision to trope forces that place one in a passive position; an absence of mastery, or a decision to trope the impossibility of mastery—these features distinguish Strand's engagements with nuclear apocalypse from those of the Stevens texts considered in the body of this study. A similar stance emerges in the poetry of John Ashbery. At the climax of "A Wave," for example, Ashbery describes

> The cimmerian moment in which all lives, all destinies
> And incompleted destinies were swamped
> As though by a giant wave that picks itself up
> Out of a calm sea and retreats again into nowhere
> Once its damage is done. (*AW* 81)

This passage echoes an earlier part of the poem, in which Ashbery tells us that

> all of a sudden the scene changes:
> It's another idea, a new conception, something submitted
> A long time ago, that only now seems about to work
> To destroy at last the ancient network
> Of letters, diaries, ads for civilization.
> It passes through you, emerges on the other side
> And is now a distant city, with all
> The possibilities shrouded in a narrative moratorium.
> The chroniqueurs who bad-mouthed it, the honest
> Citizens whose going down into the day it was,
> Are part of it, though none
> Stand with you as you mope and thrash your way through time,
> Imagining it as it is, a kind of tragic euphoria
> In which your spirit sprouted. And which is justified in you.
>   (AW 68–69)

In the second passage in particular, Ashbery appears to describe something like what M. H. Abrams calls an "apocalypse of the imagination," the sort of cultural upheaval that Stevens attempts to resist in his wartime essays and poems, an upheaval that here does not just threaten to but actually does "destroy" a whole tradition of both private ("letters, diaries") and public (in the debased form of "ads for civilization," and, perhaps, "letters" too in a "belle-lettristic" sense) modes of discourse. If the "you" addressed in the passage is an aspect of Ashbery's self—and given the slipperiness of Ashbery's pronouns that guess seems as good as any—then the poet is granted some sort of minimal version of the romantic poet's conventional, melancholy isolation ("none / Stand with you as you mope") and special status (the "tragic euphoria" is "justified" in him). The one thing Ashbery's addressee *cannot* do is establish any sort of resistance to or mastery over the disaster: it "passes through" him and leaves him to "mope and thrash [his] way through time" rather than granting him any sort of privileged overview or understanding; his work can "justif[y]" but not resist the catastrophe. It is tempting to compare this passage, on the assumption that it, too, presents a wavelike "cimmerian moment," to the wavelike force of nobility of Stevens's "The Noble Rider," which functions as a locus of resistance to "an ever-enlarging incoherence" (*NA* 17), to "the collapse of our system" (*NA* 20). In Ashbery's poem, the wave *is* the "ever-enlarging incoherence," the force that undoes "the ancient network," and there is no resistance to it. It might be fair to say that Ashbery's poetry is already shaped by that force, that its astonishing shifts of tone, diction, and figuration come from a world where the "ancient network" has already collapsed, that the energies that drive its long, complex sentences onward are the energies of "an ever-enlarging incoherence." In fact, if the characteristic syntax of Ashbery's work at this period in his career remains undisturbed by the apocalyptic forces that roll through the Ashberian sentence, it may be because such forces are already operating in Ashbery's poetry: a poetics as open as Ashbery's will absorb everything, even an apocalyptic vision, with the same equanimity.

One might make similar claims about the Strand poems discussed above, though the scenario of nuclear war necessitates certain complications or qualifications. I have claimed that Strand does not invest in figurations of mastery, but in his two apocalyptic poems he has, in a sense, mastered the unmasterable—not simply because he has made it into poetry, but because he has absorbed it into a poetry in which the characteristic Strandian thematics, topoi, tropes, and so on, continue to operate undisturbed. Both poems embody, for example, the "erotics and politics of passivity" (97) that Linda Gregerson rightly identifies as one of Strand's perennial concerns, a politics in which "ultimate power resides with one who is only acted upon" (97); they also embody what Bloom refers to as Strand's "perpetual vision of loss, central emblem of the self unable to bear the self" ("Dark" 137). There would be good reasons, too, to read both the speaker and the neighbor of "The Way It Is" as aspects of Strand's self, another version of his recurring topos of the divided self. And both poems, despite differences in syntax, maintain the characteristic Strandian voice and tone, an almost painful absence of affect, as though the voice somehow remained unmarked by the horrific situation of and from which it speaks. These comments appear to be leading toward a criticism similar to Charles Altieri's complaint that Strand, in his "Elegy for My Father," demonstrates "moral bad taste" (*Self* 82) in "so easily reduc[ing]" father's death and life "to metaphor" (83). But my point, in fact, is more or less the opposite of Altieri's: the issue is not so much that Strand is solipsistically concerned only with "the symbolic and metaphoric effects the poet can wrest" (82) from disaster, nor even that he has "adapted" his symbolic and other effects to this subject matter, making the absence of resistance, the strange neutrality of voice, the sense of passivity function positively in relation to the possibility of nuclear holocaust. Rather, it is that such adaptation—if that is the right word—has taken place because Strand's poetics are already so thoroughly marked by his self-described sense "of impotence in the contemporary world" (Dodd 58), by his tendency, as a result, perhaps, of living with that sense of impotence, "to dramatize certain weaknesses that I have, a certain incapacity" (58).

Finally, though, any attempt to summarize the differences between Stevens's and Strand's engagements with apocalypse must involve something more than a comparison between, on the one hand, Stevens's wartime and postwar investment in figures of mastery and, on the other, Strand's refusal to provide such figurations; it must also involve something more than a comparison between that refusal on Strand's part and a similar refusal in some of Stevens's late poetry—as in, for example, the "exertion that declines" (OP 123) in "The Course of a Particular," the "horse [that] walks home without a rider" (OP 125) in "Farewell without a Guitar," the acknowledgment that a ferryman "could not bend against [the] propelling force" (CP 533) of "The River of Rivers in Connecticut," or Stevens's own risk of poetic indigence in lines like "Their indigence is an indigence / That is an indigence of the light" (CP 505). Nor would it be enough to remember that Stevens's tropes of self-emptying are the ones that exerted the strongest influence on Strand, though, as Christopher R. Miller notes, Strand "seems to have taken this ethos to a further extreme" (135). An account of the two poets' differences on this issue would need to account for Stevens's refusal to "adapt" his poetry to the "Atomic Age" and the apparent ease with which Strand adapts his own. The impossibility of mastery and resistance, or at least of creating viable fictions and figurations of mastery and resistance, are, for Strand, the givens of his cultural situation and of his poetics in a way that they are not givens for Stevens. Stevens's comments in the letter could be read as an acknowledgment that his wartime figurations of resistance cannot function in the face of nuclear holocaust, but the poetry's silence on the subject may suggest an unwillingness to figure this absolute loss of mastery *as* a loss of mastery. Stevens's figurations of the absence of mastery figure the absence of a mastery that is still possible, that can still be conceived as a possibility; Strand figures the absence as absolute, as part of "The Way It Is." Yet it would be folly to suggest that Strand makes no investment in poetic power. The investments he makes, however, leave one with another paradox, since he invests in the power of being able to lose everything or having already lost, in the severe self-discipline of "Giving Myself Up" (*SP* 52); for Strand, "ultimate power," as Linda Gregerson observes, "resides with one who is only acted upon" (97). Perhaps the difference between Strand's and Stevens's engagements with apocalypse involves a shift in the locus or mode of mastery or resistance, rather than in the mere presence or absence of such values.

Readers may have begun to predict several paragraphs ago that this study would end by categorizing the differences between Stevens and these last two poets in terms of the differences between modernism and postmodernism, though it would have to be acknowledged that Strand's and Ashbery's apocalyptic modulations do not have the same celebratory or emancipatory rhetoric as the examples from Lyotard, Derrida, and others that were explored in my second chapter. But I wish to suspend that question here, and instead pose some others—questions about why, or how, or whether it matters that these differences be understood as the differences between modernism and postmodernism. The issue at stake here is not simply the multiplicity of existing "definitions" of postmodernism (not to mention of modernism)—Ashbery, for example, would be postmodern according to Altieri's and Perloff's understandings of the term, but not according to Hutcheon's. My main concern has more to do with statements like the one that opens Charles Altieri's *Postmodernisms Now: Essays on Contemporaneity in the Arts*: "All the instruments agree that 'postmodernism' is no longer a vital concept for the arts. No artist or writer is eager to ally with it, and even critics in the humanities now find affiliations with the term a little embarrassing. Daniel O'Hara, editor of *boundary 2*, the journal that first popularized the concept, now remarks that the very notion of 'post' seems to have become little more than the kind of self-promoting rhetorical gesture we find in a university press titling a book series 'Post-Contemporary Interventions'" (1). Similar points are made in Linda Hutcheon's epilogue (subtitled "The Postmodern . . . in Retrospect") to the recent (2002) reprinting of her *Politics of Postmodernism*. But Hutcheon's observation that "literary historical categories like modernism and postmodernism are, after all, only heuristic labels that we create in our attempts to chart cultural changes and continuities" (181) needs to be weighed against Fredric Jameson's complaint concerning the regular misuse of "postmodernism" in "various partisan expressions of value, mostly turning on the affirmation or repudiation of this or that version of pluralism" (cited in Altieri, *Postmodernisms* 1)—or better yet against Hutcheon's own consistent awareness that the concept of "finding" or "discovery" embedded in the term "heuristic" is always and necessarily compromised by the circular process by which such concepts as "postmodern" are generated, defined, and ceaselessly redefined. These considerations, in other words, return me to a point made in my introduction— namely, that categorizations of Stevens as either modern or postmodern so often seem part of a project to divide the literary goats from the literary sheep. There are unmistakable differences between the way Stevens, on the one hand, and Strand and Ashbery, on the other, deal with the persistence of apocalyptic discourse, or in the ways that discourse retains a vestigial presence or force in their work; there are yet further or different differences between the ways these three poets and Jorie Graham engage with that discourse. It may well be that these differences can be mapped in relation to each other as characteristically modern, postmodern, and "post-postmodern" engagements with the discourse of the End, though I hope that whatever gestures I have made toward such charting have resisted the temptation to "misuse" the terms along the lines Jameson has described. Perhaps what this study should claim to have offered, then, before arriving at its own end, is a preliminary mapping of a hitherto neglected aspect of the history of the End—namely, its persistence in the attempts of writers at different points in the last century to conceptualize, validate, sustain and defend the aesthetic dispensations that shape their work.

Notes

1 Fowler's understanding of "mode" differs considerably from that set forth by Frye in his treatment of the five "fictional modes" (myth, romance, high mimesis, low mimesis, irony) in *Anatomy of Criticism.* Of these five modes, only romance clearly derives from a single existing genre; high mimesis appears to draw together features of tragedy, epic, and other genres, and irony clearly invokes a trope rather than a genre.

2 A page later, Löwith offers a corollary to this statement, a corollary which gives a different configuration to the relationship between end and meaning: "The claim that history has an ultimate meaning implies a final purpose or goal transcending the actual events" (6). This is a common enough point, of course; it informs all of Kermode's *The Sense of an Ending* and finds the following succinct formulation in A. E. Harvey's *Jesus and the Constraints of History:* "Unless we postulate an end towards which our efforts are tending, or which will relieve us from our suffering, our life becomes meaningless and even unendurable" (72). This theme appears in some apocalyptic texts. For example, 2 Bar. 21:17 tells us that "if a consummation had not been prepared for all, in vain would have been their beginning." (This citation and all succeeding citations from intertestamental apocalypses are taken from R. H. Charles's *The Apocrypha and Pseudepigrapha of the Old Testament.*) A later passage in the same work elaborates on this theme at some length: "He who travels by a road but does not complete it, or who departs by sea but does not arrive at the port, can he be comforted? Or he who promises to give a present to another, but does not fulfil it, is it not robbery? Or he who sows the earth, but does not reap its fruit in its season, does he not lose everything? Or he who plants a plant unless it grows till the time suitable to it, does he who planted it expect to receive fruit from it?" (22:3–7).

3 Amos N. Wilder's "The Rhetoric of Ancient and Modern Apocalyptic" speaks of a disruptive force in apocalyptic utterance: "we are dealing with acts of the imagination and of language which break with the cultural patterns of their particular period" (439). For Wilder, apocalypse returns to a *"precultural"* (441) origin of language, though he also notes that the apocalyptic writer may turn to existing mythic and religious discourse in order to express this experience (441).

4 Gura discusses the violence incited by and visited upon the Fifth Monarchists in England (136–44).

5 Cohn observes that according to Augustine, the millennium did not lie in the future but had already begun with the Incarnation and was continuing through the work of the church on earth (*Pursuit* 29). *The City of God* 20.6–11 is particularly relevant here; chapter 6 discusses the "first resurrection" as a spiritual event in the present life of the Christian, and chapter 7 gives Augustine's interpretation of the millennium. Cohn has argued, in *The Pursuit of the Millennium*, that although Augustine's interpretation became official church doctrine, a literal understanding of apocalypse persisted throughout the early Middle Ages and gained considerable fresh impetus from the writings of the twelfth-century Calabrian abbot Joachim of Fiore (30–35; 108–10). A brief summary of the history of the interpretation of apocalypse—up to 1903—appears in Frank C. Porter's entry on Revelation ("Revelation, Book of") in James Hastings *A Dictionary of the Bible* (4:241–44). Sturm's "Defining the Word 'Apocalyptic'" provides a more recent view. See also Beasley-Murray's *Jesus and the Last Days* for an exhaustive account of the history of the interpretation of the "little apocalypse" of Mark 13. Abrams's studies of romanticism listed in my bibliography deal with the interiorization of apocalypse in nineteenth-century literature and philosophy. Thomas Altizer, in "Imagination and Apocalypse," interprets this phenomenon as a consequence of the rift between the divine and the worldly, and between subject and object, which emerges in postmedieval Western culture.

6 Bloom refers to the "highly anti-apocalyptic virtue of patience" in relation to the conclusion of Stevens's *Notes toward a Supreme Fiction* III, vi ("*Notes*" 93).

7 Obviously, Parker and Robinson both rely on Derrida's writings, but do not comment on this essay or the more recent "No Apocalypse, Not Now" in the body of their texts, since these essays appeared either after or during the completion of their books. Robinson discusses "Of an Apocalyptic Tone" in a long note (251 n. 1).

8 The mystagogues Kant attacks attempt to bypass the "labour of thought" (Norris 236) necessary to philosophy and, for Derrida, deconstruction; "the overlord reaches with a leap and through feeling what is immediately given him" (Derrida, "Apocalyptic" 70), and the mystagogues cause "the voice of reason" "to derail or become delirious" (71). They make "a leap from concepts to the unthinkable or the irrepresentable, an obscure anticipation of the mysterious secret come from the beyond" (72).

9 This issue is also crucial to Derrida's "Violence and Metaphysics," which demonstrates the impossibility of Emmanuel Levinas's attempt to transcend or break with metaphysics in his *Totality and Infinity*.

2: AN EVER-ENLARGING INCOHERENCE: WAR, MODERNISMS, AND MASCULINITIES

1 Kermode offers a detailed treatment of this relationship throughout *The Sense of an Ending*. Robinson treats the topic more briefly, offering a more general but still useful formulation of the issue when he writes that "an author's image of the end of the world invariably leads one to consider the author's image of the end of the *text*" (7).

2 Richard Jackson provides a contrast to these two critics' use of the heart/head division as a means of explaining the tensions in Stevens's concept of temporality. Jackson reads Stevens as a poet of "radical time," one concerned with "a temporality that always evades us" (10), but places him in a poetic tradition which attempts to "subvert the spatiability of time, and yet achieve a sort of transcendental, spatialized vision" (9); Stevens finds that "the spatial metaphor can never be fully abandoned" (11). Jackson seems more faithful to the complexity of Stevens's poetry in *not* arranging these tendencies within a traditional head/heart paradigm.

3 Here, the fact that Stevens does not see this state as a preparation for something better also suggests a homology with Kermode's observation that *his* time's apocalyptic break with the apocalyptic past has left Western culture in "a period of perpetual transition" (*Sense* 28). Stevens foresees only a permanent impermanence: "The disclosures of the impermanence of the past suggested, and suggest, an impermanence of the future" (*NA* 20–21).

4 I shall return to the question of nostalgia in a later chapter, but here wish to clarify Jameson's distinctions between modernist and postmodern nostalgias, which add an important complication to Lyotard's more straightforward opposition between a nostalgic modernism and antinostalgic postmodernism. Jameson opposes himself to the

> complacent eclecticism of postmodern architecture, which randomly and without principle but with gusto cannibalizes all the architectural styles of the past and combines them in overstimulating ensembles. Nostalgia does not strike one as an altogether satisfactory word for such fascination (particularly when one thinks of the pain of a properly modernist nostalgia with a past beyond all but aesthetic retrieval), yet it directs our attention to what is a culturally far more generalized manifestation of the process in commercial art and taste, namely the so-called nostalgia film (or what the French call *la mode rétro*). (*Postmodernism* 19–20)

5 Quoted, to use Stevens's words, "from Croce's Oxford lecture of 1933."

6 Stevens quotes Wordsworth's remarks in the preface on "the real language of man" on pp. 13–14 of "The Noble Rider" as part of his own review of changes in poetic language. But the prime difference for Stevens involves

"the pressure of reality" (*NA* 13): "The Napoleonic era is regarded as having had little or no effect on the poets and the novelists who lived in it. But Coleridge and Wordsworth and Sir Walter Scott and Jane Austen did not have to put up with Napoleon and Marx and Europe, Asia and Africa all at one time. It seems possible to say that they knew of the events of their day much as we know of the bombings in the interior of China and not at all as we know of the bombings of London, or, rather, as we should know of the bombings of Toronto or Montreal" (*NA* 21).

7 Jenkins, as the latter comments suggest, moves beyond purely aesthetic concerns to explore the textual politics implicit in Stevens's formalism; she argues quite convincingly that in Stevens's essay formalist poetics strain against his rhetoric of engagement, and she suggests more generally that "Stevens' poetry from 1939 to 1942 displays a *tension between* attraction to the autotelic world of the poem and desire for engagement, for intervention, in the wider world" (55).

8 Cf. his reading of "The Auroras of Autumn," pp. 239 ff. in *Metaphysician in the Dark*.

9 The pervasiveness of the shift toward pluralities in this field is witnessed not just by the number of works devoted to "masculinities" but by the *range* of works that take this approach to the issue. These works include the social constructivist viewpoint of writers such as R. W. Connell (cited above) and David S. Gutterman, who insists on the need for a "reimagination of masculinity that is open to a cornucopia of contingent, shifting identities" (63); the peculiar, Marx-informed middle ground occupied by John MacInnes, who says, in *The End of Masculinity*, "that masculinity exists only as various ideologies or fantasies, about what men *should* be like" (2) while arguing against the pluralizing of "masculinity"; Michael Kimmel's solid, culturally and historically specific empirical investigation, in *Manhood in America*, of the "tension between the multiplicity of masculinities that collectively define American men's actual experiences and this singular 'hegemonic' masculinity" (6); and, finally, Victor Seidler's somewhat quixotic attempt "to learn from [postmodernism's] more complex notions of the fluidity and fragmentation of identities while refusing the erasure of emotional and spiritual depth and experience" (xii).

10 Glen MacLeod identifies the painting in *Wallace Stevens and Modern Art* (p. 209 n. 24).

11 Riddel, for example, writes that Stevens "returns to his subman not as creator of portents and statues, but as the vital being itself and chokes off his poem with a plea for the absolutely irrational, a commitment to the sheer 'gaudium of being'" (*Clairvoyant* 134). For Patke, the poem comes to "a curious close, lacking the courage of its own invention" (68).

12 Les Entretiens de Pontigny, a ten-day seminar series held at Mount Holyoke,

was modeled on a similar event held annually for some thirty summers before the war at a medieval monastery in Pontigny, France. For a detailed account, see Filreis, *Wallace Stevens and the Actual World*, 98–100. Filreis argues that much of the essay's rhetoric of unity, wholeness, and so on demonstrates a consciousness of the specific audience to whom the paper was addressed. Such a context may indeed account for some of the heightening of this aspect of the earlier paper's rhetoric, though what is of interest for me is the fact that Stevens chooses to develop it in relationship to the same concern with the imagination's continuing validity and ability to survive its own disconfirmations of its products.

3: WHAT COULD NOT BE SHAKEN: MEDITATION IN A
TIME OF WAR

1 The poem's references to a "booming wintry and dull" (*CP* 214), Filreis writes, presage only the arrival of a spring whose colors will soon "burst into flames" (*CP* 214). Filreis's reading does not clarify why this booming, if it is the booming of spring, has apparently replaced or drowned out, with its "Massive drums and leaden trumpets," the "fluters' fortune" (*CP* 214) of spring. His reading may be motivated by his desire to narrate Stevens's progress from an initial isolationist stance to full support for America's involvement in the war in Europe—a Stevens unconcerned with omens of war in 1938 (or with the Spanish civil war) proves more consistent with a disengaged Stevens (and America) during the early years of World War II.

2 Mary Doyle Springer, in "Closure in a Half Light," comments briefly on the "abrupt deviational effect" (171) of Stevens's dashes in the last of his "Six Significant Landscapes" and in "World without Peculiarity." As I have just suggested, though, her reading captures only one aspect of their force.

3 Here I am referring to the longer cadenza usually included between the end of the recapitulation and the beginning of the coda in the first movement of a classical concerto.

4 Stevens gives one of his most beautiful versions of this paradox in canto x of "An Ordinary Evening in New Haven," in a notable antiapocalyptic passage which makes change a guarantee of continuity. Here, he writes that our spirit resides

> In a permanence composed of impermanence,
> In a faithfulness as against the lunar light,
>
> So that morning and evening are like promises kept,
> So that the approaching sun and its arrival,
> Its evening feast and the following festival,

This faithfulness of reality, this mode,
This tendance and venerable holding-in
Make gay the hallucinations in surfaces. (*CP* 472)

5 Ramazani, in "Stevens and the War Elegy," and Jenkins, pp. 37–64 of *Wallace Stevens: Rage for Order*, offer useful explorations of this motif in Stevens's war poetry.

6 Bloom, for instance, writes that this work takes a "pugnacious and polemical . . . stand against the past" (*Climate* 219) but finds continuity with the past in the apparent overcoming of "divergence" (*CP* 293) in the final couplet (*Climate* 221). For Filreis, who reads the poem as a response to Allen Tate's "Ode to the Confederate Dead," the poem's "unmistakable conclusion" reveals "a new sense of likeness between past and present [that] supports 'these violent marchers of the present'" (*Actual* 120–21). Filreis is particularly concerned with the element of *personal* identification in Stevens's relationship to his "semblables"; he contrasts this with Alan Tate's desire for historical objectivity and his rejection of romantic and subjective interpretations of the past.

7 Some other Stevens poems pit the rhetoric of the "centre" against teleological and apocalyptic thinking; see, for example, the contrast between "final belief" and "the central good" (*CP* 250, 251) in "Asides on the Oboe" (1940), or "Of Ideal Time and Place" (1947), in which "the last man," maker of "the final choice" at an "exultant terminal" (*NA* 88–89), will turn away from his terminal situation and look back to the past—Stevens's own present—as "the *center* of ideal time" (*NA* 89, my emphasis). For other readings of the function of Stevens's rhetoric of the "centre," see Harold Bloom's "The Central Man," Riddel's "Stevens on Imagination," or La Guardia 22–28. Carroll discusses Stevens's concern with the center throughout *Wallace Stevens' Supreme Fiction* and gives a particularly useful account of two senses of "centre" in Stevens on pp. 199–200 of that book. But his reading of the center is marred by a determination to find a transcendental and metaphysical aspect in Stevens's poetry. He attempts to place all of Stevens's references to the center within a dialectical progression toward an almost mystical end: "Stevens' purpose is to render himself the medium through which 'the central mind' comes to knowledge of itself" (4), "to become the medium through which God achieves knowledge of himself" (27). David R. Jarraway, in contrast, sees Stevens deconstructing the notion of center in "From the Packet of Anacharsis": "The poem thus displaces the representation of meaning away from the center and locates it in the production or repetition of meaning as meaning recedes in a quickening of rings" (189). Jarraway also reads the desire to breathe "at the azury centre of time" in "This Solitude of Cataracts" as an ironically self-destructive desire (260–61).

8 Stevens's etymological wordplay on "divergence" is characteristically complex. "Steep" and "down" clearly ask us to think of *vergere* as "to incline" ("diverge," *OED*), and all this downturning certainly seems in keeping with the reference to those who were "defeated at last and lost / In an ignorance of sleep with nothing won" (*CP* 291). There may also be a grim joke concerning the present location of Stevens's ancestors and the fact that Stevens himself will follow them down to a similar place sooner or later. Other aspects of the poem's rhetoric, as I hope to show, ask us to think of *vergere* as "bend, turn."

9 Lodge takes his point of departure from ideas first set forth by Roman Jakobson in "Two Aspects of Language and Two Types of Linguistic Disturbances," which postulated that verbal structures may be ordered according either to metonymic principles (in which elements are related on the basis of spatial or temporal contiguity) or metaphoric ones (in which elements are related on the basis of similarity or shared features).

4. THE REFUGE THAT THE END CREATES: PASTORAL AND APOCALYPTIC MODES IN "CREDENCES OF SUMMER"

1 Berger notes that "the sense of an ending pervades 'Credences'" (84).

2 The examples found in the Old Testament are generally held to belong to the genre of prophetic eschatology, rather than apocalypse, though Stevens seems not to distinguish between the two. In "Wallace Stevens' 'Puella Parvula' and the 'Haunt of Prophecy,'" for example, I have shown that Stevens combines allusions to OT eschatological prophecy and NT apocalypse in a single passage, or reads the former in the light of the latter, as though they did not differ in essence. Prophetic eschatology promises fulfillment on *this* earth, whereas the later, more "properly" apocalyptic passages see such fulfillment occurring only in a "new heaven and new earth," and only at the cost of great destruction. One might see a kind of double substitution taking place in the history of this topos throughout the Bible: what was already a figure of substitution—desirable future for undesirable present—itself undergoes another substitution, as the *place* of that future changes from a transformed "here" to a transcendent "there."

3 Kermode makes a similar point: "The end, Apocalypse, is traditionally held to resume the whole structure, which it can only do by figures predictive of that part of it which has not been historically revealed" (*Sense* 6–7). However, Lynen also sees this way of thinking as characteristic of American Puritanism in general, as is made evident when he writes that the Puritan outlook "accustomed the imagination to conceive experience in terms of the purely present in relation to a total history or conspectus of all times" (35–36). Lynen bases this conclusion on his analysis of a number of early American Puritan texts and historical documents which, while not specifically

apocalyptic in their general concerns, show a strong tendency to relate events to both the whole of history and the end projected by Revelation.

4 Stevens echoes biblical visions of the throne room of God; cf., for example, 1 Kings 22:19, Dan. 7:9–10, Rev. 4:9, 5:1, and others. Bauckham discusses this figure in *The Theology of the Book of Revelation*, pp. 31–34.

5 See Büchsel and Herntrich's discussion in Kittel's *Theological Dictionary of the New Testament* (3:921–54). God makes his judgement in Rev. 20:11–15, and is described as κριτης in 2 Tim. 4:8, Heb. 12:23, and James 4:12 and 5:9.

5: MOURNFUL MAKING: APOCALYPSE AND ELEGY IN "THE AURORAS OF AUTUMN"

1 See, for example, ll. 1082–1137 of "Autumn" in James Thomson's *The Seasons*, where observers naively interpret an auroral display as an omen of war and even as an eschatological sign. A brief account of these folkloric interpretations of the aurora appears on pp. 6–9 of Asgeir Brekke and Alv Egeland's *The Northern Light: From Mythology to Space Research*.

2 "The speaker in a confession usually takes two steps forward for every one step backward; his progress by reversion is designed to secure the proper balance of closure and delay. *In Memoriam* reverses this formula: for every one step forward the elegist inches two steps backward" (Shaw 59).

3 According to Vendler, "Credences of Summer" and "The Auroras of Autumn" "represent the wresting of Stevens' naturally elegiac style into a temporally topographical poetry" (*Extended* 232).

4 "It still ought to surprise us when we realize how thoroughly [Stevens] has excised the eschatological dimension from the elegy" (Berger 112).

5 Joseph Carroll, reading the passage in relation to *In Memoriam* 123, writes that "the central issue for [Stevens], as for Tennyson, is whether the world contains a teleological principle that would give shape and meaning to the spectacle of phenomenal change" (250). For Jarraway, "There is, consequently, no fixed or determinable teleology at back of change, save for the 'misted rock' of change itself" (242).

6 In a postmodern gesture of the kind he might not be willing to claim as his own, Jameson both uses and abuses the word "nostalgia" when applying it to postmodern art: "Nostalgia does not strike one as an altogether satisfactory word for such fascination (particularly when one thinks of the pain of a properly modernist nostalgia with a past beyond all but aesthetic retrieval)" (19). Postmodern "nostalgia," for Jameson, can only reconstruct a past of "pseudohistorical depth, in which the history of aesthetic styles displaces 'real' history" (20):

> This historical novel can no longer set out to represent the historical past; it can only "represent" our ideas and stereotypes about that past

(which thereby at once becomes "pop history"). Cultural production is thereby driven back inside a mental space which is no longer that of the old monadic subject but rather that of some degraded collective "objective spirit": it can no longer gaze directly on some putative real world, at some reconstruction of a past history which was once itself a present; rather, as in Plato's cave, it must trace our mental images of that past upon its confining walls. (25)

Jameson, it seems, is observing the same phenomenon as Hutcheon; however, unlike Hutcheon, Jameson does not interpret this "nostalgia" as a highly and deliberately politicized problematizing of representation and historicity (as Hutcheon does), but rather as a symptom of "multiple historical amnesias" (171) which mark "the loss of such ideological missions" as are characteristic, at least in the visual arts, of "painting's older (modernist) Utopian vocations" (173). Postmodern memory is strangely founded on forgetting. Despite Jameson's differences from Hutcheon, his understanding of postmodern "nostalgia" would still lead me—as indeed it leads Jameson (cf. *Postmodernism* I, 16, or pp. 176–91 of his article in Axelrod's and Deese's *Critical Essays on Wallace Stevens*)—to read Stevens as more modern than postmodern.

7 For Canon Aspirin, cf. Berger 53, Bloom, *Climate* 267, and Vendler, *Extended* 258. Bloom also associates the father in "Auroras," who resembles "one that is strong in the bushes of his eyes" (*CP* 414), with the "lasting visage in a lasting bush" of *Notes* III, iii (266). Carroll makes the associations with Whitman and "Crude Foyer" (246); for the angel of *Notes* III, vii, cf. Carroll 245, Jarraway 245–46, Vendler, *Extended* 258.

8 Some of these associations reappear in canto vi of "An Ordinary Evening in New Haven"; there, "the hierophant Omega" becomes "stooping, polymathic Z, / He that kneels always on the edge of space" (*CP* 469). For previous readings of the Jahweh figure, cf. Arensberg, "White Mythology" 166, Bloom, *Climate* 266, and Vendler, *Extended* 258.

9 Shaw titles this section of his fifth chapter "Breakdown or Breakthrough? From Elegy to Apocalypse." Other critics of "The Auroras of Autumn" have certainly noted a major shift in tone between cantos iv and v. Berger, for instance, writes that in this canto "nostalgia soon turns to disgust" (55). Vendler provides the most severe assessment: "The autumnal wind has blown pretenses away, and the creator-father becomes, in consequence, the object of contempt, the 'fetcher' of negresses and clawing musicians and slavering herds, the hospitalier of a disorderly riot" (*Extended* 259). Even critics such as Bloom and Leggett, who take exception to these accounts of the poem, note a significant difference between cantos iv and v; Bloom, for example, describes it as "a total undoing of the father's optimism

and of the son's poetry" (*Climate* 268). Leggett finds Vendler *and* Bloom "too strong in their condemnation of the father, and they ignore the inevitable direction of the poem's initial five cantos, in which the opening image of form gulping after formlessness is traced progressively through the realms of matter, mind or feeling, and, finally, art" (*Poetic Theory* 182). But Leggett's reading does not account for the very different tone of canto v.

10 Stevens's obvious pleasure in arranging such fetchings emerges in a letter to Rosamund Bates Cary, dated May 6, 1935: "I thought it might be amusing to send you a little money, and ask you to make up a box of things that you thought that Holly might like and send it to her, so that she would have the thrill of receiving a box from Japan" (*LWS* 281). On December 27 of the same year, Stevens reported to Mrs. Cary that Holly "very distinctly appreciates the delicacy of the little dolls sent by you, and their silk dresses" (*LWS* 304) and that she "is frightfully steamed up about the doll festival. She very much wants you to buy a set of the classical figures of which you write" (*LWS* 304). The following letter to Leonard van Geyzel, Stevens's correspondent in Ceylon, dated September 14, 1937, provides some further detail: "For my daughter there should be a considerable number of little things: not toys, because she has outgrown toys. There might be one or two small carved figures; in her case, too, a necklace might do very well. I am sure that she would be interested in having some colored postcards; if there are any strange things to eat that would pack and carry well, she would be glad to have them. But what would go over best with her would be a miscellany" (*LWS* 324).

11 Barbara M. Fisher makes a similar point when she notes that "Stevens uses parody to establish a link with traditional sources—the 'romantic tenements' of aesthetic form and poetic utterance, the confluence of poetry and religion in a sacred text. But Stevens is also using parody to separate himself, to maintain distance from these same sources" (*Intensest* 24). The seriousness of "Puella Parvula"—at no point does it strike the note of parody one finds in earlier antidoctrinal poems like "The Bird with the Coppery, Keen Claws" (1921) or "A High-Toned Old Christian Woman" (1922)—already indicates, perhaps, the greater force with which the past weighs upon this poem.

12 Vendler, for example, complains that the canto begins "in the arid vein of *Description without Place*, in a toying with the philosophical mode" (*Extended* 267). In her view, the poem's crucial turn consists of "gestures of willed assertion" (266), and the whole canto proves to be "a centaurlike poem, half abstract discussion, half wish-fantasy" (267). Berger, comparing the discovery of innocence in the auroras to the more cautious "It must be visible or invisible" (*CP* 385) of *Notes* I, vi, writes that "when it is a question of innocence [Stevens] grows more insistent, if not more convincing"

(65). Leggett, too, is puzzled here, and notes: "Curiously, the existence of innocence is proven by the visible northern lights" (*Poetic Theory* 190).

13 "In the narrative of male sexual paranoia, 'Woman' must be constructed as that known object to which male anxiety can be transferred" (Carpenter 117). Carpenter, after discussing the false prophetess, Jezebel (Rev. 2), and the "woman clothed with the sun" (Rev. 12), notes that "only later, in the figure of the Whore, is female power successfully reduced to the single element of sexuality, which can be represented as wholly foul and polluting, and then wholly destroyed" (118). Her reading of Revelation emphasizes the text's misogyny, insisting that its violent sexual imagery (particularly the whore of Babylon in Rev. 17) does not merely function as the vehicle of a political metaphor, but rather constitutes a literal attack on women. Martin Jay's commentary on the Whore (in "The Apocalyptic Imagination and the Inability to Mourn" in *Force Fields*) is more psychoanalytic in emphasis, as the following passage indicates: "Cast out of the psyche rather than symbolically integrated, the identified-with mother returns, as it were, as the avenging 'whore of Babylon' and 'mother of harlots' so ferociously reviled by John of Patmos and his progeny" (96).

14 Cf. Arensberg, "White Mythology," 164–65; Berger 48–49; Bloom, *Climate* 265; La Guardia 132; Vendler, *Extended* 256. The relationship to the muse is more implicit than explicit in La Guardia and Vendler.

15 Stevens's question to the "Timeless mother" (*CP* 5) of "In the Carolinas" (1917)—"How is it that your aspic nipples / For once vent honey?" (*CP* 5)—offers an earlier and deeply ambivalent image of the mother; the "return to birth, a being born / Again in the savagest severity, / Desiring fiercely" (*CP* 321) of "Esthétique du Mal" x presents another reunion, though one that differs greatly in tone from "Auroras" iii. But these do not focus on the mother's face, and it is unclear in these cases whether the mother is possessed by or possesses her children. The "one of the fictive music," "Sister and mother and diviner love" (*CP* 87), whom Stevens once asked to give back "The imagination that we spurned and crave" (*CP* 88), remains a somewhat more distant and elusive figure, hardly one that Stevens could claim to "possess." Arensberg gives a Freudian reading of some of Stevens's mother figures in pp. 23–27 of "'A Curable Separation': Stevens and the Mythology of Gender." C. Roland Wagner's "Wallace Stevens: The Concealed Self" explores the notion that "ambivalent attachment to the nurturing, pre-Oedipal mother is central to our understanding of Stevens" (125), and his reading of canto iii of "Auroras" asks us to consider "whether Stevens' *wife* might be seen as the mother who 'has grown old'" (128).

16 Jarraway sees the mother as an emblem of presence, though one that reveals its own incompleteness. While "the mother's gaze yields the relation to self-presence," we eventually find that "presence is not total, and that the

house 'half dissolved' by evening is at least half about a relation to otherness, that is, 'the half [its inhabitants] can never possess'" (79–80).

17 Eleanor Cook notes Stevens's wordplay on "Descartes" ("of cards") in the poem (*OP* 137), and observes that M. Descartes has forgotten "trees and air and indeed the cards themselves (which is to say, himself) as facts rather than as principles" ("Riddles" 228).

18 Stevens's comments on Leibniz seem instructive: "The concept of this monadic creation seems to be the disappointing production of a poet *manqué*. Leibniz had a poet's manner of thinking but there was something a little too methodical about it. . . . Leibniz was a poet without flash" (*OP* 268–69).

19 For Kristeva's discussion of mourning and language acquisition, see *Black Sun* 41–43; for her discussion of melancholia in this context, see pp. 43–58 of the same work. For her, melancholic speech is set outside the symbolic order, displaying the characteristics of the semiotic text.

20 Here it is worth remembering the following passage, quoted already in my introduction, from "Of an Apocalyptic Tone Recently Adopted in Philosophy": "Truth itself is the end, the destination, and that truth unveils itself is the advent of the end. Truth is the end and the instance of the Last Judgment. The structure of truth here would be apocalyptic. And that is why there would not be any truth of the apocalypse that is not the truth of truth" (84).

6: PAST APOCALYPSE, PAST STEVENS:
JORIE GRAHAM'S *The Errancy*

1 See, for example, Vendler, *Given* 107, "Married" 237, 240, "Fin-de-Siècle" 244; Gardner 186; Longenbach, "Jorie Graham's" 102, 104–6. Longenbach sees the desire for closure in Graham's work as a force that Graham herself does not fully acknowledge, at least not in her published interviews and prose writings; Vendler and Gardner, on the other hand, both assume that Graham's poetic territory consciously and deliberately includes this desire as one of its operating principles.

2 This is not simply a matter of disagreement among different critics, but of uncertainty within the work of individual readers of Graham's poetry. Bonnie Costello, for example, sees the Graham of *Erosion* as a poet who "reassert[s] modernist values and ambitions" ("Jorie Graham" 374) but finds a "temporal, postmodern aesthetic" (395) in her later work, despite the fact that Graham "has never entirely surrendered . . . the pursuit of the timeless, the impersonal, the beautiful over the brutality and flux of history" (374). For Longenbach, her work demonstrates a certain modernist ambitiousness ("Jorie Graham's" 99); "resist[ing] the narratives we usually bring to postmodern poetry while, at the same time, inviting us

to consider her poetry in relationship to those narratives" (101), Graham's oeuvre "weakens links that readers of postmodern poetry almost always take for granted" (102). Charles Molesworth (277) and Willard Spiegelman (256) present similarly divided views; only Vendler (see, e.g., "Married" 242) and Gardner (see pp. 168–169 and 188 for examples) treat Graham as an unequivocally postmodern poet.

3 In all of her work on Graham, Vendler has given considerable emphasis to Graham's tendency to work through a logic of binary conceptual pairs.

4 Winthrop uses the phrase more as a warning than as a celebration of the Puritans' godly purpose: "for wee must Consider that wee shall be as a Citty upon a Hill, the eies of all people are uppon us; soe that if wee shall deale falsely with our god in this worke wee have undertaken and soe cause him to withdrawe his present help from us, wee shall be made a story and a by-word through the world, wee shall open the mouthes of enemies to speake evill of the wayes of god and all professours for Gods sake" (295). Sacvan Bercovitch's *The Puritan Origins of the American Self* remains a classic study of the eschatological dimension of the Puritan sense of nationhood (see pp. 50–58 in particular for an exposition of the basic terms of the argument; Tichi 15–18 offers another useful summary).

5 See, for example, Derrida's discussion of folds in "The Double Session" (*Dissemination* 173–286).

6 Here, I am indebted to graduate students Anna Lidstone and Allison Crawford, whose term papers on Graham reminded me of the importance of the body as a source of knowledge in her work.

Bibliography

Abrams, M. H. "Apocalypse: Theme and Romantic Variations." In *The Revelation of St. John the Divine*, edited by Harold Bloom, 7–33. New York: Chelsea, 1988.

———. "English Romanticism: The Spirit of the Age." In *Romanticism Reconsidered*, edited by Northrop Frye, 26–72. New York: Columbia University Press, 1963.

———. *Natural Supernaturalism: Tradition and Revolution in Romantic Literature*. New York: Norton, 1971.

Adamson, Joseph. "Apocalyptic Hysteria in Stevens." *Wallace Stevens Journal* 11, no. 1 (spring 1987): 3–11.

Alpers, Paul J. *What Is Pastoral?* Chicago: University of Chicago Press, 1996.

Alter, Robert. "The Apocalyptic Temper." *Commentary* 41 (June 1966): 61–66.

Altieri, Charles. *Postmodernisms Now: Essays on Contemporaneity in the Arts*. University Park: Pennsylvania State University Press, 1998.

———. *Self and Sensibility in Contemporary American Poetry*. Cambridge: Cambridge University Press, 1984.

———. "Why Stevens Must Be Abstract; Or, What a Poet Can Learn from Painting." In *Wallace Stevens: The Poetics of Modernism*, edited by Albert Gelpi, 86–118. Cambridge: Cambridge University Press, 1985.

Altizer, Thomas J. J. "Imagination and Apocalypse." *Soundings* 53 (winter 1970): 398–412.

Aquinas, St. Thomas. *Summa Theologica*. Translated by Fathers of the English Dominican Province. Vol. 20. London: Burns, Oats and Washbourne, 1932.

Arensberg, Mary B. "'A Curable Separation': Stevens and the Mythology of Gender." In *Wallace Stevens and the Feminine*, edited by Melita Schaum, 23–45. Tuscaloosa: University of Alabama Press, 1993.

———. "White Mythology and the American Sublime: Stevens' Auroral Fantasy." In *The American Sublime*, edited by Mary Arensberg, 153–72. Albany: State University of New York Press, 1986.

"Ares." In *Oxford Classical Dictionary*. 3d ed. Edited by Simon Hornblower and Antony Spawforth. Oxford: Oxford University Press, 1996.

Ashbery, John. *Selected Poems*. New York: Penguin, 1985.

———. *A Wave*. New York: Noonday Press/Farrar, Straus and Giroux, 1984.

Ashton, John. *Understanding the Fourth Gospel.* Oxford: Clarendon Press, 1991.

Auden, W. H. *Collected Poems.* Edited by Edward Mendelson. New York: Vintage, 1991.

Auerbach, Erich. "'Figura.'" In *Scenes from the Drama of European Literature*, 11–76. Minneapolis: University of Minnesota Press, 1984.

Augustine, Saint. *The City of God.* Translated by Marcus Dods. 2 vols. Edinburgh: T & T Clark, 1913.

———. *The Confessions.* Translated by J. G. Pilkington. In *Basic Writings of Saint Augustine*, edited by Whitney J. Oates, 1:3–256. 2 vols. New York: Random House, 1948.

Bahti, Timothy. "End and Ending: On the Lyric Technique of Some Wallace Stevens Poems." *Modern Language Notes* 105, no. 5 (December 1990): 1046–62.

Banta, Martha. "American Apocalypses: Excrement and Ennui." *Studies in the Literary Imagination* 7, no. 1 (spring 1974): 1–30.

Bauckham, Richard. *The Climax of Prophecy: Studies on the Book of Revelation.* Edinburgh: T & T Clark, 1993.

———. *The Theology of the Book of Revelation.* Cambridge: Cambridge University Press, 1993.

Beasley-Murray, George R. *Jesus and the Last Days: The Interpretation of the Olivet Discourse.* Peabody, Mass.: Hendrickson, 1993.

Beehler, Michael. *T. S. Eliot, Wallace Stevens, and the Discourses of Difference.* Baton Rouge: Louisiana State University Press, 1987.

Benamou, Michel. *Wallace Stevens and the Symbolist Imagination.* Princeton, N.J.: Princeton University Press, 1972.

Bercovitch, Sacvan. *The Puritan Origins of the American Self.* New Haven, Conn.: Yale University Press, 1975.

Berger, Charles. *Forms of Farewell: The Late Poetry of Wallace Stevens.* Madison: University of Wisconsin Press, 1985.

Bernstein, Charles. *A Poetics.* Cambridge: Harvard University Press, 1992.

The Bible. Authorized King James Version. Introduction and notes by Robert Carroll and Stephen Prickett. Oxford: Oxford University Press, 1997.

Bloom, Harold. "The Central Man: Emerson, Whitman, Wallace Stevens." *Massachusetts Review* 8 (1966): 23–42.

———. "Dark and Radiant Peripheries: Mark Strand and A. R. Ammons." *Southern Review* 8, no. 1 (January 1972): 133–49.

———. Introduction to *The Revelation of St. John the Divine*, edited by Harold Bloom, 1–5. New York: Chelsea House, 1988.

———. "*Notes toward a Supreme Fiction.* A Commentary." In *Wallace Stevens: A Collection of Critical Essays*, edited by Marie Borroff, 76–95. Englewood Cliffs, N. J.: Prentice-Hall, 1963.

————. *Wallace Stevens: The Poems of Our Climate*. Ithaca: Cornell University Press, 1976.

Blumenberg, Hans. *The Legitimacy of the Modern Age*. Translated by Robert M. Wallace. Cambridge, Mass.: MIT Press, 1983.

Boethius, Anicius Manlius Severinus. *The Consolation of Philosophy*. Translated by Richard Green. Indianapolis: Bobbs-Merrill, 1962.

Booker, Keith M. "'A War Between the Mind and Sky': Bakhtin and Poetry, Stevens and Politics." *Wallace Stevens Journal* 14, no. 1 (spring 1990): 71–85.

Borroff, Marie. "An Always Incipient Cosmos." In *Wallace Stevens*, edited by Harold Bloom, 89–108. New York: Chelsea House, 1985.

————. "Introduction: Wallace Stevens: The World and the Poet." In *Wallace Stevens: A Collection of Critical Essays*, edited by Marie Borroff, 1–23. Englewood Cliffs, N.J.: Prentice-Hall, 1963.

Bozeman, Theodore Dwight. *To Live Ancient Lives: The Primitivist Dimension in Puritanism*. Chapel Hill: University of North Carolina Press, 1988.

Brekke, Asgeir, and Alv Egeland. *The Northern Light: From Mythology to Space Research*. Berlin: Springer, 1983.

Brogan, Jacqueline Vaught. *Stevens and Simile: A Theory of Language*. Princeton, N.J.: Princeton University Press, 1986.

————. "Stevens in History and Not in History: The Poet and the Second World War." *Wallace Stevens Journal* 13, no. 2 (fall 1989): 168–90.

Brooks, David. "A Conversation with Mark Strand." *Ontario Review* 8 (1978): 23–33.

Browning, Robert. *The Poems*. Edited by John Pettigrew. Supplemented and Completed by Thomas J. Collins. 2 vols. New Haven, Conn.: Yale University Press, 1981.

Büchsel, Friedrich, and Volkmar Herntrich. "κρίνω." In *Theological Dictionary of the New Testament*, edited by Gerhard Kittel and translated by Geoffrey W. Bromiley, 3:921–54. Grand Rapids, Mich.: Wm. B. Eerdmans, 1964.

Bull, Malcolm. "On Making Ends Meet." In *Apocalypse Theory and the Ends of the World*, edited by Malcolm Bull, 1–17. Oxford, Mass.: Blackwell, 1995.

Butler, Judith. *Gender Trouble: Feminism and the Subversion of Identity*. 1990. New York: Routledge, 1999.

Carpenter, Mary Wilson. "Representing Apocalypse: Sexual Politics and the Violence of Revelation." In *Postmodern Apocalypse: Theory and Cultural Practice at the End*, edited by Richard Dellamora, 107–35. Philadelphia: University of Pennsylvania Press, 1995.

Carroll, Joseph. *Wallace Stevens' Supreme Fiction: A New Romanticism*. Baton Rouge: Louisiana State University Press, 1987.

Charles, R. H. "Apocalyptic Literature." In *A Dictionary of the Bible: Dealing with Its Language, Literature, and Contents Including the Biblical Theology,* edited by James Hastings, 1:109–10. New York: Charles Scribner's Sons, 1903.

———. *A Critical and Exegetical Commentary on the Revelation of St. John.* 2 vols. New York: Charles Scribner's Sons, 1920.

———. "Eschatology of the Apocryphal and Apocalyptic Literature." In *A Dictionary of the Bible: Dealing with Its Language, Literature, and Contents Including the Biblical Theology,* edited by James Hastings, 1:741–49. New York: Charles Scribner's Sons, 1903.

———. *Eschatology: The Doctrine of a Future Life in Israel, Judaism and Christianity: A Critical History.* 1899. New York: Schocken Books, 1963.

———, ed. *The Apocrypha and Pseudepigrapha of the Old Testament.* 2 vols. Oxford: Clarendon Press, 1913.

Cixous, Hélène. "Castration or Decapitation?" In *Out There: Marginalization and Contemporary Culture,* edited by Russell Ferguson et al., 345–56. New York: New Museum of Contemporary Art and Massachussets Institute of Technology, 1990.

Cleghorn, Angus J. *Wallace Stevens' Poetics: The Neglected Rhetoric.* New York: Palgrave, 2000.

Cohn, Norman. *Cosmos, Chaos, and the World to Come: The Ancient Roots of Apocalyptic Faith.* New Haven, Conn.: Yale University Press, 1993.

———. *The Pursuit of the Millennium: Revolutionary Millenarians and Mystical Anarchists of the Middle Ages.* 3d ed. London: Pimlico, 1993.

Collins, Adela Yarbro. "The Power of Apocalyptic Rhetoric—Catharsis." In *The Revelation of St. John the Divine,* edited by Harold Bloom, 73–94. New York: Chelsea House, 1988.

Collins German-English, English-German Dictionary. London: Collins, 1980.

Collins, John J. "Introduction: Towards the Morphology of a Genre." *Semeia* 14 (1979): 1–20.

Connell, Robert W. *Masculinities.* Cambridge, U.K.: Polity Press, 1995.

Cook, Eleanor. *Poetry, Word-Play, and Word-War in Wallace Stevens.* Princeton, N.J.: Princeton University Press, 1988.

———. "Riddles, Charms, and Fictions in Wallace Stevens." In *Centre and Labyrinth: Essays in Honour of Northrop Frye,* edited by Eleanor Cook et al., 227–44. Toronto: University of Toronto Press, 1983.

———. "Stevens and Catullus: A Note." *Wallace Stevens Journal* 23, no. 1 (spring 1999): 73–74.

———. "Wallace Stevens and the King James Bible." *Essays in Criticism* 41, no. 3 (July 1991): 240–52.

Costello, Bonnie. "Jorie Graham: Art and Erosion." *Contemporary Literature* 33, no. 2 (summer 1992): 373–95.

Cullmann, Oscar. *Christ and Time: The Primitive Christian Conception of Time and History*. Translated by Floyd V. Filson. Rev. ed. London: SCM Press, 1962.

Daniélou, Jean. *The Theology of Jewish Christianity*. Translated and edited by John A. Baker. London: Darton, Longman & Todd, 1964.

Dante Alighieri. *The Divine Comedy*. Vol. 1, *The Inferno*. Translated by Mark Musa. 1971. New York: Penguin, 1985.

Deleuze, Gilles. *The Fold: Leibniz and the Baroque*. Translated by Tom Conley. Minneapolis: University of Minnesota Press, 1993.

Derrida, Jacques. *Dissemination*. Translated by Barbara Johnson. Chicago: University of Chicago Press, 1981.

———. "Ellipsis." In *Writing and Difference*, translated by Alan Bass, 294–300. Chicago: University of Chicago Press, 1978.

———. "Force and Signification." In *Writing and Difference*, translated by Alan Bass, 3–30. Chicago: University of Chicago Press, 1978.

———. "From Restricted to General Economy: A Hegelianism without Reserve." In *Writing and Difference*, translated by Alan Bass, 251–77. Chicago: University of Chicago Press, 1978.

———. "No Apocalypse, Not Now (full speed ahead, seven missiles, seven missives)." Translated by Catherine Porter and Philip Lewis. *Diacritics* 14, no. 2 (summer 1984): 20–31.

———. "Of an Apocalyptic Tone Recently Adopted in Philosophy." Translated by John P. Leavey, Jr. *Semeia* 23 (1982): 63–97.

———. *Of Grammatology*. Translated by Gayatri Chakravorty Spivak. Corrected ed. Baltimore: Johns Hopkins, 1998.

———. "Violence and Metaphysics: An Essay on the Thought of Emmanuel Levinas." In *Writing and Difference*, translated by Alan Bass, 79–153. Chicago: University of Chicago Press, 1978.

———. "White Mythology: Metaphor in the Text of Philosophy." In *Margins of Philosophy*, translated by Alan Bass, 207–71. Chicago: University of Chicago Press, 1982.

Dewey, Joseph. *In a Dark Time: The Apocalyptic Temper in the American Novel of the Nuclear Age*. West Lafayette, Ind.: Purdue University Press, 1990.

Doggett, Frank. *Stevens' Poetry of Thought*. Baltimore: Johns Hopkins Press, 1966.

Doggett, Frank, and Dorothy Emerson. "A Primer of Possibility for 'The Auroras of Autumn.'" *Wallace Stevens Journal* 13, no. 1 (spring 1989): 53–66.

Edelstein, J. M. *Wallace Stevens: A Descriptive Bibliography*. Pittsburgh: University of Pittsburgh Press, 1973.

Eliade, Mircea. *Cosmos and History: The Myth of the Eternal Return*. Translated by Willard R. Trask. New York: Harper and Row, 1959.

Eliot, T. S. *Collected Poems*. London: Faber and Faber, 1963.

Emerson, Dorothy. "Wallace Stevens' Sky That Thinks." *Wallace Stevens Journal* 9, no. 2 (fall 1985): 71–84.

Endo, Paul. "Stevens and the Two Sublimes." *Wallace Stevens Journal* 19, no. 1 (spring 1995): 36–50.

Ermarth, Elizabeth Deeds. *Sequel to History: Postmodernism and the Crisis of Representational Time*. Princeton, N.J.: Princeton University Press, 1992.

Filreis, Alan. *Modernism from Right to Left: Wallace Stevens, the Thirties, and Literary Radicalism*. Cambridge: Cambridge University Press, 1994.

———. *Wallace Stevens and the Actual World*. Princeton, N.J.: Princeton University Press, 1991.

Fisher, Barbara M. "Ambiguous Birds and Quizzical Messengers: Parody as Stevens' Double Agent." *Wallace Stevens Journal* 9, no. 1 (spring 1985): 3–14.

———. *Wallace Stevens: The Intensest Rendezvous*. Charlottesville: University Press of Virginia, 1990.

Foster, John Wilson. "A Redefinition of Topographical Poetry." *Journal of English and German Philology* 69 (1970): 394–406.

Foucault, Michel. *The Archaeology of Knowledge and the Discourse on Language*. Translated by A. M. Sheridan Smith. New York: Pantheon, 1972.

———. *The Order of Things*. London: Tavistock, 1970.

Fowler, Alastair. *Kinds of Literature: An Introduction to the Theory of Genres and Modes*. Oxford: Clarendon Press, 1982.

Frank, Joseph. "Spatial Form in Modern Literature: An Essay in Two Parts." *Sewanee Review* 53, no. 2 (spring 1945): 221–40 and 53, no. 3 (summer 1945): 433–56. Reprinted in *The Idea of Spatial Form* by Joseph Frank, 5–66, New Brunswick, N.J.: Rutgers University Press, 1991.

Freeman, Barbara Claire. *The Feminine Sublime: Gender and Excess in Women's Fiction*. Berkeley: University of California Press, 1995.

Freud, Sigmund. "Mourning and Melancholia." In *On Metapsychology: The Theory of Psychoanalysis; Beyond the Pleasure Principle; The Ego and the Id and Other Works*, edited by Angela Richards, 247–68. Vol. 11 of the Penguin Freud Library. Harmondsworth: Penguin, 1984.

Frost, Stanley Brice. *Old Testament Apocalyptic: Its Origins and Growth*. London: Epworth Press, 1952.

Frow, John. *Marxism and Literary History*. Oxford: Blackwell, 1986.

Frye, Northrop. *Anatomy of Criticism: Four Essays*. 1957. Princeton, N.J.: Princeton University Press, 1971.

———. *The Great Code: The Bible and Literature*. Toronto: Academic Press Canada, 1982.

———. "The Realistic Oriole: A Study of Wallace Stevens." *Hudson*

Review 10 (autumn 1957): 353–70. Reprinted in *Critical Essays on Wallace Stevens*, edited by Steven Gould Axelrod and Helen Deese, 63–77. Boston: G. K. Hall, 1988.

Gardner, Thomas. *Regions of Unlikeness: Explaining Contemporary Poetry.* Lincoln: University of Nebraska Press, 1999.

Genette, Gérard. *The Architext: An Introduction.* Translated by Jane E. Lewin. Berkeley: University of California Press, 1992.

———. *Palimpsests: Literature in the Second Degree.* Translated by Channa Newman and Claude Doubinsky. Lincoln: University of Nebraska Press, 1997.

Ginzberg, Louis. "Cabala." In *The Jewish Encyclopedia: A Descriptive Record of the History, Religion, Literature, and Customs of the Jewish People from the Earliest Times*, edited by Isidore Singer, 3:456–79. New York: Ktav, 1964.

Graham, Jorie. *The End of Beauty.* Hopewell, N.J.: Ecco, 1987.

———. *The Errancy.* Hopewell, N.J.: Ecco, 1997.

———. "An Interview with Jorie Graham." Interview by Thomas Gardner. *Denver Quarterly* 26, no. 4 (spring 1992): 79–104

———. Introduction to *The Best American Poetry, 1990*, xv–xxxi. New York: Collier-MacMillan, 1990.

———. *Materialism.* Hopewell, N.J.: Ecco, 1993.

———. *Region of Unlikeness.* New York: Ecco Press, 1991.

———. *Swarm.* New York: Ecco Press, 2000.

Gregerson, Linda. "Negative Capability." Review of *Selected Poems*, by Mark Strand. *Parnassus. Poetry in Review* 9, no. 2 (fall/winter 1981): 90–114.

Gura, Philip F. *A Glimpse of Sion's Glory: Puritan Radicalism in New England, 1620–1660.* Middletown, Conn.: Wesleyan University Press, 1984.

Gutterman, David S. "Postmodernism and the Interrogation of Masculinity." In *The Masculinities Reader*, edited by Stephen M. Whitehead and Frank J. Barrett, 56–71. Cambridge: Polity, 2001.

Halliday, Mark. *Stevens and the Interpersonal.* Princeton, N.J.: Princeton University Press, 1991.

Hammer, Langdon. "Afterword: Last Words on Stevens and Apocalypse." *Wallace Stevens Journal* 23, no. 2 (fall 1999): 194–96.

Hanson, Paul D. *The Dawn of Apocalyptic: The Historical and Sociological Roots of Jewish Apocalyptic Eschatology.* Rev. ed. Philadelphia: Fortress Press, 1979.

Hardy, Thomas. *The Complete Poetical Works of Thomas Hardy.* Edited by Samuel Hynes. 5 vols. Oxford: Clarendon Press, 1982.

Harrap's Standard German and English Dictionary. 4 vols. London: Harrap, 1974.

Hartman, Geoffrey H. *Wordsworth's Poetry: 1787–1814.* New Haven, Conn.: Yale University Press, 1964.

Harvey, A. E. *Jesus and the Constraints of History.* London: Duckworth, 1982.

Heffernan, James A. W. "The Temporalization of Space in Wordsworth, Turner, and Constable." In *Space, Time, Image, Sign: Essays on Literature and the Visual Arts,* edited by James A. W. Heffernan, 1:63–77. New York: Peter Lang, 1987.

Hines, Thomas J. *The Later Poetry of Wallace Stevens: Phenomenological Parallels with Husserl and Heidegger.* Lewisburg, Pa.: Bucknell University Press, 1976.

Hobbs, Michael. "'Gusts of Great Enkindlings': Spectral Apocalypse in 'The Auroras of Autumn.'" *Wallace Stevens Journal* 23, no. 2 (fall 1999): 126–40.

Hollander, John. "The Sound of the Music of Music and Sound." In *Wallace Stevens: A Celebration,* edited by Frank Doggett and Robert Buttel, 235–55. Princeton, N.J.: Princeton University Press, 1980.

Hopkins, Gerard Manley. *The Poetical Works of Gerard Manley Hopkins.* Edited by Norman. H. Mackenzie. Oxford: Clarendon Press, 1990.

Huston, Dennis J. "'Credences of Summer': An Analysis." *Modern Philology* 67 (1970): 263–72.

Hutcheon, Linda. *A Poetics of Postmodernism: History, Theory, Fiction.* New York: Routledge, 1988.

———. *The Politics of Postmodernism.* 2d ed. London: Routledge-Taylor and Francis, 2002.

———. *A Theory of Parody: The Teachings of Twentieth-Century Art Forms.* New York: Methuen, 1985.

Irwin, Mark. "Kite's Body, and Beyond." Review of *The Dream of the Unified Field: Selected Poems, 1974–1994,* by Jorie Graham. *Denver Quarterly* 31, no. 1 (summer 1996): 60–67.

Jackson, Richard. *The Dismantling of Time in Contemporary Poetry.* Tuscaloosa: University of Alabama Press, 1988.

Jameson, Fredric. *Postmodernism, or, The Cultural Logic of Late Capitalism.* Durham, N.C.: Duke University Press, 1991.

———. "Wallace Stevens." In *Critical Essays on Wallace Stevens,* edited by Steven Gould Axelrod and Helen Deese, 176–91. Boston: G. K. Hall, 1988.

Jardine, Alice A. *Gynesis: Configurations of Woman and Modernity.* Ithaca, N.Y.: Cornell University Press, 1987.

Jarraway, David R. *Wallace Stevens and the Question of Belief: Metaphysician in the Dark.* Baton Rouge: Louisiana State University Press, 1993.

Jay, Martin. *Force Fields: Between Intellectual History and Cultural Critique.* New York: Routledge, 1993.

Jenkins, Lee M. *Wallace Stevens: Rage for Order*. Brighton: Sussex Academic Press, 2000.

Johnson, Samuel. *The Lives of the Poets*. London: George Bell & Sons, 1890.

Kant, Immanuel. *Critique of Judgement*. Translated by J. H. Bernard. New York: Hafner, 1951.

Keeling, John. "The Moment Unravels: Reading John Ashbery's 'Litany.'" *Twentieth Century Literature* 38 (summer 1992): 125–51.

Kermode, Frank. *The Sense of an Ending: Studies in the Theory of Fiction*. New York: Oxford University Press, 1967.

———. "Waiting for the End." In *Apocalypse Theory and the Ends of the World*, edited by Malcolm Bull, 250–63. Oxford: Blackwell, 1995.

Kimmel, Michael S. *Manhood in America: A Cultural History*. New York: Free Press, 1996.

Klink, Joanna. "To Feel an Idea." Review of *Swarm*, by Jorie Graham. *Kenyon Review* n.s. 24, no. 1 (winter 2002): 188–201.

Kristeva, Julia. *Black Sun: Depression and Melancholia*. Translated by Leon S. Roudiez. New York: Columbia University Press, 1989.

———. *Desire in Language: A Semiotic Approach to Literature and Art*. Edited by Leon S. Roudiez. Translated by Thomas Gora et al. New York: Columbia University Press, 1980.

———. "Women's Time." Translated by Alice Jardine and Harry Blake. *Signs: Journal of Women in Culture and Society* 7, no. 1 (1981): 13–25.

Kronick, Joseph G. "Of Parents, Children, and Rabbis: Wallace Stevens and the Question of the Book." *Boundary* 2, no. 10 (1982): 125–54. Reprinted in *Critical Essays on Wallace Stevens*, edited by Steven Gould Axelrod and Helen Deese, 102–29. Boston: G. K. Hall, 1988.

La Guardia, David M. *Advance on Chaos: The Sanctifying Imagination of Wallace Stevens*. Hanover, N.H.: University Press of New England, 1983.

Leggett, B. J. *Early Stevens: The Nietzschean Intertext*. Durham, N.C.: Duke University Press, 1992.

———. *Wallace Stevens and Poetic Theory: Conceiving the Supreme Fiction*. Chapel Hill: University of North Carolina Press, 1987.

Lensing, George S. "'Credences of Summer': Wallace Stevens' Secular Mysticism." *Wallace Stevens Journal* 1 (1977): 3–9.

Lentricchia, Frank. *Ariel and the Police: Michel Foucault, William James, Wallace Stevens*. Madison: University of Wisconsin Press, 1988.

Lessing, Gotthold Ephraim. *Laocoon*. Translated by Robert Phillimore. London: George Routledge and Sons, 1905.

Lewicki, Zbigniew. *The Bang and the Whimper: Apocalypse and Entropy in American Literature*. Westport, Conn.: Greenwood Press, 1984.

Lewis, Wyndham. "A Review of Contemporary Art." *Blast* 2 (July 1915), 38–47. Rpt. Santa Rosa: Black Sparrow Press, 2000.

Lincoln, Eleanor Terry. Introduction to *Pastoral and Romance: Modern Essays in Criticism*, edited by Eleanor Terry Lincoln, 1–6. Englewood Cliffs, N.J.: Prentice-Hall, 1969.

Lipking, Lawrence. *The Life of the Poet: Beginning and Ending Poetic Careers*. Chicago: University of Chicago Press, 1981.

Litz, A. Walton. "Space and Time in 'Notes toward a Supreme Fiction.'" *Wallace Stevens Journal* 17, no. 2 (fall 1993): 162–67.

Lodge, David. *The Modes of Modern Writing: Metaphor, Metonymy, and the Typology of Literature*. London: Arnold, 1977.

Lombardi, Thomas F. "Wallace Stevens and the Haunts of Unimportant Ghosts." *Wallace Stevens Journal* 7, no. 1–2 (spring 1983): 46–53.

Longenbach, James. "Jorie Graham's Big Hunger." *Denver Quarterly* 31, no. 3 (winter 1997): 97–118.

———. *Modernist Poetics of History: Pound, Eliot, and the Sense of the Past*. Princeton, N.J.: Princeton University Press, 1987.

———. *Wallace Stevens: The Plain Sense of Things*. New York: Oxford University Press, 1991.

———. "The World after Poetry: Revelation in Late Stevens." *Wallace Stevens Journal* 23, no. 2 (fall 1999): 187–93.

Longinus. *On the Sublime*. Translated and edited by W. Rhys Roberts. Cambridge: Cambridge University Press, 1899.

Lowance, Mason I., Jr. *The Language of Canaan: Metaphor and Symbol in New England from the Puritans to the Transcendentalists*. Cambridge, Mass.: Harvard University Press, 1980.

Löwith, Karl. *Meaning in History*. Chicago: University of Chicago Press, 1949.

Lynen, John F. *The Design of the Present: Essays on Time and Form in American Literature*. New Haven, Conn.: Yale University Press, 1969.

Lyotard, Jean-François. *The Postmodern Condition: A Report on Knowledge.* Translated by Geoff Bennington and Brian Massumi. Minneapolis: University of Minnesota Press, 1984.

MacCaffrey, Isabel G. "The Other Side of Silence: 'Credences of Summer' as an Example." *Modern Language Quarterly* 30 (1969): 417–38.

Macdonald, D. L. "The Return of the Dead in 'Large Red Man Reading.'" *Wallace Stevens Journal* 12, no. 1 (spring 1988): 21–34.

MacInnes, John. *The End of Masculinity: The Confusion of Sexual Genesis and Sexual Difference in Modern Society*. Buckingham, Eng.: Open University Press, 1998.

MacLeod, Glen G. *Wallace Stevens and Modern Art: From the Armoury Show to Abstract Expressionism*. New Haven, Conn.: Yale University Press, 1993.

Marinelli, Peter V. *Pastoral*. London: Methuen, 1971.

Masel, Carolyn. "'Cloudless the morning. It is he': The Return of the Figural in Stevens' Apocalypses." *Wallace Stevens Journal* 23, no. 2 (fall 1999): 111–25.

May, John R. *Toward a New Earth: Apocalypse in the American Novel.* Notre Dame, Ind.: University of Notre Dame Press, 1972.

McCann, Janet. *Wallace Stevens Revisited: "The Celestial Possible."* New York: Twayne, 1995.

Metzger, Lore. *One Foot in Eden: Modes of Pastoral in Romantic Poetry.* Chapel Hill: University of North Carolina Press, 1986.

Miller, Christopher R. "Mark Strand's Inventions of Farewell." *Wallace Stevens Journal* 24, no. 2 (fall 2000): 135–50.

Miller, J. Hillis. "Impossible Metaphor: Stevens' 'The Red Fern' as Example." *Yale French Studies* 69: 150–62.

———. *The Linguistic Moment: From Wordsworth to Stevens.* Princeton, N.J.: Princeton University Press, 1985.

———. *Poets of Reality: Six Twentieth-Century Writers.* Cambridge: Harvard University Press, Belknap Press, 1965.

Miller, Tyrus. *Late Modernism: Politics, Fiction, and the Arts between the World Wars.* Berkeley: University of California Press, 1999.

Milton, John. *The Poetical Works of John Milton.* Edited by Helen Darbishire. Vol. 1. Oxford: Clarendon Press, 1952.

Mitchell, W. J. T. "The Politics of Genre: Space and Time in Lessing's *Laocoon.*" *Representations* 6 (spring 1984): 98–115.

———. "Spatial Form in Literature: Toward a General Theory." *Critical Inquiry* 6 (spring 1988): 339–67. Reprinted in *The Language of Images,* edited by W. J. T. Mitchell, 271–99. Chicago: University of Chicago Press, 1980.

Molesworth, Charles. "Jorie Graham: Living in the World." *Salmagundi* 120 (fall 1998): 276–83.

Monroe, Robert Emmett. "Figuration and Society in 'Owl's Clover.'" *Wallace Stevens Journal* 13, no. 2 (fall 1989): 127–49.

Moore, Marianne. *The Complete Poems of Marianne Moore.* New York: Macmillan / Viking, 1981.

Morrison, Paul. "'Sepulchres of the Fathers': 'Notes Toward a Supreme Fiction' and the Ideology of Origins." *Wallace Stevens Journal* 13, no. 1 (spring 1989): 15–26.

Muret-Sanders Enzyklopädisches englisch-deutsches und deutsch-englisches Wörterbuch. 2 vols. Berlin-Schöneberg: Langenscheidtsche Verlagsbuchhandlung, 1910.

Norris, Christopher. "Versions of Apocalypse: Kant, Derrida, Foucault." In *Apocalypse Theory and the Ends of the World,* edited by Malcolm Bull, 227–49. Oxford: Blackwell, 1995.

Oepke, Albrecht. "καλύπτω." In *Theological Dictionary of the New Testament*, edited by Gerhard Kittel and translated by Geoffrey W. Bromiley. 3:556–92. Grand Rapids, Mich.: Wm. B. Eerdmans, 1964.

Otten, Thomas J. "Jorie Graham's _____s." *PMLA* 118, no. 2 (March 2003): 239–53.

Parker, Patricia A. *Inescapable Romance: Studies in the Poetics of a Mode.* Princeton, N.J.: Princeton University Press, 1979.

Patke, Rajeev S. *The Long Poems of Wallace Stevens: An Interpretive Study.* Cambridge: Cambridge University Press, 1985.

Patterson, Annabel. *Pastoral and Ideology: Virgil to Valéry.* Berkeley: University of California Press, 1987.

Pearce, Roy Harvey. "Wallace Stevens: The Last Lesson of the Master." *English Literary History* 31 (March 1964): 64–85. Reprinted in *The Act of the Mind: Essays on the Poetry of Wallace Stevens*, edited by Roy Harvey Pearce and J. Hillis Miller, 121–42. Baltimore: Johns Hopkins Press, 1965.

Perloff, Marjorie. *Poetry On & Off the Page: Essays for Emergent Occasions.* Evanston, Ill.: Northwestern University Press, 1998.

———. "Revolving in Crystal: The Supreme Fiction and the Impasse of Modernist Lyric." In *Wallace Stevens: The Poetics of Modernism*, edited by Albert Gelpi, 41–64. Cambridge: Cambridge University Press, 1985.

Peucker, Brigitte. "The Poem as Place: Three Modes of Scenic Rendering in the Lyric." *PMLA* 96, no. 5 (October 1981): 904–13.

Pons Großwörterbuch Englisch-Deutsch. Stuttgart: Klett, 1978.

Porter, Frank C. "Revelation, Book of." In *A Dictionary of the Bible: Dealing with Its Language, Literature, and Contents Including the Biblical Theology*, edited by James Hastings, 4:239–66. New York: Charles Scribner's Sons, 1903.

Pound, Ezra. "*Affirmations*: As for Imagisme." *The New Age*, January 15, 1915. Reprinted in *Selected Prose 1909–1965*, edited by William Cookson, 374–77. New York: New Directions, 1973.

———. *Selected Prose 1909–1965.* Edited by William Cookson. New York: New Dimensions, 1973.

Quinby, Lee. *Anti-Apocalypse: Exercises in Genealogical Criticism.* Minneapolis: University of Minnesota Press, 1994.

Quinn, Justin. "Jorie Graham and the Politics of Transcendence." *P.N. Review* 24, no. 6 (July–August 1998): 22–25.

Quinn, Sister M. Bernetta. *The Metamorphic Tradition in Modern Poetry: Essays on the Work of Ezra Pound, Wallace Stevens, William Carlos Williams, T. S. Eliot, Hart Crane, Randall Jarrell, and William Butler Yeats.* New Brunswick, N.J.: Rutgers University Press, 1955.

Ramazani, Jahan. "Stevens and the Self-Elegy: Making Alpha of Omega." *Essays in Literature* 18, no. 1 (spring 1991): 93–105.

————. "Stevens and the War Elegy." *Wallace Stevens Journal* 15, no. 1 (spring 1991): 24–36.

Reddish, Mitchell G. Introduction to *Apocalyptic Literature: A Reader*, edited by Mitchell G. Reddish, 19–38. Peabody, Mass.: Hendrickson, 1995.

Reguiero, Helen. *The Limits of Imagination: Wordsworth, Yeats, and Stevens.* Ithaca, N.Y.: Cornell University Press, 1976.

————. "The Rejection of Metaphor." In *Wallace Stevens*, edited by Harold Bloom, 51–60. New York: Chelsea House, 1985.

Ricks, Christopher. "Geoffrey Hill 1: The Tongue's Atrocities." In *The Force of Poetry*, by Christopher Ricks, 285–318. Oxford: Clarendon Press, 1984.

Ricoeur, Paul. *Time and Narrative.* Translated by Kathleen McLaughlin and David Pellauer. 3 vols. Chicago: University of Chicago Press, 1985.

Riddel, Joseph N. *The Clairvoyant Eye: The Poetry and Poetics of Wallace Stevens.* Baton Rouge: Louisiana State University Press, 1965.

————. "The Climate of Our Poems." *Wallace Stevens Journal* 7, no. 3–4 (fall 1983): 59–75. Reprinted in *Critical Essays on Wallace Stevens*, edited by Steven Gould Axelrod and Helen Deese, 145–62. Boston: G. K. Hall, 1988.

————. "Metaphoric Staging: Stevens' Beginning Again of the 'End of the Book.'" In *Wallace Stevens: A Celebration*, edited by Frank Doggett and Robert Buttel, 308–38. Princeton, N.J.: Princeton University Press, 1980.

————. "Stevens on Imagination—the Point of Departure." In *The Quest for Imagination: Essays in Twentieth Century Aesthetic Criticism*, edited by O. B. Hardison, Jr., 55–85. Cleveland: Press of Case Western Reserve University, 1971.

Robinson, Douglas. *American Apocalypses: The Image of the End of the World in American Literature.* Baltimore: Johns Hopkins University Press, 1985.

Rotella, Guy L. *Reading & Writing Nature: The Poetry of Robert Frost, Wallace Stevens, Marianne Moore, and Elizabeth Bishop.* Boston: Northeastern University Press, 1991.

Rowland, Christopher. *The Open Heaven: A Study of Apocalyptic in Judaism and Early Christianity.* London: SPCK, 1982.

————. "'Upon Whom the Ends of the Ages Have Come': Apocalyptic and the Interpretation of the New Testament." In *Apocalypse Theory and the Ends of the World*, edited by Malcolm Bull, 38–57. Oxford: Blackwell, 1995.

Rowley, H. H. *The Relevance of Apocalyptic: A Study of Jewish and Christian Apocalypses from Daniel to the Revelation.* Rev. ed. New York: Association Press, 1964.

Sacks, Peter M. *The English Elegy: Studies in the Genre from Spenser to Yeats.* Baltimore: Johns Hopkins University Press, 1985.

Salmond, S. D. F. "Eschatology." In *A Dictionary of the Bible: Dealing with*

Its Language, Literature, and Contents Including the Biblical Theology, edited by James Hastings, 1:734–41. New York: Charles Scribner's Sons, 1903.

Schaum, Melita. *Wallace Stevens and the Critical Schools*. Tuscaloosa: University of Alabama Press, 1988.

Scholem, Gershom. *The Messianic Idea in Judaism and Other Essays on Jewish Spirituality*. New York: Schocken Books, 1971.

Seidler, Victor. *Man Enough: Embodying Masculinities*. London: Sage, 1997.

Shakespeare, William. *Hamlet*. In *The Complete Signet Classic Shakespeare*, edited by Sylvan Barnet, 917–61. New York: Harcourt Brace Jovanovich, 1972.

———. *King Lear*. In *The Complete Signet Classic Shakespeare*, edited by Sylvan Barnet, 1182–1228. New York: Harcourt Brace Jovanovich, 1972.

Shaviro, Steven. "'That Which Is Always Beginning': Stevens' Poetry of Affirmation." *PMLA* 100, no. 2 (March 1985): 220–33.

Shaw, David. *Elegy and Paradox: Testing the Conventions*. Baltimore: Johns Hopkins University Press, 1994.

Shelley, Percy Bysshe. *The Selected Poetry and Prose of Shelley*. Edited by Harold Bloom. 1966. New York: New American Library, 1978.

Smith, Barbara Herrnstein. *Poetic Closure: A Study of How Poems End*. Chicago: University of Chicago Press, 1968.

Spears, Monroe Kylendorf. *Space against Time in Modern Poetry*. Texas Christian University Press, 1972.

Spiegelman, Willard. "Jorie Graham's 'New Way of Looking.'" *Salmagundi* 120 (fall 1998): 244–75.

Spivak, Gayatri Chakravorty. Translator's preface to *Of Grammatology*, by Jacques Derrida. Corrected ed., ix–xc. Baltimore: Johns Hopkins University Press, 1998.

Springer, Mary Doyle. "Closure in a Half Light: Wallace Stevens' Endings." *Wallace Stevens Journal* 16, no. 2 (fall 1992): 161–81.

———. "Repetition and 'Going Round' with Wallace Stevens." *Wallace Stevens Journal* 15, no. 2 (fall 1991): 191–208.

Steiner, Wendy. "*Res Poetica*: The Problematics of the Concrete Poem." *New Literary History* 12 (1981): 529–45.

Stevens, Wallace. *The Collected Poems of Wallace Stevens*. 1954. New York: Vintage Books, 1990.

———. *Letters of Wallace Stevens*. Edited by Holly Stevens. New York: Knopf, 1970.

———. *The Necessary Angel: Essays on Reality and the Imagination*. New York: Vintage Books, 1951.

———. *Opus Posthumous*. Revised, enlarged, and corrected ed. Edited by Milton J. Bates. New York: Vintage Books, 1990.

Strand, Mark. *Blizzard of One.* New York: Knopf, 1998.

———. "A Conversation with Mark Strand." *Ohio Review* 13, no. 2 (winter 1972): 54–71.

———. *Selected Poems.* 1980. New York: Knopf, 2000.

Sturm, Richard E. "Defining the Word 'Apocalyptic': A Problem in Biblical Criticism." In *Apocalyptic and the New Testament: Essays in Honour of J. Louis Martyn,* edited by Joel Marcus and Marion L. Soards, 17–48. Sheffield: JSOT Press, 1989.

Sukenick, Ronald. *Wallace Stevens: Musing the Obscure: Readings, an Interpretation, and a Guide to the Collected Poetry.* New York: New York University Press, 1967.

Teres, Harvey. "Notes toward the Supreme Soviet: Stevens and Doctrinaire Marxism." *Wallace Stevens Journal* 13, no. 2 (fall 1989): 150–67.

Tennyson, Alfred. *In Memoriam.* Edited by Robert H. Ross. New York: Norton, 1973.

Tichi, Cecilia. *New World, New Earth: Environmental Reform in American Literature from the Puritans through Whitman.* New Haven, Conn.: Yale University Press, 1979.

Toliver, Harold E. *Pastoral: Forms and Attitudes.* Berkeley: University of California Press, 1971.

Turner, James. "The Matter of Britain: Topographical Poetry in English, 1600–1660." *Notes and Queries* 25 (1978): 514–24.

——— *The Politics of Landscape: Rural Scenery and Society in English Poetry, 1630–1660.* Oxford: Blackwell, 1979.

Vaughan, Henry. *Complete Poems.* Edited by Alan Rudrum. Harmondsworth: Penguin, 1983.

Vendler, Helen Hennessy. *The Breaking of Style: Hopkins, Heaney, Graham.* Cambridge: Harvard University Press, 1995.

———. "Fin-de-Siècle Poetry: Jorie Graham." In *Soul Says: On Recent Poetry,* 244–56. Cambridge: Harvard University Press, Belknap Press, 1995.

———. *The Given and the Made: Strategies of Poetic Redefinition.* Cambridge: Harvard University Press, 1995.

———. "Mapping the Air: Adrienne Rich and Jorie Graham." In *Soul Says: On Recent Poetry,* 212–34. Cambridge: Harvard University Press, Belknap Press, 1995.

———. "Married to Hurry and Grim Song: Jorie Graham's *The End of Beauty.*" In *Soul Says: On Recent Poetry,* 235–43. Cambridge: Harvard University Press, Belknap Press, 1995.

———. *On Extended Wings: Wallace Stevens' Longer Poems.* Cambridge, Mass.: Harvard University Press, 1969.

———. *Wallace Stevens: Words Chosen Out of Desire.* Knoxville: University of Tennessee Press, 1984.

Virgil. *Eclogues*. Translated by David Ferry. New York: Farrar, Straus, and Giroux, 1999.

Voros, Gyorgyi, *Notations of the Wild: Ecology in the Poetry of Wallace Stevens*. Iowa City: University of Iowa Press, 1997.

Wagar, W. Warren. *Terminal Visions: The Literature of Last Things*. Bloomington: Indiana University Press, 1982.

Wagner, C. Roland. "Wallace Stevens: The Concealed Self." *Wallace Stevens Journal* 12, no. 2 (fall 1988): 83–101. Reprinted in *Wallace Stevens and the Feminine*, edited by Melita Schaum, 117–39. Tuscaloosa: University of Alabama Press, 1993.

White, Hayden. *Metahistory: The Historical Imagination in Nineteenth-Century Europe*. Baltimore: Johns Hopkins University Press, 1973.

Whitman, Walt. *Complete Poetry and Collected Prose*. Edited by Justin Kaplan. New York: Literary Classics of the United States, 1982.

Wilder, Amos N. "The Rhetoric of Ancient and Modern Apocalyptic." *Interpretation* 25 (1971): 436–53.

Williams, Raymond. *The Country and the City*. London: Chatto and Windus, 1973.

Winthrop, John. "A Modell of Christian Charity." In *Winthrop Papers*, vol. 2, 1623–1630, edited by Stewart Mitchell, 282–95. Boston: Massachusetts Historical Society, 1931.

Woodland, Malcolm. "Wallace Stevens' 'Puella Parvula' and the 'Haunt of Prophecy.'" *Wallace Stevens Journal* 23, no. 2 (fall 1999): 99–110.

Wordsworth, William. *The Prelude, or Growth of a Poet's Mind*. Edited by Ernest de Selincourt, 2d ed. Revised by Helen Darbishire. Oxford: Clarendon Press, 1959.

———. *Selected Poems and Prefaces*. Edited by Jack Stillinger. Boston: Houghton Mifflin, 1965.

Index

Bernhardt, Sarah, 63–64

Bernstein, Charles, 206–7

Bible: 1 Corinthians, 174, 210; 2
Corinthians, 13, 28, 172; Daniel,
7, 8, 60, 121, 226n4; Ezekiel, 8,
121, 140, 158; Haggai, 74–75;
Hebrews, 74–75, 226n5; Isaiah,
7, 10, 74–75, 111, 121; James,
226n5; Joel, 8, 111; 1 Kings,
226n4; Luke, 14; Mark, 7, 10, 13,
28, 172; Matthew, 7, 10, 121, 140,
176; Obadiah, 8; 2 Peter, 10;
Revelation, 7, 15, 17, 21–22, 111,
112, 121, 136, 140, 155, 226n4,
226n5, 229n13; 1 Thessalonians,
10; Timothy, 226n5; Zechariah,
7, 8, 10

Bloom, Harold, xii, xiii, xiv, 6, 14,
86, 112, 114, 134, 145, 147, 154, 214,
220n6, 224n6, 227n9

Bozeman, Theodore, 15

Brazeau, Peter, 62

Brightman, Thomas, 15

Bull, Malcolm, 16

Burke, Kenneth, 86

Butler, Judith, 50, 55, 156

Carpenter, Mary, 155, 229n13

Carroll, Joseph, xiv, 6, 103, 224n7,
226n5

Charles, R. H., 7, 12–13, 14

Cixous, Hélène, 156, 165

Cleghorn, Angus, xiv, 5

Cohn, Norman, 13, 17, 220n5

Coleridge, Samuel Taylor, 57

Collins, Adela Yarbro, 15, 136

Collins, J. J., 7, 8

Connell, R. W., 50–51, 222n9

Cook, Eleanor, xii, xiii, 6, 25, 86,
115, 118, 140–41, 152, 207, 230n17

Costello, Bonnie, 230n2

Crane, Hart, 45

Cullmann, Oscar, 11, 13

De Chirico, Giorgio, 85

Deleuze, Gilles, 182, 201–2

Derrida, Jacques: on apocalypse, 11,
12, 20–21, 32–33, 35, 155, 166,
230n20; on apocalyptic desire,
24–25, 115, 136; deconstruction
of apocalypse by, 22–23; on
metaphor, 174; on paradox of
antiapocalypse, 22–23, 125–26,
183, 220n9; on teleology, 16; on
writing, 127

Donne, John: "The Break of Day,"
187; "The Sun Rising," 187

elegy: 226n2; antiapocalyptic force
of, 136–38; mourning and
melancholia in, 164–66. *See
also* Stevens, Wallace: and
apocalyptic-elegiac modulations

Eliot, T. S.: "The Waste Land," 178

Les Entretiens de Pontigny, 222n12

eschatology. *See* apocalypse:
history of

Filreis, Alan, 69, 70, 116, 222n12,
223n1, 224n6

Fisher, Barbara M., 121, 228n11

Foucault, Michel, xvi, 22, 33,
96–97

Fowler, Alastair, xvi, 7–10, 23–24,
219n1

Freeman, Barbara, 49

Freud, Sigmund, 165

Frow, John, 10

Frye, Northrop, 15, 219n1

Gardner, Thomas, 175–76

gender, 50

genre, 7–8, 9; and antigenre,
23–24; and gender, 69

Goldsmith, Oliver: "The Deserted Village," 132

Graham, Jorie, 146; and aesthetic eras, 169–70; allusions to Wallace Stevens's poetry by, 169, 186–90, 192–94, 196–98; antiapocalyptic stance of, xv, 169–75, 177, 192–93, 195, 196–97; and apocalypse, xv, 169–75, 179–81, 185–86, 187–90, 203–4, 208–9; and apocalyptic desire, 170–72, 193–94, 197, 200; compared to Wallace Stevens, 172–73, 179, 186, 190–92, 202–4; and deconstruction, 173–74; and the feminine, 180, 195, 197–98; and gender, 172–73; and historicopolitical context, 190–92; and imaginative autonomy, 177–78; and inside/outside figuration, 177–79, 182–85; and irony, 201; and masculinity, 186, 192–95; and modernism, 173, 175, 186, 198–200, 204–5, 230n2; and narrative "gap" or "delay," 182–85; and nostalgia, 172–73, 198–201; and postmodernism, xv, 173–75, 177, 200–5, 208, 230n2; poststructuralist thinking in, 179–82; and Puritan millennarianism, 176–77, 178, 185–86; and subjectivity, 201–2; and teleology, 179–81

Graham, Jorie, poetic works: "Annunciation," 174; "Annunciation with a Bullet in It," 184–86; "The Break of Day," 184–85; "Concerning the Right to Life," 184; *The End of Beauty*, 170, 177, 183; "The End of Progress Aubade," 194–95, 196; *The Errancy*, xv, 169, 174, 175–77, 180, 182, 194–95, 202; "The Errancy," 180; "Eschatological Prayer," 170, 176; "Event Horizon," 184; "The Guardian Angel of Not Feeling," 182; "The Guardian Angel of Point-of-View," 177, 197; "The Guardian Angel of Self-Knowledge," 180; "The Guardian Angel of the Little Utopia," 177–79, 195; "The Guardian Angel of the Private Life," 178, 198; "The Guardian Angel of the Swarm," 178, 182, 201–2; "In the Pasture," 195; "Le Manteau de Pascal," 177, 187, 198; "Manifest Destiny," 170; *Materialism*, 177, 183–84; "Noli Me Tangere," 192–93; "Oblivion Aubade," 199, 201; "Of the Ever-Changing Agitation in the Air," 196–97, 198; "The Phase after History," 170; "Pollock and Canvas," 180; "Red Umbrella Aubade," 197; "The Scanning," 177, 197; "Self-Portrait as Both Parties," 174; "Self-Portrait as the Gesture between Them," 192–93, 198; "Self-Portrait as Hurry and Delay," 194; "The Sense of an Ending," 170; "So Sure of Nowhere Buying Times to Come," 179–82, 188, 199; "Spelled from the Shadows Aubade," 186–90, 194, 195; "Studies in Secrecy," 198; *Swarm*, 183; "The Veil," 199; "What the End is For," 170

Graham, Jorie, prose and interviews: "Interview" (with Thomas Gardner), 170–73, 194, 195, 196, 197, 201; "Introduction"

Norris, Christopher, 22, 220n8

Parker, Patricia, 14, 17, 19–20, 136, 220n7
pastoral, xiv, 69, 76, 110–11; and elegy, 132–33; and epic, 110; *locus amoenus* in, xiv
Patke, Rajeev S., 222n11
Patterson, Annabel, 76, 110
Pearce, Roy Harvey, 128
Perloff, Marjorie, 36, 37, 41–42, 70, 216
Plato, 51, 55–56
postmodernism, xi, xiii, xiv, xvii, 25; and aesthetic form, 35–36; and closure, 163–64; compared to modernism, 33–34, 104–5, 149–50, 206, 216–17; and discursive power, 104–5; and gender, 155–56; historical process in, 96–97; and irony, 41–42, 149–50; and late modernism, xi–xii; and mastery, 104–5, 147; and nostalgia, 33–34, 146, 221n4, 226n6; and parody, 149–50; as radical break with past, 32–33; and subjectivity, 39–40, 150; and writing, 127; and World War II, 34
poststructuralism. *See* postmodernism
Pound, Ezra: and modernist rhetoric of energy, 44; and modernist rhetoric of purification, 173–74; and postmodernism, 207; and virility, 61

Quinby, Lee, 11

Ramazani, Jahan, 86, 98
Ricoeur, Paul, xvi, 35
Riddel, Joseph N., 5, 104, 121, 222n11

Robinson, Douglas, 11, 17, 30–31, 113, 136, 220n7, 221n1
Rowland, Christopher, 13

Salmond, S. D. F., 7–8
Scholem, Gershom, 13, 17–18, 116
Seidler, Victor, 222n9
self-elegy, xvii
Shakespeare, William: *Hamlet*, 64; *King Lear*, 8; *Romeo and Juliet*, 187; *The Tempest*, 151
Shaw, David, 135–37, 151, 226n2, 227n9
Shelley, Percy Bysshe, 132; "Ode to the West Wind," 151
Smith, Barbara Herrnstein, 162–63
Spenser, Edmund, 19; "November" (*The Shepheardes Calender*), 138
Spiegelman, Willard, 230n2
Spivak, Gayatri Chakravorty, 33
Stevens, Wallace: and abstraction, 153; and aesthetic form, 36–38, 97; and apocalypse, xvi–xvii, 3–6, 23, 26, 69, 78, 88–91, 134–35, 225n2; and apocalyptic desire, 6, 18, 25, 103–4, 115–17, 121–22, 124, 125–29, 131–32; and apocalyptic elements in anti-apocalypse/postapocalypse, 25, 98–99, 115–17, 118, 120–29, 133, 139–46; and apocalyptic-elegiac modulations, 162; and apocalyptic-pastoral modulations, 112–13, 117–19, 132–33; and belief, 48–49; and closure, 162–65; and communism, 3–5, 190–91; continuity within the oeuvre of, 79–81, 87, 98; and the Depression, 3; and desire, xvi, 54, 80–83, 113–15; and discursive power, xvi, 18, 31, 90–91, 95–96, 104–5, 107–9, 119–22, 124–26,

131–33, 134, 162, 203; and elegy, xvii, 98, 105–6, 132–33, 134, 139, 226n3; and the ends of cultural/aesthetic eras, 29–30, 64–67, 69, 70, 71, 75, 78, 87, 97–98, 135, 145–46, 150–51, 208; and fascism, 3, 5, 70, 190–91; as father, 228n10; and the feminine, 49, 52–54, 67–68, 76, 85, 106–7, 156–61, 164, 229n15; and formalism, 38–39, 222n7; and gender, xvii, 27–28, 64, 106–7; and genealogy, 87–88, 108; and historical continuity, 78, 83–84, 88, 92–98, 224n6; and imaginative autonomy, 40–41, 72; and imaginative power, 37–38, 45, 64–67, 80; imaginative self-protection in, 38–40, 71–74, 76–77, 98; inside/outside figuration in, 38–41, 71–74, 75–77, 85; and irony, 29, 42–49, 67, 104, 149–53; and Last Judgment, 140–41; and literary tradition, 36–38, 70, 78–79, 86–87, 94–95, 97–98, 105, 147, 162, 166; and masculinity, xvi, 26, 27–28, 49–64, 67, 77–78, 80–82, 87–91, 98–99, 105–9, 120–24, 134, 147–49, 151–52, 154, 155–56, 158–59, 161–62, 203, 227n7; and masculinity's internal contradictions, 54–56, 67–68, 82–87, 105, 109, 117, 122–24; mastery in, 134, 154, 203, 215–16; and metaphor, 93–94; and metonymy, 93–94; as modernist, xiii, xvi–xvii, 27, 33–35, 38–39, 42–49, 57–58, 64, 104–5, 149–53, 164, 207–8, 217; muse figures in, 71, 76, 84–85, 106–7, 156–59, 229n14, 229n15; nobility in, 42–45, 51–56, 152;

and nostalgia, 33–34, 55, 65, 90, 93, 98, 146, 163–64; and nuclear war, 209–10, 215–16; and parody, 228n11; and pastoral, xvii, 46–47, 48, 70, 72–73, 74–77, 78, 103–4, 106–7, 109, 110–11, 113–15, 129–31; on philosophy and poetry, 62–64, 158–59; and political power, 59–61; and postmodernism/poststructuralism, 27, 31–32, 39–40, 42–45, 49, 65–67, 75–76, 95–99, 104–5, 126–27, 149–52; as postmodernist/poststructuralist, xiii, xiv, xvi, 43–44, 66–67, 72, 97–98, 134, 159–60, 217; and prophecy, xvi, 91, 109; and self-elegy, xvii, 133, 135, 139, 146–51; and self-parody, 131–32, 151–52; and subjectivity, 39, 58; and the sublime, 45, 73, 130–31, 133, 143, 145; and topographical poetry, 113, 139, 226n3; and vocal tropes, 126–27; and World War II, xv, xvi, 3, 26, 92–93, 103, 141, 143; and World War II's cultural/aesthetic impact, 27, 29, 34, 36–38, 46–48, 56, 61, 64–67, 69–71, 72–74, 78–79, 81–88; World War II and post-war poetry, 105–9; and World War II's impact on concepts of masculinity, 27–28, 51–54, 56

Stevens, Wallace, poetic works: "Analysis of a Theme," 65; "Asides on the Oboe," 128–29; "The Auroras of Autumn," xvii, 127, 129, 133, 134–35, 138–66, 187, 194, 196, 198; "Bantams in Pine-Woods," 59–60, 114; "The Bird with the Coppery, Keen Claws," 59; "The Comedian as the Letter C," 6, 55; "A Completely New

Set of Objects," 96; "Contrary Theses (I)," 70, 72–73; "Country Words," 58–61; "The Course of a Particular," 132, 215; "Credences of Summer," xiii, xiv, xvii, 59, 103–29, 131–33, 134, 193; "Cuisine Bourgeoise," 94; "Depression before Spring," 60; "Description without Place," 3–4, 5, 96; "Disillusionment of Ten O'Clock," 60; "The Dove in the Belly," 106; "A Duck for Dinner" (*Owl's Clover*), 3–6; "Dutch Graves in Bucks County," 69, 87–94, 95, 96, 98, 187–89, 198, 224n6; "The Emperor of Ice Cream," 54; "Esthétique du Mal," 73, 114, 152, 229n15; "Examination of the Hero in a Time of War," 150, 211; "Extracts from Addresses to the Academy of Fine Ideas," xvi, 3–4, 46–49; "Extraordinary References," 105–6, 110–11; "Fabliau of Florida," 24; "Farewell without a Guitar," 215; "Final Soliloquy of the Interior Paramour," 157; "Forces, the Will & the Weather," 114; "Gigantomachia," 44, 211; "Girl in a Nightgown," 69, 70–72, 74–77, 223n1; "The Green Plant," 203; "The Idea of Order at Key West," 45; "In the Carolinas," 229n15; "The Irish Cliffs of Moher," 203; "Last Looks at the Lilacs," 59–60; "Le Monocle de mon Oncle," 55; "Lebensweisheitspielerei," 203, 215; "Life on a Battleship," xiv; "Long and Sluggish Lines," 203; "Looking across the Fields and Watching the Birds Fly," 127,

203; "Man and Bottle," 84, 85–87, 116–17; "The Man with the Blue Guitar," 55, 65, 211; "Martial Cadenza," 69, 70, 77–84, 85, 86, 117, 188–89, 198; "Men Made Out of Words," 87; "More Poems for Liadoff," 105–6; "Mountains Covered with Cats," 106, 110–11; "Mr. Burnshaw and the Statue" (*Owl's Clover*), 5; "Not Ideas about the Thing But the Thing Itself," 203; *Notes toward a Supreme Fiction*, 45, 55, 59, 70, 86, 107, 133, 147, 149, 157, 174, 202; "Of Ideal Time and Place," 128–29; "Of Modern Poetry," 36, 65, 84, 149, 174; "An Ordinary Evening in New Haven," xii, xiii, 141, 223n4, 227n8; "Outside of Wedlock" ("Five Grotesque Pieces"), 73, 94–95; "The Owl in the Sarcophagus," 65; "Peter Quince at the Clavier," 55, "Poetry Is a Destructive Force," 117; "Presence of an External Master of Knowledge," 127; "Prologues to What Is Possible," 202; "Puella Parvula," 45, 71; "A Quiet Normal Life," 159, 202; "Recitation after Dinner," 87; "The Region November," 127–28; "Repetitions of a Young Captain," xvi, 56, 64–68, 73–74, 106; "The River of Rivers in Connecticut," 215, 203; "The Rock," xii; "The Role of the Idea in Poetry," 97; "Sailing after Lunch," xiv; "Saint John and the Back-Ache," xii; "The Snow Man," 132; "Solitaire under the Oaks," 159, 230n17;

"Sombre Figuration" (*Owl's Clover*), 56, 222n11; "St. Armorer's Church from the Outside," 203; "Sunday Morning," xvi; "Things of August," 104, 129–31, 193; "To an Old Philosopher in Rome," 203; "To the One of Fictive Music," 229n15; "Two Figures in Dense Violet Night," 60; "Two Illustrations That the World Is What You Make of It," 203; "A Woman Sings a Song for a Soldier Come Home," 106–7, 110–11; "The Woman That Had More Babies Than That," 49; "Variations on a Summer Day," 70; "Yellow Afternoon," 84–85

Stevens, Wallace, essays: "A Collect of Philosophy," 63, 159, 230n18; "The Figure of the Youth as Virile Poet," xvi, 49, 56–59, 61–64, 67, 83–84, 87, 158; "The Noble Rider and the Sound of Words," xvi, 26–27, 28–30, 34–35, 36–41, 42–45, 51–56, 57, 64, 69, 73, 83–84, 96, 116–17, 152, 153, 213–14; "Two or Three Ideas," 30

Stevens, Wallace, letters: 26, 47, 209. *See also* individual authors

Strand, Mark: and apocalyptic mode, 209–12, 215–16; compared to Wallace Stevens, 211, 215; "Eating Poetry," 212; "Elegy for My Father," 214–15; "Five Dogs," 212; "Giving Myself Up," 216; historical and political context, 212; and masculinity, 209–12; and mastery, 210, 212, 214–16; and nuclear war, 209–12, 214–15; "The Way It Is," 209, 210–12, 214, 216; "When the Vacation Is Over for Good," 209–10

Sturm, Richard E., 220n5

sublime, 49–50

Tennyson, Alfred: *In Memoriam*, 136–38

Teres, Harvey, 5

Thomson, James: "Autumn" (*The Seasons*), 226n1

Toliver, Harold, 110, 112, 130

Vaughan, Henry: "Distraction," 178

Vendler, Helen, 103, 107, 134, 149, 174–75, 226n3, 227n9, 228n12

Verrocchio, 51–52, 55–56

Virgil, 132

Wagner, C. Roland, 229n15

Wallace Stevens Journal, xiii

Weiss, Paul, 62–63

Whitman, Walt; and muse/mother figure, 45, 49, 157; "When Lilacs Last in the Dooryard Bloom'd," 78–79

Wilder, Amos N., 219n3

Williams, William Carlos, 45; and modernist rhetoric of purification, 173–74; and apocalypse, xvii

Winthrop, John, 176, 231n4

Wordsworth, William: apocalypse in, 16; preface to *Lyrical Ballads*, 37–38; "The Ruined Cottage," 132

World War II: and aesthetic form, 36; and cultural change, 29–30, 36, 107

Yeats, William Butler: 86; "The Lake Isle of Innisfree," 115; "A Prayer for My Daughter," 70, 153